DEEP ROOTS,
BROKEN BRANCHES

DEEP ROOTS,

BROKEN BRANCHES

A History and Memoir

Victoria Bynum

University Press of Mississippi / Jackson

Willie Morris Books in Memoir and Biography

The University Press of Mississippi is the scholarly publishing agency of
the Mississippi Institutions of Higher Learning: Alcorn State University,
Delta State University, Jackson State University, Mississippi State University,
Mississippi University for Women, Mississippi Valley State University,
University of Mississippi, and University of Southern Mississippi.

www.upress.state.ms.us

The University Press of Mississippi is a member
of the Association of University Presses.

This work depicts actual events as truthfully as recollection permits
and/or can be verified by research. The names and identifying details
of some individuals may have been changed to respect their privacy.

All photographs are from the collection of the author.

Library of Congress Cataloging-in-Publication Data

Names: Bynum, Victoria E., author.
Title: Deep roots, broken branches : a history and memoir / Victoria Bynum.
Other titles: Willie Morris books in memoir and biography.
Description: Jackson : University Press of Mississippi, [2025] | Series:
Willie Morris books in memoir and biography | Includes bibliographical
references and index.
Identifiers: LCCN 2024051359 (print) | LCCN 2024051360 (ebook) | ISBN
9781496855619 (hardback) | ISBN 9781496855626 (epub) | ISBN
9781496855633 (epub) | ISBN 9781496855640 (pdf) | ISBN 9781496855657
(pdf)
Subjects: LCSH: Bynum, Victoria E. | Huckenpoehler, Mary Daniel. |
Historians—United States—Biography. | Families—United States.
Classification: LCC D15.B9 A3 2025 (print) | LCC D15.B9 (ebook) | DDC
929.20973—dc23/eng/20241211
LC record available at https://lccn.loc.gov/2024051359
LC ebook record available at https://lccn.loc.gov/2024051360

British Library Cataloging-in-Publication Data available

CONTENTS

PREFACE

*Follow that thread as far as you can and you'll find that it does
not end, but weaves into the unimaginable vastness of life.*
—Parker Palmer

I am a true Cold War baby, born in 1947, the same year as the so-called Truman Doctrine, which promised US military intervention wherever international conflicts threatened to expand communism. World War II enabled my parents, Stan and Margaret Bynum, to escape the wrenching poverty of Depression-era childhoods and join the lower middle class of postwar America. My maternal grandparents, William and Mary Huckenpoehler, pressed on in small-town Waconia, Minnesota, where William was born and where his and Mary's marriage began during World War I. Mary, though born and raised in an elegant Minneapolis home, knew poverty longer than she knew wealth.

Writing this memoir/history reminded me of the once popular feminist phrase "The personal is political," shorthand in the 1970s for identifying patriarchal norms as the source of the inequality, personal abuse, and unhappiness of so many women. When "liberation" became associated with the decade's more carefree mantra "If it feels good, do it," feminism grew more confusing. In a conversation during those years with Lisa, a friend and feminist colleague, I discussed the attitudes of two history professors famous for their seduction of female students as well as their grade-yourself classes. "Ask them about women's liberation," Lisa joked, "and they'll tell you they just love liberated women." I knew exactly what she meant. Gender, we agreed, was a necessary category of analysis, along with class and race, for analyzing a power structure that was male, rich, and white. In the decades that followed, many scholars of nineteenth-century America, including me, contributed studies that examined the plight of women, ethnic minorities, and the poor during America's checkered rise to nationhood, the Civil War, ill-fated Reconstruction, and Industrial Revolution.

I continue along that path here with a study that is both biographical and autobiographical. Often written in the first-person voice, *Deep Roots, Broken Branches* reveals personal stories that are more detailed and complex but no less political than those of my previous works. My grandmother traded the comforts of an upper-middle-class life for marriage to a working-class man who did not share her culture, religion, or level of education. In my twenties, I envisioned writing a history solely about her and her ancestors, using her unpublished family history/memoir as the centerpiece. Over time and with training as a historian, I decided to include my mother as well as myself to analyze our interconnected lives in a depth that would have been impossible for me as a young woman.

The result is a highly personal yet broadly researched history that begins in Wales as a nineteenth-century rags-to-riches immigrant story and later pivots to a twentieth-century American riches-to-rags saga. The lives of multiple generations of women linked by DNA and intertwined histories reveal the roots of our family's transition from Gilded Age wealth to Depression-era poverty to Cold War militarism, alcoholism, and adultery. Well before the socially torn and politically volatile 1950s and 1960s of my youth, my grandmother's and mother's scars from the Great Depression and World War II dictated the terms on which I entered the world.

ACKNOWLEDGMENTS

I'm deeply indebted to my grandmother, Mary Daniel Huckenpoehler, who planted the seed for *Deep Roots, Broken Branches* when she gave me her family history drafts, notes, and vintage photographs. Several of our kin later contributed letters, photographs, and memories. My mother, Margaret Huckenpoehler Bynum, supplied photograph albums from the 1940s and 1950s, while my aunt, Jeanne Huckenpoehler Van Sise, provided more than a decade of family letters. My cousin, Mary Van Sise Champagne, who shares my passion for history, contributed important, insightful perspectives. Cousin Inga Huckenpoehler McArdle provided photocopies of Mary Daniel Huckenpoehler's photograph album, documents, and family letters written between the 1950s and the 1970s. I am grateful for all that these women shared with me.

Throughout the writing of this history, I've endeavored to tell the stories of people I knew well with a frankness tempered by sympathy. Regarding relatives I knew slightly or not at all, I combined historical objectivity with critical analysis. In writing the complicated and painful life story of my mother's sister, Mary Jo Huckenpoehler Drumm, I gained crucial insights from three of Mary Jo's grandchildren through Jane, her birth daughter: Sandy Grapper Troyer, Daniel Drumm, and Deanne Drumm. I offer heartfelt thanks to these cousins for sharing details of childhoods scarred by their grandmother's and mother's mental disorders and addictions.

Family members and colleagues alike helped me to complete the most challenging book I've ever written. Several conversations with Jim Bynum enriched the chapters about our childhood. Thanks go to Dierdre Payne for introducing me to the inspiring writings of Parker Palmer. Mary Champagne, Erika Pierce, Randy Pierce, and Sandy Troyer read the book's early drafts, and Gregg Andrews, Elizabeth Cobbs, and Ann Elwood provided thorough critiques of those drafts. I'm deeply grateful to acquisitions editor Lisa McMurtray and senior project editor Valerie Jones at the University Press of Mississippi for taking on this manuscript and skillfully guiding it toward publication. I also thank the press's three anonymous readers for helping me to synthesize and clarify my analysis, senior book designer Jennifer Mixon for the book's evocative cover, and copyeditor Ellen Goldlust for her meticulous editing of the entire manuscript. Finally, I offer special thanks to Gregg Andrews, my loving partner, who shares my fascination with the past while bringing comfort and joy to the present.

DEEP ROOTS, BROKEN BRANCHES

PROLOGUE

Discovering Mary Daniel

In the spring of 1958 I sat with my parents, brothers, and grandparents at a long dining table in a spacious room bathed in light from the surrounding windows. Not quite eleven years old, I had never been to this stately house in the prestigious Kenwood suburb of Minneapolis, Minnesota. Nor had I ever met the elderly woman who hosted us. Come to think of it, I had never attended a formal dinner party. The strangeness of bourgeois elegance lit up my senses. The meal's courses were served one after another, but all I remember is the sculptured dessert with its golden meringue base, swirled and baked to perfection and crowned with a creamy, whipped lime confection. My experience with desserts consisted mainly of Mom's delicious pies, served mostly during the holiday season and topped with store-bought ice cream or home-whipped cream. The dinner's staid and inexplicably tense atmosphere inspired me to giggle nervously and blurt out that the dessert was "a masterpiece," as though it were a sculptured artifact. Feeling witty, I repeated myself and laughed louder, looking to my brothers for reinforcement. They ignored me. Nor did our hostess or my mother smile. Feeling foolish, I quietly commenced eating the masterpiece.

My well-meant but ill-timed outburst reflected self-consciousness and unfamiliarity with gracious, mannerly dining as well as my uncertainty about where we were and why we were there. My family was in the middle of an important transition—the most important of my young life. Dad, a tech sergeant in the US Air Force, had been transferred from Florida to California. Allotted thirty days travel time, we visited relatives along the way. In between, we gawked at famous tourist sites—Yellowstone National Park, Mount Rushmore, the Badlands—and took pictures with our trusty Kodak. Best of all, Dad hardly drank on this trip, and he and Mom never once fought the way they did back home.

Our first destination after leaving Florida was Jones County, Mississippi, Dad's birthplace. We pulled up to his brother Oran's farm. No sooner had I exited the car than a short, robust man with a lined, sunburned face grabbed me and hugged me hard. He proclaimed his joy at seeing his "only niece" after so many years. After spending a few hours with Uncle Oran, we drove to the home of Aunt Merle, Dad's only sister, where we spent about a week. Married to Grover Breazeale, a hard-drinking tenant farmer, Merle was the poorest of our Bynum kinfolk. To supplement Grover's income, she served lunches at the local school cafeteria. Although the Breazeales worked hard to eke out a living, their ramshackle farmhouse, outdoor toilet, and country ways marked them as "poor whites" to a suburban kid like me. Dad had long since shed his southern accent and—except for eating grits, pickled pig's feet, and tomato gravy—many of his southern ways. His career as an air force sergeant had lifted our family into a lower-middle-class lifestyle.

My Minnesota grandparents were likely about as poor as the Breazeales. Grandma and Grandpa Huckenpoehler rented the upstairs portion of an old two-story home that did not contain a full bathroom, much less a dining room. Guests washed up at the bathroom sink and dined at a kitchen table located in the living room. Yet somehow Grandma was central to the high-class dinner we attended in Minneapolis. It turned out that the dignified lady who hosted us was her sister, Margaret Daniel Jones, called Marge. And though I didn't know it at the time, I was eating dinner—for the first and last time—in the very home in which Grandma, Mary Daniel, was born and raised.

Years passed before I fully grasped that my grandmother had been raised in privilege by a well-educated family that took great pride in its accomplishments and social standing. Except for when she visited our family in Florida in 1955–56, this one evening at her childhood home was the only time I saw her outside the small-town, German American family she married into at age thirty. Huckenpoehler, not Daniel, was my mom's family name. I didn't recall

The Bynum family with Mary and Harrigan Huckenpoehler at their home, Waconia, Minnesota, 1958.

Mom ever mentioning her Daniel cousins from Minneapolis, but several years after that dinner, I learned more about the Daniel side of Mom's family during another visit to my grandparents' home. I don't remember the exact year or my age, only that I was alone in what Grandma called her "rumble room" doing what I loved to do—rifling through her boxes of saved letters, magazines, and ancient knickknacks. I stumbled on the Civil War letters of my great-grandfather, Roderick E. Daniel. Reading them, I got caught up in the words of a young soldier navigating a new relationship that soon turned to talk of marriage. Excited by my discovery, I couldn't wait to ask Grandma about the letters.

Grandma, pleased that I was interested in her stuff, explained that these were her very own father's love letters to her mother. I don't believe I had ever heard the names of either of my maternal great-grandparents before that day. Nor did it hit me that I had opened a window onto my grandmother's life story. My interest in Roderick Daniel must have meant a lot to her, because several years later, in 1971, she passed on to me the yellowed draft of her unfinished history of the Daniel-Lewis family that she had begun writing in the 1940s. In addition to the typed manuscript, she gave me various drafts and notes, typed and handwritten over the years in notebooks and on scraps of paper, used envelopes, and the backs of old letters. She also handed me her entire cache of Roderick's letters, a portion of a journal she kept in the 1920s, and a collection of Daniel family studio portraits.

Grandma's memories of herself as the young Mary Daniel intrigued me from the first moment that I began to read her unpublished memoir/history. The conservative Victorian traditions that persisted at the time of her birth in 1887 influenced her throughout her life, especially in her intense quests for religious faith and the comforts of a nurturing, orderly family life. At the same time, she yearned for a career as an artist or a writer. The tensions between her needs for emotional security and for creative expression appeared rooted in the circumstances of her birth. I learned that during the precise moments when my grandmother was entering the world, her mother hemorrhaged to death. "That must have been a very desolate Christmas for the Daniel family," she wrote. Then she added, "I wonder whether they pitied me for the fact that my mother had never, and would never, held me in her loving arms? Or did they, quite understandably, resent me as the cause of their terrible loss?" The torment of feeling resented and unlovable followed her into adulthood.[1]

By age twenty-two, Mary Daniel embodied the college-educated "New Woman" of early twentieth-century America. Although her family forced her to choose the more conventional female profession of teaching over commercial art or creative writing, Mary loved college. Between 1909 and 1911, she lived in a boardinghouse with other students while attending teachers college. Lonely and scared upon arrival, she immediately developed a "violent crush" on Hazel McQuay, "a very beautiful senior girl" to whom Mary wrote poems and presented bouquets of flowers. Mary expressed no embarrassment over the intensity of her feelings for another woman. Such crushes were common among upper-middle-class women, most of whom were educated and socialized in largely female worlds. She remembered Hazel with fondness but noted with amusement that no sooner did she get over the crush than an incoming student developed an equally intense crush on her. By age twenty-five, Mary was a grade-school teacher in Waconia, Minnesota, who shared a lively social life with her female colleagues. But she still felt unwanted and in the way when she returned to Kenwood during summers and at Christmas.[2]

At age thirty, Mary made the most significant choice of her life. In the grip of lifelong alienation from the Daniel family, she committed her supreme act of rebellion by marrying William B. Huckenpoehler, known as Harrigan, the grandson of German American Catholic farmers. The New

Woman exchanged her professional status for the traditional role of home-maker, or what German Americans referred to as *kinder, kuche,* and *kirche* (children, kitchen, and church). For the rest of her long life, Mary Daniel Huckenpoehler struggled to be a good wife, mother, and grandmother and a devout Catholic while remaining true to the intellectual and artistic interests of her youth.

I have pored over my grandmother's collections and research materials end-less times in the fifty-plus years since I first read her unpublished memoir. From the beginning, I was eager to "do something" with the materials, but I lacked the necessary resources and education. I was not raised to consider attending college, and I did not have the experience necessary to understand the personal and historical significance of what I read. In a family fractured by alcoholism, violence, and adultery, I entered my teens insecure and over-sexualized by what I had seen and experienced as a child. Pregnant at age sixteen in California, I dropped out of high school to marry twenty-year-old air force airman Burt Pierce. In 1971, when Grandma gave her papers to me, I was twenty-four years old, poorly educated, and the mother of two children, Randy and Erika.

Not that I let that stop me. Despite my family responsibilities, I studied Grandma's papers and traced our family lines. By now, Burt had left the air force and we lived in Seaside, California, where we got around on bicycles to enable Burt to afford college on his veterans' benefits. Seaside's tiny pub-lic library had to suffice for my research. The library carried only self-help guidebooks to published genealogy records, but its two librarians eagerly helped me navigate the interlibrary loan system. The tiny white-haired chief librarian, her tall, blonde assistant, and I were often the only people in the library. Together, we ordered all the published works I wanted from the Sutro Genealogical Library in San Francisco, and I pursued my new hobby, amateur genealogy. Considering my lack of historical training, there was little I could do beyond creating family charts and scrapbooks, but for the time being I felt satisfied with all I accomplished.

I left the helpful Seaside librarians behind when we moved to Chico, California, where Burt decided to attend college alongside my brother Bill. Soon after we arrived, I discovered that the town maintained a "Mormon

Stake" from which I could order and read microfilmed records from the Church of the Latter-day Saints in Salt Lake City. My research skills kicked up a notch. Now I was reading copies of original manuscript censuses and local county records rather than published transcriptions.

Less than a year later, we were again on the move. Caught between our desire for Burt to earn a college degree and the need to make a living, we exchanged Northern California for Southern California in April 1973. While Burt sought work as a carpenter, I discovered San Diego's large downtown library, which contained a genealogy room of published records as well as numerous historical works. Occasional full days at the library allowed me to pore over published tax records, censuses, and county histories. In turn, library work made me yearn to attend college. As Burt's and my goals diverged, our marriage suffered. We separated in 1974. I immediately enrolled full-time at San Diego City College. Despite my developing love of history, I majored in art. At last, I imagined, I would develop my drawing talents and maybe even achieve my grandmother's failed quest to become a commercial artist.

I still had a lot to learn about myself, but after two successful years at City College, I was determined to earn a bachelor's degree. San Diego State University was too far away for a single mother who did not own a car and barely knew how to drive. Nor was downtown San Diego a safe place to raise children. In the fall of 1976, a college friend and I transferred up north to Sonoma State College in Rohnert Park. History quickly became my favorite subject, especially after I took a course in the Civil War. While reading a footnote in a Civil War history textbook during a long bus ride to my parents' home in Monterey, I learned that my dad's Mississippi birthplace had been dubbed the Free State of Jones after its people revolted against the Confederacy. As had been the case with my great-grandfather's Civil War letters years earlier, I again realized that history was directly connected to my own life.

By now, Burt had remarried and moved to Iowa to grow soybeans and raise geese. I consented to let the kids live with him while I transferred to Chico State University, where I earned a bachelor's degree in history in the spring of 1978. Eager to further my history education, I entered graduate school at the University of California, San Diego in the fall. Randy and Erika spent another year in Iowa while I completed my master's degree. When they returned, we moved into student housing, and I worked on a PhD in history.

These were life-changing years in which I experienced the joy of being a morning person. To meet the demands of history seminars, I often set my alarm clock for 4:00 a.m. and read for two hours. By 7:00, I was ensconced in a library carrel, ready to work, with a giant cup of coffee, a doughnut, and my book bag. In 1982, when I conducted research at the North Carolina State Archives for my doctoral dissertation, the peaceful solitude I felt while transcribing nineteenth-century court, county, and government records revealed an introverted side of myself that I had barely been aware of before I entered college.

I did not forget Grandma's memoir. I considered annotating and analyzing it under the direction of a supervising professor, but I was drawn to studying the political context in which ordinary people in the South struggled during the Civil War and its aftermath. My genealogical experience with federal censuses and county court records led directly to the dissertation that became my first book. Grandma's manuscript remained tucked away.

Over the next twenty-five years, I honed my skills as a historian, producing three books and many articles. A curious thing happened along the way. Studying women, free people of color, and white farmers on North Carolina's Civil War home front for *Unruly Women: The Politics of Social Control in the Old South* led me back to the Free State of Jones and the doorstep of my father's family history. My broadened interest in history drew me closer to my own history—all the way to my southern roots in Mississippi. Jones County's war within a war became the topic of my second book, *The Free State of Jones: Mississippi's Longest Civil War*, and the inspiration for the 2016 movie of the same name. At this point, it seemed unlikely that I would ever return to my grandmother's manuscript, but in retirement, I did. Today, I marvel at how Roderick Daniel's letters, which I read so many years ago on a cozy afternoon as I mined Grandma's papers, whetted my appetite for a broader understanding of Mary Daniel and led me down the path of lifelong self-discovery.

PART I

Origins

1

The Welsh Roots of an American Civil War Love Story

Although my grandmother learned Welsh history as a child from her family—and got in trouble in school for criticizing the British version—she skipped over that history in her memoir and went right to her parents' budding romance during the raging Civil War. As though writing a Harlequin romance, she described her father Roderick as bedazzled by a fellow soldier's photograph of his "kissing cousin," Mary Ellen Lewis. With the soldier's permission, Roderick wrote Mary Ellen a letter and was delighted to receive one in return. She, in turn, savored the attention of this brave young soldier fighting for the Union against the Confederate States of America.[1]

After reading their letters, I was charmed by my Welsh American great-grandparents and eager to learn more. I became even more so after an older cousin loaned me a professionally researched chart of Mary Ellen's Welsh ancestors that he had commissioned. The chart's personal names and place-names, especially "Rees Davies of Blaen Cowny" and "Susannah Jones of Pant Glas," reached back into the eighteenth century and particularly intrigued me. Later, while sifting through Grandma's loose papers, I found the name and address of Jane Jones, a relative of Mary Ellen's who lived in Abergele, Wales. The year was 1971, and the address was from the 1940s, but I took a chance and wrote to Jane anyway. I soon heard back from her nephew, Frank Jones of

Thomas Davies(?) (*left*; cousin of Mary Ellen Lewis) and   Mary Ellen Lewis, ca. 1860.
Roderick Evan Daniel, ca. 1861–65.

Cardiff, who told me that his aunt, Jennie Frances Jones, had died three and a half years earlier at age ninety-five. Over the next few months, Frank and his wife, Nancy, exchanged family information and photos with me. I learned that my distant American cousin, Daisy (Margaret Ullmann), had sent care packages as well as letters to Jennie during World War II, which explained how Grandma had Jennie's address, which provided me with a starting point for connecting with our Old World roots. Sharing my excitement, Mom bought me a beautiful book of photography featuring Welsh scenery that looked lovely on Burt's and my coffee table. Occasionally, I opened the book and stared at scenes of the rugged, beautiful country whose history I shared but knew nothing about.[2]

Grandma knew only that her grandparents had been among thousands of emigrants who left Wales in the 1840s in search of a fresh start in America. Roderick, she wrote, had arrived when he was four years old, and Mary Ellen had been the first in her family to be born in America. I yearned to know the experiences that precipitated that generation's daring journey across the ocean, but the research required was not yet within my grasp. Instead, I began college full time, and my beautiful book of Welsh photography gave way to a coffee table strewn instead with college texts and notebooks. The ensuing decades of teaching history and writing about the American South took precedence over researching my family history. Only after I retired and began writing for myself did the reverse become true. With time on my hands and Grandma's memoir on my mind, I began to study my ancestors' history in Wales and in America. In the following pages, my historian's voice replaces that of a granddaughter.

Around 2019, a poorly translated excerpt from a 1918 article in the Welsh American newspaper *Y Drych* (*The mirror*) circulated on several Davies family Ancestry pages. The storyteller, a Davies relative, claimed that my great-great-great-grandmother, the same Susannah Jones of Pant Glas who appeared in my cousin's genealogy, was friends with the nationally revered hymnist and Nonconformist intellectual Ann Griffiths. The author further mentioned that the two young women occasionally walked together to the market town of Bala, some twenty-five to thirty miles away from their village. I was intrigued but skeptical—not just about the distance, but also because researchers of family history often exaggerate their ancestors' associations with famous people. I became less skeptical, however, after I studied Ann's life. I learned that she was not famous until after her death and that she and Susannah had been born in the parish of Llanfihangel-yng-Ngwynfa in Montgomeryshire, North Wales, only four years apart. Even after Susannah married my great-great-great-grandfather, Rees Davies, and moved to Llangadfan, the women lived within eight miles of one another. I also learned that Ann had indeed visited Bala and crossed the Berwyn Mountains, as did thousands of others, to attend Calvinistic Methodist meetings. By the early nineteenth century, Ann's home had become the gathering spot for discussions among Calvinistic converts. The baptismal records of Rees and Susannah's six children reveal that they too embraced Calvinistic Methodism.[3]

It's easy to believe that Ann and Susannah sought a greater understanding of life together. They lived during years of turmoil in Wales, propelled by the same international forces of commerce, industrialization, and religious/cultural upheaval that produced the American and French Revolutions. The expansion of worldwide markets reshaped the lives of Welsh farmers and artisans. As was the case elsewhere in Europe and in America, religious revivalism swept through Wales and particularly Montgomeryshire. Although Welsh Calvinistic Methodism emerged alongside Wesleyan Methodism in opposition to the Church of England, the two denominations differed significantly. Emphasizing feelings and personal experience as signs of one's salvation, the Welsh Methodists believed in predestination and the infallibility of Scripture. Reading the Bible, preaching, and writing and singing hymns were enthusiastically encouraged, causing literacy rates to rise among Wales's rural folk.

Whatever the exact nature of Ann and Susannah's relationship, their lives ended abruptly and too soon, in a way all too familiar in their era. Both died shortly after giving birth to children who died alongside them. Susannah's widowed husband, Rees Davies, married Gwen Davies in 1821 and continued in the Welsh Methodist faith. In 1840, Rees and Susannah's son William married the sister of the Reverend Thomas Jones, the first Welsh missionary to visit India, whose family studied Calvinistic Methodism with Ann. By the spring of 1844, however, Rees was a desperate man who at age sixty-four had grown old and infirm. By then, poor harvests and low grain prices had made paupers of tenant farmers like him throughout Great Britain. Workhouses now dotted the landscape of the United Kingdom, though Wales had fewer than most. The Llanfyllin Union Workhouse, located just thirteen miles northeast of Rees's village, appeared to be Rees and his large family's destination as the specter of dependency loomed before him.[4]

With his two wives, Rees fathered seventeen children, six of whom were under the age of twelve in 1844. Several emigrating neighbors urged him to come with them to America. The United States, they assured him, was a powerful, thriving nation that promised abundant land and good jobs to those brave enough to cross the ocean. Rees thought long and hard about leaving the only world he knew and decided, yes, that's what he would do. But sadly, after auctioning off his modest possessions, he had only half the needed capital to transport his family to America. And that cache would soon be depleted if he stayed in Wales, leaving him at the mercy of Llanfyllin Workhouse.

In desperation, Rees appealed to Llangadfan's parish rector for help. The Reverend Griffiths Howell took pity and appealed directly to the Poor Law Commissioners of London, urging them to supplement the Davies family's voyage expenses. The commissioners were persuaded to grant the funding by two considerations: first, funding the Davieses' voyage to America would be cheaper than supporting his family for years to come; second, several of Rees's grown children from his first marriage, including a married daughter, had already settled there and could assist his family's adjustment. The daughter was Margaret Davies Lewis, Mary Ellen Lewis's mother.[5]

Margaret and her husband, John D. Lewis, had boarded the SS *Orpheus* in Liverpool with their four daughters and landed in New York City on 1 June 1841. The family immediately settled in Utica, Oneida County, New York, where John found work as a carpenter. Exactly three years to the day later, the Rees Davies family joined them in Utica, by then known as the Welsh cultural capital of the world. Even earlier, Utica had gained fame as a hothouse for the religious fervor that drove the nation's Second Great Awakening (1790–1840). As Welsh Calvinistic Methodists, the Davieses shared the evangelical convictions that underlay that era's moral reform and abolitionist movements and caused the region later to be dubbed the Burned-over District.[6]

The history of the Welsh in America began long before the nineteenth century. Among the earliest European colonizers of North America, they, like the English, came over as farmers and merchants, masters and servants. Others ventured elsewhere, participating in the Atlantic slave trade or settling in England's West Indies colonies. Between 1500 and 1870, enslaved Africans produced sugar, coffee, and tobacco for international export. Back home in Wales, eighteenth-century miners of the southern valleys produced copper like never before to meet Europe's demand for slave shackles, ships, and steamboats. Sheep farmers in Montgomeryshire, the heart of Wales's woolen industry, exploited the labor of poor tenants to meet British enslavers' demands for "Negro Cloth." The tentacles of the commercial revolution that transformed medieval fiefdoms into modern networks of production and trade stretched far and wide. Nor could that commercial revolution be separated from the religious upheavals that accompanied it. When the Reverend Thomas Jones (brother-in-law of my great-great-great-uncle William R. Davies) entered the Khasi Hills of northeastern India in 1840 under the auspices of the Welsh Calvinistic Methodist Foreign Missionary Society, he intended to plant a distinctively Welsh-village form of Christianity in opposition to that of the Anglican London Missionary Society. Rev. Jones mixed among the Khasi people, teaching literacy as well as Christianity. In the end, however, British imperialists appropriated and sabotaged his work to serve the ends of empire.[7]

Depending on circumstances, time of arrival, and place of settlement, Welsh immigrants to America joined in the planting of colonies and the dispossession of Indigenous peoples as well as participated on both sides of the American Revolution. Many became farmers, some using enslaved labor, as revealed in records from the 1701 "Welsh Tract" of present-day Delaware and its splinter community, "Welsh Neck" of 1736 South Carolina. Others among the Welsh were progressive forces for education, abolitionism, and egalitarian government. Welsh Quakers of Pennsylvania were prominent anti-Crown activists. Morgan John Rhys opposed slavery even before he migrated from Wales in 1794. Protestant Nonconformist Richard Price migrated only as far as London to condemn slavery and advocate for American independence. A close friend of Benjamin Franklin, Price published *Observations on the Nature of Civil Liberty* (1776), a pamphlet that anticipated the Declaration of Independence and won him an invitation to visit America.[8]

Beginning in 1838, the Welsh American press of Utica and New York City played a critical role in fomenting abolitionist ideas among Welsh immigrants. In 1840, minister and antislavery activist Robert Everett founded *Y Cenhadwr Americanaidd* (The American messenger), which won the approval and admiration of Black abolitionist Frederick Douglass as a "purely anti-Slavery Paper." In addition, Everett preached against slavery from his pulpit and canvassed Utica neighborhoods with other abolitionists to raise awareness of slavery's evils. He and his cohorts were occasionally hissed at, booed, and pelted with eggs for their efforts. Nevertheless, Everett and his Welsh American contemporary, William Thomas, echoed William Lloyd Garrison's insistence that Congress end slavery and grant equality to Blacks. Like Garrison, they renounced the antislavery colonization movement as wrongheaded and fundamentally racist.[9]

Welsh American presses continued their antislavery work right up to the Civil War. In 1844, Everett supported the abolitionist Liberty Party's candidate, James G. Birney, for president. The following year, Utica's Welsh Baptist newspaper, *Y Seren Orllewinol* (The western star), called for slavery's immediate abolition and the ouster of pro-slavery politicians from office. Shortly after Harriet Beecher Stowe's *Uncle Tom's Cabin* appeared in 1852, several Welsh presses, including Everett's, arranged to have it published in the Welsh language. Thanks to their efforts, alongside those of preachers and schoolteachers, the Welsh of New York, Pennsylvania, Ohio, and Wisconsin became increasingly antislavery.[10]

As the abolitionist movement gained traction in the United States, emigration from Great Britain again surged. The British Parliament's repeal of the Corn Laws that protected farmers' profits gave the final push to Roderick Daniel's father, Evan Daniel, a farmer and blacksmith from Llangeitho, Cardiganshire, South Wales. In 1848, twenty-five-year-old Evan and his twenty-year-old wife, Mary Evans Daniel, gathered up their sons (Roderick, age four, and Thomas, age two), along with Mary's parents, Roderick and Catharine Evans, and her sister, Deborah, and sailed to New York City. After debarking, they headed straight to Racine, in the newly admitted state of Wisconsin, where a vibrant Welsh community awaited them. There, they joined the Welsh Presbyterian Church (also called the Calvinist Methodist Church).[11]

Wisconsin's verdant lands and growing communities held great promise for farmers and artisans. Treaty by treaty, the US government cleared the path for immigrant settlements by acquiring the lands of the state's Menominee, Ojibwe (Chippewa), Potawatomi, and Ho-Chunk (Winnebago) peoples. Few white settlers, including the Welsh, questioned the government's right to do so. I assume they adhered to the popular and convenient assumption of many Europeans that Indigenous peoples were irredeemable "savages" and barriers to the "productive" use of land. The promise that America's vast frontier would end the Welsh nightmare of displacement predisposed them and other immigrants to assume that the dispossession of Native peoples was inevitable.

While most white settlers welcomed government policies that sealed the Native Americans' fate, memories of lost Welsh homelands complicated the feelings of some. Interviewed in 1920, several Welsh pioneers in Albany, Wisconsin, remembered with sympathy that displaced peoples continued to plant corn and fish in their ancestral home. Indigenous people and encroaching settlers also frequently traded with each other. Some Welsh Americans recalled pilgrimages made by "long trains of Indians" each summer to visit the "beloved waters" and "effigy mounds of their clans." One woman described Native Americans visiting the Rock and Sugar Rivers of Wisconsin fifty years after their expulsion because, as one told her, the Rock River is "the home of my spirit."[12]

Although Welsh immigrants' overall acceptance of Native dispossession contradicted their widespread opposition to Black slavery, self-interest influenced both attitudes. The Welsh knew only too well that Great Britain's sugar and tobacco colonies, with their dependence on enslaved labor, had fueled the oppressive industrial system that led to Welsh displacement. They did not want American enslavers to engross lands or crowd out free labor. As Welsh editor and poet J. P. Harris wrote in 1843, having experienced economic impoverishment themselves, the "Sons of Wales" must never support the "evil Enchantress of the South."[13]

Despite the promise of cheap land and well-paying artisan and industrial jobs, economic and cultural struggles awaited my ancestors. Roderick Daniel's mother, Mary, died just a few years after the family's arrival in Racine, prompting his father, Evan, to abandon farming and return to blacksmithing. In 1850, Evan lived and worked in the home and workshop of Lewis Jones, a Welsh-born shoemaker. With no mother to care for them, Roderick and Tom often stayed at their maternal grandparents' farm. They grew up among Welsh American bricklayers, carpenters, and tailors.[14]

In Utica, New York, Rees and Gwen Davies lived even more precariously. Their rented home included thirteen people, four of whom were wage-earning young men and most of whom were kinfolk. Rees's daughter Margaret lived a good distance away, and I found no evidence of contact between her and Rees in the United States. The bonds between Rees and the five children from his first marriage may have loosened after their mother's death in 1819. Only seven years old when Susannah and her newborn daughter died, Margaret would have keenly felt the loss and perhaps even been neglected when Rees married Gwen less than two years later and immediately began a second family. As Margaret grew older, she likely helped care for her younger siblings. In 1835, Margaret married John D. Lewis, and they moved to the nearby village of Cefn Coch and began their own family. The Lewises farmed for six years but failed to prosper and immigrated to America, where John succeeded as a carpenter. Fifteen of Margaret's siblings and half-siblings followed but took disparate paths to success. Some remained in New York, while others journeyed to Pennsylvania, Ohio, Illinois, and Wisconsin and worked as farmers, carpenters, foundry workers, dressmakers, and music teachers. Rees and Gwen remained in Utica until Rees's death in 1858, at which time Gwen and three of her unmarried daughters moved to New York City's Sixteenth Ward.[15]

Reflective of their different generations, Gwen Davies and her stepdaughter Margaret Lewis carved out strikingly different lives in America. Both lived into their nineties—Gwen almost to one hundred—and witnessed the transformation of the northern United States from a largely rural society fueled by cheap immigrant labor to an industrial colossus built on wage labor. Like many first-generation immigrants, Gwen clung firmly to her Welsh heritage. She reminisced all her life about her early years in Montgomeryshire. Her American grandchildren and great-grandchildren heard glorious tales about Wales's heroic past and Gwen's childhood fears of being kidnapped by "Bonie" (Napoleon Bonaparte). Even after more than fifty years in the United States, she spoke very little English, remaining faithful to the "old Cymric tongue" until her death in 1895. Margaret, eighteen years younger than Gwen, adopted a more cosmopolitan approach to life in the United States. She became fluent in English, traveled frequently, and encouraged her children to assimilate rapidly into American society while retaining their Welsh culture and religion.[16]

In 1849, John and Margaret Lewis moved to Berlin, Wisconsin, about 130 miles north of Racine, where their daughter Mary Ellen's future husband, Roderick Daniel, grew up. By the time Mary Ellen began exchanging letters with Roderick, her family was comfortably established in their new community. The older of John and Margaret's two sons, John Jr., followed his father into carpentry and later settled in California. Two Lewis daughters died young, but the four who survived became well-known in the Welsh community as talented singers. All of them married upwardly mobile men, two from elite, non-Welsh backgrounds.

The growing US crisis over slavery dramatically affected all of their lives. As cotton production soared in the South's Black Belt and beyond, slavery expanded, pushing southern farmers who did not use enslaved labor into less fertile regions. The greater prosperity of northern and midwestern farmers generated a contest between North and South over land in the Far West. In 1837, South Carolina senator John C. Calhoun had pronounced slavery a "positive good" for all society. Hoping to appease small farmers of the South with the promise of fresh western lands in the 1840s and 1850s, he and other regional leaders insisted that the US Constitution protected slavery's expansion. Antislavery northerners argued otherwise. In 1848, former Democratic president Martin van Buren sought to regain the office on the Free Soil ticket. Warning of a "slaveocracy" intent on engrossing lands nationwide, the Free Soil Party won major support from farmers of the North and Midwest. Only after Free Soilers united with abolitionists and antislavery Whigs to create the Republican Party, however, was the pro-slavery Democratic Party successfully challenged.[17]

As slavery brought the nation to the brink of war, personal events dramatically changed the Daniels' lives in Racine. In 1858, Evan Daniel's Welsh neighbor, Erasmus James, died, leaving a widow and two sons. With lightning speed, Evan married Erasmus's widow, Elizabeth, and moved into the spacious James home. Evan immediately set up his own blacksmithing enterprise, and the teenaged Roderick became his first apprentice. Although my grandmother knew her Grandpa Evan well, she never mentioned his second marriage. A clue as to why appears in Elizabeth James Daniel's will. When she died in 1878, Evan received a home for life, but his heirs were not permitted to receive any of her estate. Elizabeth and Evan's marriage was likely one of convenience, providing him with a business and a comfortable home but leaving his sons to make their own way in the world.[18]

The Civil War soon took charge of the brothers' immediate futures. In 1856, Racine's Welsh Calvinistic Methodist Tabernacle announced its support for John C. Frémont, the Republican Party's first presidential candidate. The Tabernacle proudly flew the party's banner, "Free speech, free soil, free press, and Frémont." New York City's *Y Drych*, long a critic of radical abolitionism, changed its position in 1857 to support antislavery guerrillas in Kansas. In 1859, Welsh Republicans declared radical abolitionist John Brown a martyr after his execution for instigating a biracial revolution against the institution. There must be no more compromises over slavery, they asserted, as the nation moved toward war.[19]

Racine's Welsh community strongly supported Republican candidate Abraham Lincoln in 1860 and favored ending slavery above all other political goals. When the South responded to Lincoln's election by seceding from the Union, most Racine citizens eagerly supported the Union cause. On 12 August, the city's voters passed a series of resolutions that affirmed their ethnic identity as well as their "duty to stand by this government in time of need and peril and share the fortunes of the republic in victory or death." A resolution advised the Lincoln administration to declare "all slaves owned by rebel masters . . . hereafter and forever . . . free." Three days earlier, eighteen-year-old Roderick had enlisted in Company F, the Welsh "Cambrian Guards" unit of the 22nd Wisconsin Infantry. His muster role described him as 5 feet, 8 inches tall, of medium build, with a dark complexion, black hair, and hazel eyes. His ability to play the trombone won him an assignment to Company F's band. The following month, Roderick was mustered in at Camp Utley, named for its abolitionist commander, Colonel William L. Utley.[20]

The 22nd Wisconsin was first ordered to Cincinnati, then to Covington, Kentucky, where they arrived the same day the Lincoln administration crafted the Emancipation Proclamation, which freed enslaved persons only in the states that had seceded. Kentucky had not seceded, but the soldiers of the 22nd nevertheless provided refuge to several fugitives. The gathering of "contraband" began in October 1862 at Camp Wells, outside a large farm near Williamstown. According to Private Harvey Reid of Company A, George, a Black youth about seventeen years old, suddenly appeared one morning and asked to join them, and "the guard boys immediately took him into the ranks," providing him with an overcoat, a hat, and a gun. Wrote Reid, "He was a soldier as natural as life." George's enslaver soon came looking for him, but George kept his face turned away and was not recognized. His younger brother, Johnnie, and another young man, Abe, soon joined the regiment, and before long, there were "10 or 12 of them." At one point, the soldiers rescued an eighteen-year-old woman who claimed that her captors were planning to deliver her to a brothel. Colonel Utley arranged for her transportation into the protective custody of renowned abolitionist Levi Coffin.[21]

In Lexington, another enslaved teenager, Adam, "came into the lines." He was especially desperate, claiming that his enslaver, George Robertson, regularly and severely whipped him. Robertson, whom Reid contemptuously referred to as "Mr. Slaveholder," was a former chief justice of the Kentucky Supreme Court. He soon appeared in camp and demanded Adam's return, threatening to charge the 22nd Wisconsin with unlawful seizure of enslaved persons in a neutral state. Utley scoffed at the idea and taunted Robertson to "go and try to take" Adam, provoking "uproarious cheering" from the gathered soldiers. Robertson stalked off. One Welsh soldier wrote home that if President Lincoln had refused to grant "neutrality" to politicians who enslaved other humans, "this horrible rebellion would have ended long before now."[22]

Robertson knew Lincoln personally and appealed directly to the president. Utley wrote to Lincoln as well. Even after Brigadier General Quincy A. Gilmore ordered the 22nd to return enslaved people to their masters, Utley refused to budge, citing the Emancipation Proclamation. Lincoln's only recourse for overriding each state's constitutional power to approve or disapprove of slavery within its own borders was to invoke his presidential war powers, as in the case of the Emancipation Proclamation. Yet those powers were being challenged by pro-slavery congressmen: to invoke them again threatened to derail emancipation. Lincoln publicly took neither Robertson's nor Utley's side but instead offered to buy five remaining enslaved persons who accompanied the 22nd Wisconsin and to give their title to Colonel Utley. Judge Robertson objected and forced the matter into the courts, where the exigencies of war and Confederate defeat finally ran out the clock on his victory. Though Robertson won a money judgment against Utley, the refugees remained free. Congress later indemnified the colonel. Lincoln's strategy won the day, and the US government avoided a constitutional showdown between federal and state powers at a vulnerable point in the Civil War.[23]

From that point on, the 22nd Wisconsin Infantry was nicknamed the Abolitionist Regiment. Relations among the soldiers and between soldiers and formerly enslaved people, however, were not always harmonious. Reid criticized "rabid abolitionists" for "coaxing" enslaved people into camp and then "pett[ing]" and "flatter[ing]" them. He described the liberated laborers as "lazy, saucy, and lousy" instead of the "perfect beings" the abolitionists had envisioned. When the Methodist abolitionists realized the truth, according to Reid, they turned the formerly enslaved people "out of their tents in the cold."[24]

Reid's words echo common racist stereotypes of the era and reveal tensions among northern whites over Blacks, abolitionism, and the true purpose of the Civil War. In practical terms, it is hardly surprising that white soldiers (even abolitionist ones) and escaped enslaved people in cramped wartime camps might resent and misunderstand one another.

Colonel Utley proved a better abolitionist than regiment commander. In March 1863, a detachment of the 22nd Wisconsin was sent to Middle Tennessee to fight with Colonel John Coburn's forces against Major General Earl Van Dorn's Confederate forces. At a crucial point of confrontation, Utley countermanded the orders of Colonel Edward Bloodgood, whom Utley had put in command of the 22nd Wisconsin. Utley's actions wreaked havoc in the ranks, exposing several regiments, including the 22nd, to capture by Confederate forces at Thompson's Station on March 5 as well as at Brentwood on March 25. Roderick was captured at Brentwood. He and the other prisoners were sent by foot and by rail to Richmond, Virginia, where they spent two months in Libby Prison. During that journey, they passed through Chattanooga, on the eastern border of Tennessee, an area rife with southern Unionists who whispered their sympathies when guards were out of earshot.[25]

Much later, Roderick told my grandmother that the Confederate captors rode horseback while the prisoners marched for three days and two nights. Any man who fell and could not get back up was shot to death. In a letter from

29 April 1863, however, Reid, who was in a different company from Roderick, wrote that the leader of the Confederate forces, Brigadier General Nathan Bedford Forrest, was a "gentleman" and the "secesh" captors were "very kindly, letting the weary ones ride their horses while [they] would walk, and sharing their corn bread and bacon with the hungry." Reid was very sick when he was captured and after arriving in Richmond was immediately hospitalized at "one of the most comfortable hospitals in the United States—the old U.S. Naval School." But others apparently were not treated as well, and twenty-four members of other companies in the regiment died in Richmond.[26]

In May 1863, the prisoners were exchanged and released. The 22nd Wisconsin was reorganized in St. Louis and rejoined the war in Tennessee. At some point, Roderick began his correspondence with Mary Ellen Lewis. In his earliest surviving letter, written hastily on 3 April 1864 from Nashville in response to a missive from her, he requested that she send a photograph of herself and promised to send one of himself in return, though he warned that once she saw his "likeness," he might never hear from her again. Over the next three years, their correspondence chronicles their growing feelings for each other and provides glimpses into Roderick's metamorphosis from a young immigrant to an ambitious war-seasoned man, ready to make his way in the world and assume the responsibilities of a husband. Through his eyes, the vivacious Mary Ellen emerges as a young woman braving a romantic adventure with a man she had never met.[27]

In the spring of 1864, the 22nd Wisconsin was attached to the Army of the Cumberland to serve General William Tecumseh Sherman's Atlanta Campaign in northwestern Georgia. The regiment engaged in numerous skirmishes and battles—Resaca, Dallas, New Hope Church, and Allatoona Pass—between 14 May and 5 June. On 27 June, during the Siege of Atlanta, the unit's soldiers participated in the assault on Kennesaw Mountain, where the Confederate forces included the unit that my father's distant Mississippi kinfolk were forced to rejoin after their capture by Confederate Colonel Robert Lowry in the swamps of Jones County, Mississippi. Ironically, these members of Newt Knight's guerrilla band were Unionists, too.[28]

Writing letters to Mary Ellen gave Roderick an important respite from war. As he shared the danger and dramas of battlefields, the two steadily fell in love. At first, Roderick prudently addressed Mary Ellen as "dear friend," then as "My Dear Sister," and, finally, "My Darling Sister." By August 1864 he was eager to meet her and looked forward to a future together despite the uncertainty of war: "If nothing happens," he wrote, "we will be pretty well acquainted in a little over a year." Detailed as a nurse in Atlanta's 3rd Division hospital, he expressed joy at having "perused with pleasure" her latest "epistle": "If my right hand was amputated," he wrote, "I believe I would be compelled to write an answer to it tonight. But don't I wish I was situated tonight so that I could shake hands with my Sister Mary. And as bashfull as I *am*, I would 'kiss her for her mother.'" Considering that Roderick had endured imprisonment and witnessed the death of comrades, his use of phrases such as *if nothing happens* and words such as *amputated* suggest his fears.[29]

In the same letter, Roderick reported a quiet Atlanta front except for "some pretty lively skirmishes." He complained that he had not seen his regiment, including his "dearest friend in the world," for six or seven days and that he was "beginning to feel homesick, for the regiment is my home at present." After Confederate forces fled Atlanta on 1 September 1864, the 22nd Regiment served with the Army of Georgia between 15 November and 10 December, joining more than 100,000 other Union soldiers in General Sherman's infamous March to the Sea. From January to April 1865, the 22nd participated in the Carolinas Campaign.[30]

On 14 April 1865, Roderick dashed off a letter to Mary Ellen. With only a pencil and newsprint stationery from the Wisconsin Soldiers' Aid Society on hand, he excitedly wrote, "We started from Goldsboro Monday 10 and captured Raleigh on the 13th A.M. Our reg't was rear guard of the train of the Army of Georgia. We reached Raleigh this P.M. We expect to march after [General Joseph E.] Johnston ~~yesterday~~ tommorow [*sic*]." Embarrassed at his mistake," he added, "I have just visited an Insane Asylum—probably that is the reason that I confound the days of the week." He closed with, "I can write no more at the present for the mail is just going out by a man from our reg't and is going to leave us tonight, and it is getting too dark for me to see what I am writing."[31]

Three days later, Johnston surrendered to Sherman at the modest farmhouse of James and Nancy Bennett in nearby Durham. With that surrender, the Civil War was essentially over, and jubilant Union forces soon began celebrating. The 22nd Wisconsin marched through Richmond to Washington, DC. There they participated in the 23–24 May Grand Review Parade of 80,000 soldiers down Pennsylvania Avenue before throngs of cheering spectators. On 12 June 1865, Roderick and his fellow soldiers were happily mustered out of the army. According to Mary's memoir, her father then "made straight for Berlin, Wisconsin, arriving in time to take in a Welsh eisteddfod in which Mary Ellen was to sing. That was their first meeting face-to-face." Evan O. Jones, Roderick's closest friend in the 22nd Wisconsin Infantry and fellow sufferer in Libby Prison, may have accompanied him to Berlin, since Evan married Mary Ellen's older sister Jennie less than a year later.[32]

Roderick, economically less equipped than Evan to support a wife, and Mary Ellen became engaged in early 1866, but they delayed their marriage until 1867. In mid-1866, he was home in Racine, looking for work while reconnecting with family and old friends. His final five letters to Mary Ellen between 1866 and 1867 percolate with eagerness to achieve success in postwar reconstructed America. In love and happy to be alive, Roderick immersed himself in Racine society, working variously as a band director, penmanship teacher, salesman, and telegraph operator for the railroad. According to Mary, his telegraph job ended when he was fired for refusing to work on the Sabbath.[33]

On 9 June, Roderick apologized to Mary Ellen for his late response to her letter, explaining that he had been "very busy indeed for the last week" and had worked "all night one night." He was planning to attend a gathering of Welsh Calvinistic Methodist dissenters at the community's Presbyterian church in what promised to be a "big time." Roderick then ticked off a daunting list of his memberships, including a debating society, band, and musical society. And, he added, he had recently agreed to lecture at the local Sunday school. "I suppose I must shake off some of these coils after I get married," he half promised.[34]

Roderick also mentioned having seen Mary Ellen's mother, Margaret, when she visited Racine, perhaps as a guest in the home of her daughter Jennie and new son-in-law, Evan Jones. "I think more of your mother every time I see her. I love her because she is the mother of my *precious* Mary." His next line revealed a bit of nervousness: "She will probably tell you what she thinks of me when she gets home." Roderick apparently passed muster, because he and Margaret Lewis seem to have gotten on well for the rest of their lives.[35]

Evan had recently opened a butcher shop, and he wanted Roderick to "keep his books and learn the business in general and board with him." Tempted by his promise of good wages, Roderick wrote, "I have about concluded that it's the best thing I could do for it's a very profitable business and that's quite an inducement." But he offered a mock warning: if he took the job and lived with Jennie and Evan, "she will tell you what a mean fellow I am. That will make it very bad. But I believe the best way is to get married before they hardly realize what I am."[36]

Roderick soon abandoned his plan to bring his new wife to Racine when a lucrative position as a fire insurance adjustor came his way in Oshkosh, jumping at the offer to join the new corporate middle class spawned by post–Civil War industrialization. By late November 1866, he was living and working in Oshkosh, where his brother, Tom, joined him in early December after obtaining a job with the same company. "Ain't that Jolly!" Roderick exulted, "but it will be jollier when my wife and his wife live at Oshkosh and that time is nearing every day."[37]

All seemed to be falling into place. The only thing that soured Roderick's mood, he told Mary Ellen, was when he "accidently spoiled my good gold pen," as he had that very day, "and you know that always makes me cross as a bear." Perhaps feeling a bit ashamed at such an uncharacteristically ostentatious remark, he quickly backed off, denouncing materialism and greed and insisting that he had become "wiser." "Once my whole brain was engaged in scheming a way to get money," he continued, "but of course I could never get enough." Now, however, while he would not refuse a chance to make money, "I don't feel as if that was the chief end of life."[38]

In early June 1866, just weeks before his wedding, Roderick wrote his last surviving letter as a single man. In it, he teased her with mentions of other women: he had recently met "Miss Stephens," and he and Sarah Williams "took a walk to the Lake Shore Wednesday evening. I will give you the details of the journey when you come here Tuesday. But in case you don't come, all I can do will be to attempt a repetition of the aforesaid pleasant privilege." He was hoping that jealousy would persuade Mary Ellen to travel "over the water" to Oshkosh since the pressures of business prevented him from visiting her before their wedding day. But Mary Ellen likely considered a visit to his home improper, and having waited more than two years to be with her beloved, she could endure a few more days.[39]

On 27 June 1867, Roderick Daniel and Mary Ellen Lewis were properly married in Berlin by the Lewis family's Congregationalist minister. Only then did the couple travel to Oshkosh to make their new home.[40]

Although I've read and reread Roderick Daniel's Civil War letters over the years, I only recently learned that his unit was known as the Abolitionist Regiment—a surprise nearly as great as the one I experienced earlier when

I learned that several of my father's southern ancestors from Jones County, Mississippi, had fought against the Confederacy. And I was just as surprised to discover that those two groups of soldiers met on the battlefields of Kennesaw, Georgia.

These two Civil War stories have other connections as well. As I conducted research for what became *The Free State of Jones*, I realized that the War of 1812 not only helped shape an American identity among white frontier farmers but also built a firewall that kept many southerners loyal to the US government. In the North, where many immigrants still struggled to learn English, the Civil War itself was a powerful Americanizing force. For my great-grandfather Roderick, who disdained glorification of war to his daughter Mary, becoming an American sprang not from the pride of battlefield victories but rather from risking his life to transform his family's new homeland into a "more perfect union."[41]

Karl Marx viewed the Civil War as a second American Revolution: by destroying chattel slavery and disempowering the enslaver class, it paved the way for a workers' revolt against capitalism. Industrial capitalists, however, proved remarkably adept at dividing workers along ethnic and racial lines to create a new hierarchy of labor. By the 1870s, northern politicians had ceded control over the land, labor, and legislatures of the South's old ruling class in exchange for profits from the exploitation of its natural resources. Terrorization, intimidation, and segregation of Black southerners followed. Meanwhile, an industrial rather than class revolution followed, opening the way for my Wisconsin ancestors to move into the upper class while my Mississippi ancestors were left to farm their devastated lands as best they could.[42]

2

Class Matters in the Gilded Age

I'd probably be dead long ago if I had stayed in that
Minneapolis rat race. . . . I would have been either
a "social failure" or a miserable success.
—MARY DANIEL HUCKENPOEHLER, 18 July 1971

In a 1971 letter, my grandmother Mary described the family I never knew
existed before I read her parents' love letters. In both her memoir and subsequent letters, she disdained the snobs and social climbers on her mother's
side of the family. She hinted at the Lewises' aspirations when she described
her father's delay in marrying Mary Ellen until he could support her in the
manner she "expected and deserved."[1] Although there's no evidence that Mary
Ellen pressured Roderick to increase his earning ability, it is certainly true
that the Lewis clan was socially ambitious. The family enjoyed a rapid rise
to wealth and status in the post–Civil War Northwest. Roderick, thanks to a
common school education, ambition, and a few months in business school,
forged a successful career in the fire insurance industry, moving his family
from middle- to upper-middle-class status. But he never achieved the heights
reached by several of his Lewis in-laws and their children, who climbed even
higher on the golden ladder of success.

By 1872, Roderick and Mary Ellen had two sons—Roderick Llewelyn (Llew), age three, and two-year-old Lewis Franklin—and another on the way. The Daniels seemed committed to Oshkosh for the rest of their lives, especially after Mary Ellen's parents and two of her siblings left Berlin for Nekimi, an old Welsh settlement located just eight miles south of Oshkosh. The move to Nekimi did not suit the Lewises, however, and John and Margaret Lewis returned to Berlin by 1872, perhaps because life in the Welsh village was too traditional for their upwardly mobile children.[2]

With her due date approaching and her mother no longer living nearby to help, Mary Ellen and Roderick sent Llew to her parents' Berlin home. There, according to Mary Ellen's younger sister, Katie, Llew was "getting along finely" and "never wants to go home." Eighteen-year-old Katie described the child's antics, exulted over her new hat delivered by freight for an upcoming party, and marveled at the beauty of verbena and pansies coming up "thick" in the family garden. In passing, she mentioned several family members to Mary Ellen, including their brother Bill, who, Katie wrote, was doing "finely" in Chicago. With a hint of amusement, she added that Bill "tells me that if I ever need anything to just tell *him*." Mary Ellen gave birth to the Daniels' third son, Mortimer, in 1872.[3]

While all the Lewis daughters seem to have been richly possessed of charm, talent, and social graces, Elizabeth (Libby) and Anna, the two sisters closest to each other, landed particularly "fortunate" marriages. Libby was teaching music in Racine and living with her sister Jennie and her husband, Evan O. Jones, when she met Frederic Ullmann, a successful attorney. Frederic and three older brothers had left their boyhood home of Racine for Chicago, where they achieved far greater wealth than their father, a German émigré and prosperous dry goods merchant. By 1870, Henry, Daniel, and James Ullmann were wealthy Chicago bankers, while Frederic was a lawyer who represented many "big companies," including the Lehigh Valley Railroad. On a visit to Racine, Frederic fell in love with Libby, and they married on 5 January 1871 in Berlin, Wisconsin, and bought a home in Chicago.[4]

The newlyweds settled in the Windy City just in time for one of America's greatest tragedies—the Great Fire of Chicago. Ten months into their marriage, Frederic and Libby faced the horror of what blared forth in the *Chicago Tribune*'s bold front-page headline: "FIRE! Destruction of Chicago!" According to the paper, twenty-six hundred acres of buildings had been destroyed, eighty thousand people had been burned out of their homes, and hotels, banks, and offices throughout Chicago's main business district had been destroyed—and the fire raged on. More than one hundred dead bodies had been recovered from the debris. Although Frederic and Libby were not among the working poor who suffered the greatest losses, the fire nonetheless deeply affected them. A week later, Henry Ullmann's burned corpse was found at the downtown corner of Madison and Clark Streets. Mary's memoir made no mention that her aunt Libby, whom she had known well and wrote about at some length, had experienced the Great Chicago Fire at so intimate a level. Henry Ullmann's grisly death likely was never mentioned in my grandmother's presence.[5]

In 1875, the Lewis family gathered for Anna's Chicago wedding. Like all the Lewis sisters, Anna was an accomplished singer who grew up performing at local Welsh eisteddfods. She parlayed her musical background and natural talents into a professional career. After briefly teaching music in Oshkosh, Anna moved on to Evanston College for Ladies, just outside Chicago, where she taught voice between 1871 and 1874. She likely met her future husband, Mather Dean Kimball, through his close friends Libby and Frederic. Anna frequently performed at concerts sponsored by Chicago's Union Park Congregationalist Church, while Mather, a graduate of Northwestern University with illustrious New England roots, edited and copublished the *Green Bay Globe*, a lively and popular newssheet that focused on local events and personalities.[6]

By this time, John and Margaret Lewis had moved to Oshkosh, and they traveled with the Daniel family to Anna's wedding, though John did not attend. The Chicago and Green Bay newspaper society pages hailed the celebration as "one of the most interesting matrimonial events of the week," and Frederic and Libby Ullmann hosted the reception at their Vernon Avenue home.[7]

Newlyweds Anna and Mather soon had their own lovely home in Green Bay, thanks to Mather's father, Alonzo Kimball, who gifted them with the deed and lot. Katie must have been quite excited when she received an invitation to spend the Christmas holidays at the Kimballs' new home. At the crucial coming-out age of twenty-one, Katie would have relished not only the upscale festivities and lush decorations but also her introduction into Green Bay high society. The *Green Bay Press-Gazette* included her name in its announcement of which "ladies" would "present and receive friends" at the elegant Mather D. Kimball residence on New Year's Eve.[8]

Less than a month later, however, the Lewis family faced a grim reminder of how swiftly life might turn dark in Victorian America. In early January 1876, after six months of visits and travel, Katie contracted tuberculosis and died at her parents' home in Oshkosh. Popularly known as consumption and a leading killer of young and old alike in this era, the contagious illness also took the life of her father in August.[9]

The deaths occurred during a decade otherwise marked by professional and personal success for Roderick and Mary Ellen. Roderick prospered in the fire insurance business, forming several partnerships and for a time employing his brother, Tom, as a clerk. Despite his large household and increasing responsibilities, Roderick ignored his prenuptial promise to shake off the "coils" that occupied so much of his time as a single man. Music and singing remained an essential part of his life. In 1875, while he was serving as president of the Oshkosh Choral Society, the *Oshkosh Northwestern* complimented the Welsh choir's fine singing, especially of the Welsh anthem at a mass temperance meeting held in the city's Methodist Church. By 1877, he was secretary of the state musical association. He also became involved in politics, serving as a delegate to the state Republican convention from the First Ward of the Nineteenth Senatorial District in 1877 and 1879. Also that year, President Rutherford B. Hayes appointed him deputy collector for the Office of Revenue.[10]

On the home front, the Daniel family grew with the birth of Lillian in 1875 and Margaret (Marge) just days before John Lewis's August 1876 death. The newly widowed Margaret Lewis joined the Daniel household, perhaps helping with chores and with her grandchildren in the absence of live-in servants, though by 1880 she was living in Minneapolis with her daughter Susannah, who had married Thomas Baxter, a Welsh-born miller. The Daniels also likely employed outside help, but motherhood and running the household claimed most of Mary Ellen's time.[11]

In March 1882, the *Oshkosh Northwestern* announced that R. E. Daniel had dissolved the Daniel & Luscher insurance partnership to become a special agent for the Boston Underwriters and the Fire Insurance Association of London, a position that required him to traverse the states of Wisconsin, Michigan, Minnesota, and Illinois. Tom Daniel also left Daniel & Luscher to become a special agent for the North British Mercantile Insurance Company. With these changes, the Daniel brothers began eyeing Minneapolis as a more suitable home base. Roderick visited the city to scout living arrangements in

Roderick Evan Daniel, ca. 1875.   Mary Ellen Lewis Daniel, ca. 1875.

1885, but the move did not take place for another two years. In the interim, Roderick and Mary Ellen's two oldest boys, particularly Llew, won accolades for their musical talent and academic achievements at Oshkosh High School. In early 1887, Llew was serving as director and first violinist of the Keystone Orchestra, with Lewis on the clarinet. The ensemble provided musical accompaniment for a variety of special events, particularly at the high school.[12]

Llew's high school essays also garnered attention from the Oshkosh press. On 1 May 1886, eighty thousand workers, unionists, anarchists, and socialists marched down Chicago's Michigan Avenue to demand an eight-hour workday. Three days later, a bomb exploded in the city's Haymarket Square, killing numerous police officers and injuring many civilians. Eight radical labor activists were immediately rounded up, and four were convicted of the bombing. That same year, Llew presented a paper on "The Effects of the Introduction of Labor-Saving Machinery," though its contents are unknown. Given Llew's prosperous background, however, it seems doubtful that he shared the views of economist and Gilded Age reformer Henry George. In 1879, George emphasized that while labor-saving devices had greatly increased "comfort, leisure, and refinement" among the upper classes, the "lowest class" did not share in the benefits. Children still worked in factories,

Llew Daniel, ca. 1885.

and large numbers of people depended on charity or starved. George con-cluded that "it is as though an immense wedge were being forced, not under-neath society, but through society."[13]

In 1887, Llew delivered an oration on "The Negro Problem" at his high school commencement. In the speech, Llew advocated education in work-ing-class trades, echoing the conservative white Progressive approach to racial "uplift" popular between 1880 and 1914. Rather than integrate African Americans into public life with full rights of citizenship, Llew advocated training Black men for jobs that would provide them with incentives to abandon their "slothful" ways, a view typical of the northern philanthro-pists courted by Booker T. Washington during that era. Washington believed that the limited goodwill displayed by moneyed white men offered the best approach to combat the violence, segregation, and economic exploitation that Blacks suffered in the New South.[14]

Like many from the white northern middle and upper classes of the Gilded Age, Llew embraced reforms that offered only a modicum of eco-nomic and physical security to Blacks down South and that did not challenge white beliefs about Blacks' inferiority. Washington intended vocational educa-tion and menial labor to be ladders by which Blacks would one day achieve equal rights and opportunities, but Washington never lived to see that day. Segregation was nationally enshrined when the US Supreme Court approved "separate but equal" facilities for whites and Blacks—a bogus proposition on its face—in the 1896 *Plessy v. Ferguson* decision. Blacks who moved north joined an urban working class locked in a daily struggle to win higher wages and humane working conditions. Time and again, employers hired Blacks as strikebreakers while fomenting racism as a tool to destroy labor unions.[15]

Like most middle-class Americans, Llew had little knowledge of the day-to-day struggles of workers, immigrants, or Black Americans. Nor did he understand or even recognize the cultural richness of members of those groups. For example, trained in Welsh classical music, the Daniels and Lewises considered Black ragtime music to be trash. Their musical training as well as their racism prevented them from appreciating the syncopated beat and thumping piano that mimicked the work rhythms of the river roustabouts who created it. However, many poor working-class whites excitedly embraced ragtime music.[16]

Llew soon put aside the nation's labor and racial problems to focus on his family's upcoming move to Minneapolis. By June 1887, the family's new house in Kenwood—the same home in which my family ate dinner in 1958—was ready to be inhabited. It was an exciting if somewhat scary time for the Daniel family, especially after forty-four-year-old Mary Ellen discovered she was pregnant with her sixth child. It was her first pregnancy in nearly ten years, an indication that she and Roderick had considered their family complete after Marge's birth. The average size of middle- and upper-class families decreased after the Civil War, thanks to greater access to birth control methods including suppositories, spermicides, and condoms as well as the more common coitus interruptus (withdrawal) and douching. Abortion, common before the war, had been criminalized in virtually every state.[17]

The Daniel family's move from Oshkosh to Minneapolis dovetailed with the nation's transition from a largely rural world of farms, workshops, and local businesses to an increasingly urban industrial society. Twenty years after marrying, the Daniels had achieved solid, middle-class status with reason to hope they would rise even higher in the booming modern city. They scrambled to adjust to skyscrapers, cosmopolitan travel by rail and ship, and the rise of corporate dynasties. In exploding urban America, ambitious, upwardly mobile men aspired to become bankers, lawyers, business leaders, engineers, managers, and doctors, while their equally ambitious wives and daughters dreamed of well-appointed homes in which to raise smaller families and preside over social events, receptions, and parties. Their children enjoyed larger and more technologically advanced venues of entertainment. Amusement parks, circuses, and Wild West shows added to the excitement of modern life.[18]

Roderick's new life necessitated frequent travel to deal with difficult clients, harbingers of the hazards associated with the new urban professional lifestyle. Because of his upbringing, Roderick was temperate in his use of alcohol and tobacco, but many businessmen and politicians combined long hours of desk work, little exercise, and frequent public engagements with heavy smoking, consumption of brandy and other alcoholic beverages, and diets increasingly high in meat, butter, and sugar. Mary Daniel Huckenpoehler fondly remembered family picnics featuring iced lemonade, home-baked ham sandwiches or steaks to be broiled over an open fire, lemon or chocolate layer cakes, and—always—big, heavy freezers of ice cream. Restaurants featured not only rich meals but also convivial social gatherings known as smokers that catered to prominent men.[19]

In contrast, the wives and daughters of these professional men often joined women's clubs that offered moral guidance in the face of an increasingly complex social order. The Woman's Christian Temperance Union (WCTU), founded in Cleveland, Ohio, in 1874, combined religious and secular concerns, particularly after 1879 under the influence of Frances E. Willard, who supported labor and prison reforms and women's education and suffrage as well as temperance. More conservative socialites, however, preferred serving tea to prominent dignitaries, a sure path into the newspaper society pages, where their identities were usually obscured because they were referred to by their husbands' names. An accomplished woman who married well reveled in the distinguished identity of her successful husband. Some, however, like Mary's aunt Anna, traded on both their married and professional names. Newspapers referred to Anna as Mrs. Mather D. Kimball, except when she performed musically, when she was Anna Lewis Kimball. Anna and Mather's long association and friendship with Willard suggests that they supported the advancement of women's rights. Anna met Frances around 1871 while teaching music at the Evanston College for Ladies, where Willard served as president. Mather worked with Frances during her tenure as president of the WCTU, 1879–98, and served for ten years as editor of the WCTU magazine, *Good Form*.[20]

Anna Lewis Kimball, ca. 1890.

Unlike Anna, Mary Ellen Lewis apparently was not interested in either a career in music or social reform. Marriage to upwardly mobile Roderick Daniel made her a more typically successful Victorian woman, but she did not live to enjoy that status in old age. According to family lore, Mary Ellen had always suffered difficult pregnancies, and the birth of her sixth child was further complicated by her age and by the move to a new city and a new doctor. To complicate matters further, when she went into labor in late November 1887, a storm made the few roads to Kenwood, on the outskirts of Minneapolis, "nearly impassable." Mary Ellen's elderly new doctor sent his younger assistant to attend to her, and he panicked when she began to bleed heavily. Around midnight on 31 November, her beleaguered doctor and horrified husband watched as she bled to death. The baby survived, and Roderick named her Mary, after her mother.[21]

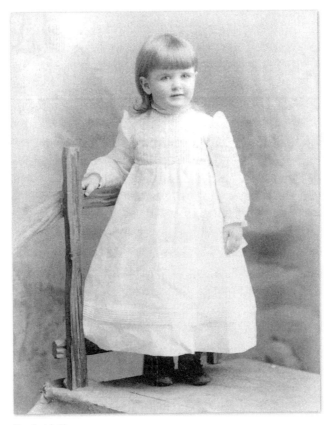

Mary Daniel, 1889.

The Daniel and Lewis families were devastated. With their families in tow, Mary Ellen's three surviving sisters—Libby Ullmann of Chicago, Anna Kimball of Milwaukee, and Susannah Baxter of Minneapolis—attended her funeral, as presumably did her mother, who now lived with Susannah. The *Oshkosh Northwestern* eulogized Mary Ellen as an "estimable Christian" who possessed a "splendid" singing voice and was a "favorite in social and musical circles."[22] Before departing Minneapolis, Libby implored Roderick to let her take her newborn niece back to Chicago and raise her as her own. In a decision of momentous importance to Mary's future, Roderick said no, insisting that he could provide for all his children and would raise Mary in the memory of her dead mother. Little more than a year later, Margaret Lewis's nephew, the eminent Reverend Francis Jones from Abergele, Wales, traveled to America on a speaking tour and baptized Mary.[23]

Despite or perhaps because of her father's firm commitment to keeping his infant daughter, Mary's birth was inextricably tied to the tragedy that marked the Daniel family's move to Minneapolis. As she noted in her memoir, she began life in a household comprised of grieving, much older siblings and a widowed father. In addition, her older brother Mortimer developed type 1 diabetes at around the same time. In February 1893, five-year-old Mary was awakened one night by the movements and voices of family members and their doctor: Mort had fallen into a diabetic coma and died. Marge, too, had a difficult adjustment, suffering eye problems accompanied by violent headaches, earaches, and toothaches.[24]

The Daniel family continued to prosper financially. By 1888, the new insurance firm of Roderick Daniel and John Hoppin employed both Roderick's brother, Tom, and second son, Lewis. Both Daniel households had live-in servants, freeing Tom's wife, Mary Trimbell Daniel, to join other elite women in attending and hosting tea, card, and supper parties. Mary and her siblings received good educations and continued to practice the musical traditions of their Welsh forebears. Llew, who studied electrical engineering, worked as a repairman for a Minneapolis electric company, while Lewis advanced in the fire insurance business. All the older children sang or played instruments. Lillian and Marge were properly introduced into society with the expectation that they would eventually marry well. And they did. Lillian wed investment broker Horace Edsell Peck in 1897, and Marge received singing lessons and taught voice at the University of Wisconsin's School of Music from 1904 to 1907 before marrying physician Herbert W. Jones when she was thirty.[25]

Despite Roderick Daniel's success in the late-nineteenth-century corporate world, his pre–Civil War artisan roots stayed with him all his life, creating a tension between the importance he assigned to manual labor and his upper-class status. He disdained snobbery and ostentatious displays of wealth. Mary remembered that "Papa had no use for Mr. Davis," a neighbor whose pink stone mansion featured a "carriage archway" with a special door and step that made it possible to enter the house without getting damp in inclement weather. Davis was a member of the Grand Army of the Republic, an organization for Union veterans of the Civil War whose most "voluble and powerful" members Roderick deemed "phonies" who likely "had never seen a day's active service." Davis's wife and daughter were "frizzly blondes with lots of ruffles and jewelry" whom Roderick believed held themselves so "proud and aloof" because their collars were so high and their corsets so stiff that they could look no other way.[26]

In keeping with his work ethic, Roderick insisted that his teenage children perform chores commonly assigned to household help, although he employed a housekeeper and a cook. In a home still lit by kerosene lamps, fifteen-year-old Marge passed through the rooms each morning, replenishing match holders and emptying burnt-match receptacles and wastebaskets. Next, she "polished and set in order" all the toiletries in the bathroom and wiped down all windowsills. Lillian cleaned the woodwork, the staircase, and the edges of the floors. Marge also was responsible for setting the table, and both girls washed dishes. Prior to his death, Mortimer and his older brothers Llew and Lewis kept the wood box filled for the kitchen cookstove and brought fuel for the coal-burning Franklin stoves that heated each room. Outdoors, the boys shoveled the walks in the winter and mowed the lawn in the summer. All the siblings pulled weeds and edged the sidewalks.[27]

As Roderick and Tom's economic and social standing rose, so did the professional opportunities for Llew and Lewis. However, upward mobility occurred more dramatically within the Lewis family, where a clear line divided the social and economic assets of the children born before 1845 and those born later. The oldest Lewis daughters—Susannah, Jennie, and Mary Ellen—married Welsh-born men who prospered in America as tradesmen, shopkeepers, or business agents, whereas younger daughters Libby and Anna married non-Welsh, US-born men with careers in politics and finance and sent their children to elite institutions of higher education.

Mary occasionally sneered at her sisters' pretensions but reserved her harshest words for what she considered the upper-class pomposity and social excesses of the Ullmanns and the Kimballs. She described her aunt Anna as a "particularly rude and vicious person to children as well as adults." Mary's favorite aunt was decidedly Susannah Lewis Baxter, whom Mary glowingly described as "black-eyed and peppy with a grand sense of humor and a social sense that must have made her a grand little wife." After the death of her first husband, Thomas Baxter, Susannah married a respectable but modest pharmacist, Robert Williams. Mary knew nothing about Jennie and speculated that she had died young.[28]

Mary had little good to say about her uncles, John Jones Lewis and William Henry Lewis. She dismissed John as a religious "crackpot" who had moved somewhere out west. She condemned Bill, an allopathic physician with a degree from Rush Medical College in Chicago, for allegedly abandoning his Irish Catholic wife, Agnes Mulcahy Lewis, and their young daughter, Agnes Margaret Lewis. Whatever their personal failings, both men fathered children who became distinguished musical performers. After her marriage to William Leon Bennett, Agnes Lewis Bennett was dubbed Minneapolis's "leading vocalist" in 1942, and she regularly received praise in the city's newspapers for her "wide range, great power, and sweetness of expression." John's son, John Arthur Lewis, was a professor of music at the University of Southern California and in 1932 directed the Xth Olympiad Chorus of Los Angeles.[29]

Mary knew much more about her aunt Libby's family and was just as critical of it. Frederic and Libby's "stylish sized family," Mary wrote with a hint of sarcasm, included three children—Bessie, Margaret (Daisy), and Frederic Jr. All received elite educations and proper social training. They enjoyed lavish excursions that distinguished them from everyday folks and made their parents glow with pride. Mary claimed that Frederic and Libby relentlessly pushed their children to succeed and that Bessie broke under the pressure. In 1897, the *Chicago Chronicle* described her as "lovely" twenty-year-old when she made her social debut at a reception hosted by her mother. A rising star of the social scene, Bessie helped arrange an event for the Musical Amateur Club the following year and appeared frequently in society pages: in January 1899, she and her mother hosted a "brilliant reception" for the daughter of Edwin F. Uhl, ambassador to Germany under President Grover Cleveland.[30]

In June 1901, the *Chicago Tribune* reported that Bessie was returning from the Wheeler School, a Providence, Rhode Island, institution for girls. Soon thereafter, Mary claimed, "something snapped" and Bessie became a "complete nervous wreck. She was unconscious for a long time and delirious. She never fully recovered." Bessie's name disappeared from the Chicago society pages after 1903.[31]

The years between 1910 and 1920 were life-changing for Anna and Libby. Both lost their husbands rather suddenly when sixty-one-year-old Mather Kimball suffered a stroke in 1910 and Frederic Ullman died of heart failure the following year at age sixty-four. The deaths drew the wealthy widows closer to each other. In 1913, they applied for passports and sailed off to Amsterdam. After their return in 1914, Libby informed the *Chicago Tribune* that she intended to sell her Hyde Park home and spend a few weeks at Chicago's Elms Hotel before heading to Florida for an extended vacation with daughters Bessie and Daisy. After their return, they relocated first to the village of Deerfield in neighboring Lake County and then around 1922 to the tony village of Winnetka, where she purchased an elegant home at 334 Ridge Avenue. In Mary's estimation, Libby used her great wealth to finance a never-ending quest for greater happiness.[32]

None of Libby and Frederic Ullmann's children married. By 1910, Fred Jr. was a lawyer with degrees from Princeton University and Northwestern School of Law whom Mary described as popular, friendly, and charming—"unlike his father."[33] Mary believed that Daisy and Fred Jr. balked at the "rat race" of high society after witnessing Bessie's breakdown and noted that Daisy, a "tomboy," rejected feminine society as well as marriage. Daisy graduated from Bryn Mawr College, where she majored in Greek and English, in 1904. She published two book-length narrative poems, *Tone-Poems* (1908) and *Pocahontas* (1912). Daisy also wrote to noted author Hamlin Garland in hopes that he could advise her on how to have her play, *The Bee Mistress*, produced by the Chicago Theatre Society.[34]

During the 1920s, Daisy attended a Woman's World Fair in Chicago, and during World War II, she wrote to and sent care packages to Jennie Frances Jones in Wales. Throughout these years, she continued to write and occasionally publish her work. At home, she raised bees and honey and tended her garden. By avoiding societal pressures to marry, Daisy had everything that was denied to Mary Daniel: an independent life fulfilled by the pursuit of creative and personal interests. Mary claimed that she lacked the "genius" to follow this path, but it seems more likely that wealth, an elite education, self-confidence, and perhaps sexual orientation guided Daisy toward choices in which marriage had no place.[35]

Yet another of Mary's cousins on the Lewis side, Margaret Baxter, bypassed marriage in favor of running a "lovely kindergarten" in her mother's Minneapolis home. Both Margaret and Daisy were prototypes of the growing number of unmarried New Women of the Progressive era (1890–1920). Mary, who gave up her fledgling teaching career shortly after her marriage, admired their independence. She wrote at length about both women in her memoir drafts, quoting Margaret Baxter's dictum that she'd rather be "sorry she didn't marry than sorry she did." And Mary quoted those words yet again in a 1971 letter to me.[36]

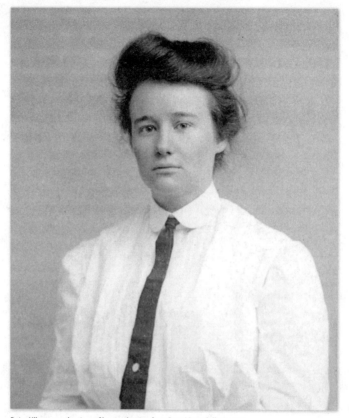

Daisy Ullmann at the time of her graduation from Bryn Mawr College, 1904.

In the terminology of the time, Daisy Ullmann and Margaret Baxter were old maids. Most of Mary's female kin, including those with careers in music, avoided that dreaded status by marrying distinguished men, but Mary was different. She married not only for love but also in rebellion against the dictates of her class. To her family, she merely married down, an act more horrifying than becoming an old maid. In her own way, Mary thumbed her nose at convention. Still, despite her thoroughgoing disdain for upper-class proprieties, I wonder if she ever speculated that had she been raised in the Ullmann home, she, like Daisy, might have built a career around her evident talents. That question might have been too painful for her to ponder.

3

Building a Family Dynasty

Roderick Daniel soon found a new wife for himself and a new mother for baby Mary. Likely while visiting old friends and the late Mary Ellen Daniel's family in Berlin, Wisconsin, in 1889, he met Jeannette May Jones, who was from the same close-knit Welsh community and was said to have greatly admired Mary Ellen. But Jeannette was twenty-one years younger than Mary Ellen and represented a new generation of educated and independent middle-class women. At age twenty-seven, she was an accomplished pianist and high school English teacher who lived with her three unmarried siblings and two maiden aunts. Her brother Alfred was a pharmacist, while another brother, Herbert, was a high school student. Her sister, Minnie, was a German-educated linguist. Like their aunts, Minnie and Jeannette showed little inclination to marry. Minnie never did, but meeting Roderick changed Jeannette's mind. She and her future husband were ethnically and culturally aligned, and his personal credentials were impressive: as my grandmother later recalled, he was "a widower with a good job earning a good salary, owning a fine big home [and] the father of a fine, big, talented, fairly comfortable and well-behaved family."[1]

And baby Mary badly needed a mother. Roderick wasted no time proposing marriage, and Jeannette said yes, breaking from the increased tendency among educated, professional women to remain single. She quickly won her new stepdaughter's love. Mary called her Mama from the beginning and admired her "ash blonde hair, fair skin, blue eyes, lovely complexion, . . . trim figure and proud erect bearing."[2]

Before their marriage took place, Roderick and Jeannette visited each other and corresponded. Despite the limits of Victorian decorum, Roderick's affection and respect for his fiancée leap from the pages of his letters. On 13 September 1889, he told "My darling Nettie" of his joy that she was "contented and happy" with their relationship as well as his "hope and expectation that that feeling will grow." Roderick then recounted his long workday, which had ended with a 129-mile train ride from Sparta to Minneapolis. It was now two o'clock in the morning, and he soon would head to Eau Claire, Wisconsin, where he had "another woman and fraud" case to investigate. Insurance frauds of all sorts, by women as well as men, were common in Gilded Age America, where the pursuit of money seemed almost a game. "I shall go there again next week and will probably stay there all the week," he wrote. "I am going to try and make life a burden to these Eau Claire women before I get through with them."[3]

Five months later, Roderick was hoping to attend a concert in Berlin with Jeannette and her family, but settling insurance losses in Minneapolis and St. Paul threatened to derail those plans. After asking Jeannette to reserve a ticket for him with the understanding that she might have to give it to someone else, Roderick speculated that he would be writing her letters "for years to come," since he was likely to continue his constant business travel. After their wedding, which was scheduled for May 1890, however, he expected to be "home Sundays nearly always." Roderick's professional responsibilities meant that the bulk of his time would be spent in trains, hotels, and restaurants, meaning that Jeannette would often be without her new husband as she got to know her six stepchildren.[4]

Roderick's letter also expounded on political events in Russia and Germany. Deploring the "trouble in this world," he denounced the "atrocities" committed under Russia's Czar Alexander III, an autocratic nationalist who persecuted Jews and imposed religious and cultural orthodoxy throughout his empire. "But I think that those made to suffer in that way now are helping the general trend toward the revolution that will benefit the race," Roderick optimistically wrote. In the next line, he applauded Germany's Kaiser Wilhelm II, predicting that "if he keeps the course that he seems to have marked out he will do an immense amount of good—and will be one of the central figures of history."[5] Mary remembered her father as an "idealist, an incipient Socialist," a kind and generous man who she thought "failed to realize that the majority of people in this world are not idealists but very selfish and self-centered people." Roderick likely admired Wilhelm II for his bellicose attitude toward Russia and his support for workers' rights, public education, and the arts and sciences. But as Mary well knew by the time she wrote her memoir, Wilhelm II proved to be an egotistical and rash emperor whose diplomatic policies were his greatest failures.[6]

When my grandmother began her memoir in the late 1940s, the world was still coming to terms with the full extent of the horrors of Hitler and the Holocaust. Likely with those events in mind, she took special care to include her memory of when Jeannette fired a teenaged governess who terrorized six-year-old Mary with tales of "Jew gardens" in which wandering children were snatched up, tortured, and killed. Jeannette also "reeducated" her stepdaughter on the equality of all humans: "Like all truly cultured and deeply religious people," Jeannette "had no narrow prejudices, racial, religious, or political."[7]

Mary likely heard other anti-Semitic slurs as a child, perhaps even from her father. His sympathy for Russian Jews coexisted alongside a personal dislike for the Jews he encountered in his travels: he chose not to spend a night in a hotel because he would have had to share a room with a Jew, opting instead to walk home. As decades of persecution pushed Jews to seek asylum in the United States, he, like many Americans, viewed them as a threat to the nation's values and principles.[8]

In the 1890s, Roderick optimistically imagined that revolution in Russia and a reformist German kaiser would cure the worst ills of Europe. Roderick died in 1908 and did not witness the eruption of World War I and Adolf Hitler's subsequent fanning of the fires of anti-Semitism to restore a defeated Germany to power.[9]

Despite having a loving, intellectual father and stepmother, Mary was a lonely and frequently angry child: by age four, her behavior alternated between violent tantrums and quiet sulking. She attributed her anger to being mocked by her teenaged siblings, who then overindulged her when she became sick. Once, while she was suffering from whooping cough, she was carried about and given "a bit of buttered bread, or a cookie and a glass of milk while sitting cuddled in someone's lap." Such indulgences, coupled with frequent teasing and admonishments, sometimes made her feel "like a pet monkey on a short leash."[10]

Attending school did not help. In fact, kindergarten gave four-year-old Mary fits of rage. The late-nineteenth-century Progressive theory of education featured small "Froebel blocks" (called gift cubes) designed to teach young children dexterity and "logical mental advancement." But Mary could not master the cubes, and one day she flung them across the room in frustration. As punishment, her teacher ordered her to stand in a corner for the rest of the session, and other students ridiculed her. Even kindergarten projects that pleased Mary, such as stringing beads or sewing with colored yarn, stimulated vivid dreams in which she relived her school day, causing her to sit up in bed, talk out loud, and flail about. According to the family doctor, she was "over-responding to her environment," and he recommended her removal from school until she was more mature. Roderick and Jeannette dutifully complied.[11]

Ten years younger than her closest sibling, Mary was too young to participate fully in family gatherings, and she felt rejected. Her isolated status changed on 15 June 1892, when Jeannette gave birth to her and Roderick's only child, Donald Herbert (Doddy) Daniel. With the addition of a younger sibling, Mary felt less like an intruder in the family.

Doddy's birth also gave Mary the chance to spend two weeks getting to know her maternal grandmother, Margaret Lewis, at her daughter Susannah's house. Mary found her stay at the Williams home pleasant and memorable. Susannah's grown daughter, Margaret Baxter, was also part of the household and conducted a private kindergarten class there. The child-friendly atmosphere and firm rules of behavior calmed Mary, who especially enjoyed the ritual of preparing for bed with her grandmother. Like most homes of the time, the Williams house lacked running water and a bathtub. Instead, a big flowered pitcher and matching china bowl filled with warm water sat atop a marble-topped commode. Once her sponge bath was completed, she and Grandma Margaret wore matching white nightgowns and sat together in rocking chairs while her grandmother soaked her feet. The "dazzlingly white" sheets, pillows, spread, and curtains contrasted with the room's walnut furniture, including the huge bed she shared with her grandmother.[12]

Fastidious in old age, Margaret Lewis wore a white lace cap with lavender bows to hide her balding crown when in the presence of company. Her steady

Margaret Davies Lewis, ca. 1890.

ways and precise rituals earned Mary's respect and affection: "Grandma smiled a lot but didn't talk much. I was very fond of her and tried to be good, but I knew she wasn't fond of children. She had raised a lot of her own and wasn't dotty about grandchildren." Because the household included Margaret Baxter's kindergarten, Mary was granted access to the school's dolls and its "wonderful" dollhouse, but with firm rules as to their use. She could move the dollhouse's furniture all she wanted but had to restore it to order when finished. Mary was permitted to dress and undress the "big doll that lay in a cradle" but could never "bring it out of the room without its clothes on." Again, she delighted in the structure imposed on her.[13]

This satisfying visit with her late mother's kinfolk put Mary in a happy frame of mind about meeting her new little brother. Doddy "had blue eyes like mine, but his hair was like light shining gold, and in lovely little curls." A pampered little boy from the beginning, Doddy was soon drinking from his own silver mug and eating with a silver spoon. His parents kept his hair long and his chubby little body in short pants until he was past the age of four.[14]

Jeannette May Jones Daniel and Doddy Daniel, ca. 1893.

Mary's memories of her maternal grandmother greatly contrasted with those of her paternal grandfather. Evan Daniel, the former blacksmith from Racine, was now an old man with piercing blue eyes and long gray beard. He lived with Roderick and Jeannette and their family for a few years prior to his death on 1 August 1895, when Mary was seven. The preceding summer, she and a friend had enjoyed building miniature towns out of discarded berry boxes: "Some we used whole for homes, schools, churches, and stores. Some we broke up into boards to make fences, walks, steps, and gates. . . . We liked to get a whole plan worked out and then hold it until the family came to admire it." But Grandpa Evan did not appreciate such activities. Whenever he came upon the girls at play, he would shoo them away, throw all their hard-gained materials in the trash, and smooth out the dirt so that no trace of the town remained.[15]

A gruff Old World grandpa, Evan would also hook her with his cane when she passed too near his rocking chair. "After his death," she wrote, "I had vivid nightmares about him in which he wagged that gray beard at me as if he knew I didn't miss him as I should." Looking back, she was unapologetic about her failure to miss him or her brother Mortimer, who had died two

Lillian Daniel, ca. 1897.

years earlier. Men dominated the Daniel household in ways she preferred to forget: "I could easily do without any of these superior beings whose only interest in me seemed to be to tease me and boss me and play tricks on me to show off their superior knowledge and strength."[16]

Mary's adolescent sisters, in contrast, modeled rituals and ideals of femininity. The need to be "dainty" required a "faint elusive fragrance," she wrote, which was achieved by placing scented sachets in bureau drawers and sewing them onto clothes hangers. Scented soaps, however, were considered vulgar: only Ivory would do. Dress shields for the underarms were standard. On hairwashing day, the Daniel women gathered and began by shaving Bocabelli castile soap (no other brand would do) into heated water and working it up into a "rich all-enveloping lather." One by one, each woman had her hair washed, her scalp massaged, and her hair rinsed three times. "Giggling and chatter" ensued as the women rolled each other's hair in curlers and applied "curling irons" and finally back-combed or ratted their tresses into the pompadours that were the height of fashion for Gay Nineties upper-middle-class ladies.[17]

Lillian Daniel excelled at such rituals. Considered the beauty of the family, she had "sparkling blue eyes," a creamy complexion, and long, wavy brown hair that she regularly fussed over. An intensely class-conscious young woman, Lillian followed her brothers' advice to eschew rouge and lipstick, the mark of a "lewd woman," and to confine perfume to her handkerchief lest someone assume she was covering up body odor. By age sixteen, she was "popular and gay," a modern young lady who played tennis, rode a bicycle, and loved to row and sail.[18]

Probably no family member frustrated Mary more than the sister nearest to her in age, Marge, and never more regularly than on Valentine's Day. Marge always "had to know how many valentines I got; . . . I couldn't keep my unpopularity to myself." In 1895, when she was seven and a half, she painstakingly made and distributed valentines among schoolmates but suffered "bitter disappointment" when she received only three in return, leading to her "first realization that the primary room of a public school is not what you could call a hot bed of rampant altruism." The heart-shaped valentine became a symbol for my grandmother's hungry heart. In her writings, she often returned to these painful memories of a sparsely filled valentine box, chronicling the humiliation she felt. And when she had her own children, she compared the number of valentines they received with the number they gave out, noting that they "never got back as many as they distributed."[19]

In June 1897, nine-year-old Mary was dazzled by Lillian's wedding to Horace Edsell Peck, a handsome, rising young businessman from an eminent family who had graduated from the University of Minnesota. In what appears to have been an effort to assure the Pecks that their son was not marrying down, the Daniels spared no expense in updating the Kenwood home. Running water, a new heating system, and a "real bathroom" with a modern toilet were installed. New hardwood floors were laid throughout the kitchen and dining areas, woodwork refurbished, floors varnished, and new curtains hung. The details of this high society event, published in the *Minneapolis Star Tribune*, included descriptions of Lillian's white satin dress, her huge bride's cake, ring bearer Doddy's lacy white suit with knee pants, the Mendelssohn wedding march played by Llew and Lewis on violins, and the huge, fragrant bouquets of American Beauty roses, lilies, and carnations that festooned the entire Daniel home.[20]

Doddy Daniel, ca. 1897.

Mary Daniel, ca. 1897.

Lillian's marriage connected the Daniels to prominent Republican families from Minnesota and Michigan. Her new husband's widowed father, Herbert N. Peck, was a successful "banker and capitalist" who traveled on business to Washington, D.C., and wintered in California. His mother, the late Sara Edsell Peck, was the daughter of Michigan state senator Wilson C. Edsell, a reformer as well as a banker. As Mrs. Horace E. Peck, Lillian's name now appeared regularly in the Minneapolis society pages. Like her aunts, Libby Ullmann and Anna Kimball, she had arrived.[21]

Two years later, on 9 August 1899, Lillian's sister-in-law, Alice Peck, had an even more elegant wedding when she married Bingley Russell Fales, a prominent Republican attorney well known for political speeches on hot-button currency issues. Despite the pedigreed sound of his name, Bingley Russell Fales was not to the manor born: he was the third of seven children of Loren C. Fales and Eliza Russell Fales of Ionia County, Michigan. After initially working as a farm laborer, Loren Fales had prospered as a farm owner following the Civil War, and by 1890, he and his two sons were active in the county's Republican politics.[22]

Prior to becoming a lawyer and trying his hand at business, Bingley had been an actor who appeared in productions at Detroit's Comedy Theater and elsewhere in the United States, including New York City. He had retired from the stage after wearying of the "nomadic life" and its "tinsel, shallow existence." When a reporter asked whether a true actor had to "live for his art," Bingley replied that most actors never achieved their "artistic ideals" because the pay was so bad: making ends meet required them to "fall from the exalted plane of the artist to the common highway of the artisan." And Bingley Fales had no desire to be a common artisan.[23]

When war broke out between the United States and Spain in 1898, Bingley enlisted in the Detroit Naval Reserves and fought on the USS *Yosemite* in the Battle of San Juan, Puerto Rico. Mustered out in August 1898, he and several other sailors were feted as heroes at Detroit's Cadillac Hotel. Employing popular imperialistic jingoism, Bingley insisted that "liberating" Cuba and the Philippines from Spain echoed the American Revolution, which had liberated his forebears from England. Two years later, however, while serving as Detroit's assistant prosecuting attorney and secretary of the Michigan League of Republican Clubs, Bingley spoke before the Frederick Douglass League and belittled the Filipino guerrillas fighting for their country's independence as "not animated by anything" approaching the American colonists' "Spirit of '76." In the wake of the Spanish-American War, the United States revealed its more modern spirit by occupying the Philippines and annexing Cuba. And in heralding the Republican Party's shift away from racial justice and toward imperialistic ventures on behalf of big business, Bingley dishonored the Black abolitionist for whom the league was named.[24]

On 15 May 1900, Bingley was elected to the board of the Detroit Naval Reserves, a position he used to attack the Naval Awards Board for having failed to award medals to the *Yosemite*'s crew. The matter was submitted to President Theodore Roosevelt for review, and by 1902, Bingley and his shipmates had their medals.[25]

It is likely that Alice and Bingley met while Alice was visiting Kalamazoo, home of her aunt Frances Peck Burrows, who was married to Michigan senator Julius Caesar Burrows, and Alice attended a Detroit event at which Bingley was present. The *Star Tribune* hailed the wedding as one of Minneapolis's "principal matrimonial events of August" and provided copious details, not only listing the guests but describing the intricate displays of flowers, ferns, palms, ribbons, and vases that adorned Herbert Peck's Hawthorn Avenue mansion.[26]

A week of parties and receptions attended by many of their illustrious out-of-town relatives preceded the Peck-Fales wedding. When the big day finally arrived, the bride entered the family drawing room at the appointed moment, cued by the appropriate music and preceded by her father and her maid—yes, her maid—perhaps standing in for Sara Peck. Alice wore a "heavy white satin" gown and carried a bouquet of American Beauty roses. Her sister Georgia, a graduate of the Lasell Seminary for Young Women near Boston, made a lovely bridesmaid, decked out in pink silk crepe adorned by silk roses. The *Star Tribune* did not describe the groom's appearance, instead noting that he was assistant district attorney for Wayne County and a popular and "active" clubman who had attended multiple "farewell dinners" with bachelor friends before arriving in Minneapolis. Large portraits of Bingley and Alice appeared side-by-side on the newspaper's society page as testimony to their exalted social status.[27]

Bingley's professional accomplishments also received extensive press coverage. In 1899, the *Detroit Free Press* splashed his dramatic courtroom prosecution of a man who had murdered his wife across its pages. And nearly four decades later, critic Virginia W. V. Shaw cited Bingley as an actor "so outstanding" that his work compared favorably with that of "leading professionals" of the 1930s.[28]

Alice had attended Carleton College in Northfield, Minnesota, but chose to marry rather than complete her degree. Marriage to Detroit's most eligible bachelor promised a more secure future than did a college degree and brought the added benefits of an exciting social life and high status. Like Mary's Lewis aunts, the Peck women had a tradition of marrying well. Alice and Bingley immediately settled in Detroit and soon began vacationing with the Burrowses as well as with her cousin Luella Peck Wadsworth, who was married to Detroit millionaire Frederick Elliot Wadsworth.[29]

The union of the Daniel and Peck/Fales family networks contributed mightily to Mary's disdain for the greed and snobbery she witnessed among her wealthy kinfolks. But Roderick's opinion of Lillian's marriage into a relentlessly wealth-seeking family is not known. He might well have found it distasteful: as a young man, he had disdained obsessions with wealth, and he later ridiculed the pretensions of his nouveau riche neighbors. And as his second wife, he chose an educated and intellectual woman. Rather than emulating her stepmother Jeannette's achievements, however, Lillian followed the model set by her maternal aunts and married a rich man.[30]

Mary was initially fond of Horace Peck, who shared her interest in drawing and painting. Once, when she fell sick, he gifted her art supplies and fresh fruit, a kindness that made her feel as though he enjoyed her company, something for which she desperately yearned. But Mary's feelings about Horace, who was no less materialistic and self-indulgent than his brother-in-law Bingley, changed over time. As a wealthy white male, Horace was free to develop his creative abilities as he pleased and with confidence in finding a venue to display his work. He became an accomplished photographer of wildlife and rural sports whose work was featured in various publications.[31]

Like President Roosevelt, Horace saw no contradiction between promoting the phenomenal growth of towns and cities while advocating the preservation of natural flora and wildlife habitats. Horace the sportsman celebrated the rugged natural beauty of the great Northwest, while Horace the businessman became rich through real estate deals that promoted the rapid economic development of wilderness areas. One fed his spirit; the other, his pocketbook.[32]

Despite their wealth and status, the Pecks and the Fales endured their share of misery and tragedy. About six months after Alice and Bingley's wedding, Alice's sister Georgia was crossing a busy street in downtown Detroit when a bicycle messenger hit her and knocked her unconscious. After lingering for twenty days and only briefly regaining consciousness, Georgia died on 2 March 1900. Announcing her death, the *Detroit Free Press* observed that "all the advantages that money and social position could attain were Miss Peck's" and that she was a talented musician whose travels in Europe and beyond had made her a "charming conversationalist." But those qualities could not prevent the Grim Reaper from claiming her.[33]

Such incidents were so common in congested turn-of-the-century American cities that bicycle messengers were nicknamed scorchers, and they constituted but one of the many dangers that accompanied urbanization. At the same time, the rise of cities was a vital component of the economic growth that catapulted families such as the Pecks and Fales to new heights of wealth. Grief stricken but undaunted, they continued to invest in America's growth. By 1905, Alice and two other investors joined her father and brother to incorporate the Trustee Loan Company of Minneapolis. The new century had just begun.

My use of the phrase *family dynasty* in this chapter's title is partly—but only partly—tongue-in-cheek. By the end of the nineteenth century, the Lewises and Daniels had worked their way up from immigrant artisans to middle- or upper-class professional status. For some, that upward mobility exceeded their wildest dreams. Talent, education, entrepreneurial ambitions, and fortunate marriages amid the Industrial Revolution all contributed to their elevation. As the twentieth century opened, some viewed themselves as a version of European royalty and eagerly acted the part. But not Mary. Despite being born to a life of status and privilege among a wide network of kin, she struggled with loneliness and alienation throughout her childhood.

4

The Misfit and the Millionaires

I had no place to go but where they sent me,
nothing to do but to earn my living the way they decreed,
however terrifying and distasteful it was to me.
—MARY DANIEL HUCKENPOEHLER, "Notes on My Life"

My grandmother's memoir reveals painful snapshots of an awkward adolescence. In 1900, at age twelve, she balked at her older sisters' insistence that she learn the social graces of her class. Fashionable Lillian, who lived with her husband, Horace Edsell Peck, in his financier father's luxurious Hawthorn Avenue mansion, and ostentatious Margaret (Marge) Daniel, who was teaching voice after studying under brilliant German singer and conductor Anna Schoen-René, were determined to refine their tall, ungainly, and self-conscious sister. First, they enrolled Mary in a dancing class, but her height discouraged boys from asking her to dance. Next, Marge proposed giving Mary private singing lessons. Forced regularly to watch Marge perform maudlin ballads such as "Fair Jessie," a Victorian dirge about a jilted young woman's suicide, Mary recoiled in horror. Writing in her memoir years later, she noted, "To this day, nothing irks me more than a high female voice lifted in solitary song. Whenever such a thing invades the radio, I rejoice in my privilege of changing to another program."[1]

Marge Daniel, ca. 1900.

Cultivating feminine charms was not for Mary. By age thirteen, she preferred outdoor sports over singing and dancing. In 1900, she repeatedly
begged the family for new skates for Christmas. Instead she received perfume, jewelry, candy, and books. Mary let loose with a tantrum of monstrous
proportions in response to what she saw as proof that her family cared only
about molding her into a proper Daniel lady: "When I opened a little jewelry
box and found a little gold and enamel sweetheart pin," she remembered, "I
was suddenly overpoweringly angry. . . . I quite lost my temper, shattering
the beautiful Christmas atmosphere with angry words, throwing the pin
across the room without a thank you." She then burst into tears and sulked
for the rest of the day.[2]

This was Mary as she approached adulthood: adventurous, intellectual,
and creative but also angry and alienated. Soon she committed her first overt
act of rebellion against her family's traditions. At age fourteen, she left the
Congregationalist church attended by the Daniels and joined the Westminster

Presbyterian church attended by her neighbors. There were no earthshaking differences between the two denominations, but Mary accomplished her goal of vexing the family. And she had set the scene for rebellions yet to come.

For now, no one took Mary too seriously. The family likely was more focused on Mary's eldest sibling, Llew, who had an identity crisis of sorts around the same time. An electrical engineer who still lived at home at age thirty, Llew headed to the Far West around 1899 and then wandered for more than a year. According to Mary, "He took his violin and said in letters that when he couldn't find congenial work, he put on a violin concert and passed the hat for fair [fare] to the next place." Traveling back toward Minnesota, Llew briefly settled in Custer County, Nebraska, where, on New Year's Day 1901, he married nineteen-year-old Margaret (Daisy) Grimes, a music teacher from the railroad village of Calloway. His wandering days over, Llew brought Daisy back to Minneapolis, where the two lived at Kenwood before seeking a home of their own.[3]

The family no doubt hoped that Mary, too, would find a suitable marriage partner—perhaps, like Lillian, a wealthy one—and settle down. Horace and Lillian Peck enjoyed a high-stepping lifestyle after moving into the Hawthorn Avenue mansion, one of at least three homes maintained by Herbert Peck. Automobiles were a particular passion of young and stylish Horace, who relished zipping around the countryside in his Apperson Jackrabbit, an expensive new model advertised as suitable for racing as well as touring. He was the quintessential outdoorsman, an avid big-game hunter renowned as a crack shot for his winning performances at shooting events. Not surprisingly, he was proficient on the golf course and on tennis courts as well.[4]

Around 1901, Horace and Herbert became enamored of the small, recently incorporated town of Kenmare, North Dakota, heavily promoted as a mecca for land-hungry farmers, merchants, and investors. Located about sixty miles northwest of Minot, near the Soo Line railroad, Kenmare was one of many "planned" western towns where, thanks to technology and railroads, goods were now mass-produced and swiftly transported to distant markets in eastern states and abroad. The town provided the perfect opportunity for Horace to combine his creative talents with a career in finance. Proficient with a camera as well as a gun, he snapped photos of hunters enjoying the rugged life amid Kenmare's pristine wilderness for publication in the *Minneapolis Journal* on 14 December 1901. His photos featured only one woman: the "Mistress" of a "Pretty Cabin on the Mouse River." The image featured a woman standing next to a small, windowless wooden cabin that presumably was all hers to tend while her husband enjoyed outdoor adventures. Women were welcome in Kenmare, but boosters pitched their ads at men who were bored with the city and seeking manly pursuits.[5]

Horace's wife would have had no interest in posing beside a "pretty cabin," much less living the rude, simple life of the "Mistress." In December 1901, Lillian Peck was focused on impending motherhood. At Christmas in the Peck mansion, she excitedly displayed her cache of "beautiful lace-trimmed" baby clothes to her sister Marge and stepmother Jeannette while Mary peeked in from the doorway. On 5 February 1902, she gave birth to the couple's only child, Roderick Daniel Peck.[6]

The new baby did not deter Horace's investment plans. He and his father decided to broker land sales to enterprising farmers by setting up shop in Kenmare. In 1902, Horace placed several newspaper ads offering to sell his four-seat steam automobile since he would soon be "leaving the city." A year later, the *Minneapolis Star Tribune* featured a full-page article extolling investment opportunities in Kenmare, where coal mining, cattle raising, dairying, and diversified farming promised great financial returns. In typical booster language, readers were assured that "all have prospered amazingly and are of one accord: that there is no place on earth like Kenmare." Accompanied by photographs and statistics, the article ended with a laudatory poem by "authoress" Mrs. Phillip Hess, who dubbed Kenmare the "Beauty Queen" of North Dakota towns.[7]

Such rhapsodizing glossed over three decades of political battles waged throughout the Northwest and Southwest over post–Civil War development and industrialization. Organized protests against railroad companies and out-of-state corporations and investment capitalists had raged since the 1870s, led first by the Farmers' Alliance and then by the People's Party. Efforts to build, buy, or lease facilities where farmers could store their products to await better market prices continued even after the demise of the People's Party. Another agricultural co-op and political organization, the American Society of Equity, founded in Indianapolis in 1902, came to North Dakota in 1907, with the group's national director, M. O. Hall, declaring, "Why, even President [Theodore] Roosevelt says, 'Organization is no less necessary for the farmer than all other classes of people.'"[8]

Horace seemed unfazed by the state's political turmoil. Shortly after Rod's birth, he moved to Kenmare, expecting Lillian and the boy to follow a year or two later. But although the Pecks officially lived in Kenmare for a decade, they also maintained an apartment on Dupont Avenue South in Minneapolis, and Lillian and Rod spent time there. Herbert Peck too lived in North Dakota for only part of the year, continuing to winter in California and maintaining Minneapolis as his home base.[9]

The promise of rich returns on the Pecks' investments was seductive, and by 1903, the banks were ready for the flow of cash. Herbert and five co-investors founded the First National Bank of Mohall, about thirty miles east of Kenmare. The elder Peck also founded the State Loan Company of Kenmare, naming himself president and Horace treasurer. Within a few years, Horace had moved up to vice president of both First National and State Loan. His profession of photo paper manufacturer took a back seat to his new profession of banking.[10]

On 20 February 1903, Lillian hosted her last elegant tea and buffet at the Hawthorn Avenue mansion, which Herbert had divided into apartments to be rented out. Horace explained his wife and son's continued residence in Minneapolis as necessary for little Rod's education, but Lillian apparently remained in Minneapolis even when school was not in session: Mary recalled spending the summers of 1910 and 1911 with them on Dupont Avenue.[11]

Kenmare provided Horace with a playground as well as with invest-ment profits. On a fine spring day in 1909, he and another photographer loaded their hunting supplies, toolboxes, and camping gear into Horace's Jackrabbit and headed west from Minneapolis to Kenmare, nine hundred miles away. The press was conveniently on hand to record their departure. Leaving behind their wives and children, the men, dressed in stylish but comfortable "leather clothing and appropriate hats and gloves," had "every appurtenance necessary to a little roughing along the roads through North Dakota." "Fast time" would be made with experienced "speed merchant" Horace behind the wheel.[12]

Within a few years, Horace was participating in shooting tournaments throughout North Dakota, where he was a great favorite among the "ladies," who "were pulling for Peck from Kenmare and appreciated his consistent shooting." He also frequently went on hunting and fishing expeditions, including a two-month junket in 1915 to Alaska and British Columbia to hunt bear and fish for king salmon along the Stikine River.[13]

Horace's talents and economic success earned him the titles of King of Finance and Millionaire of Kenmare. His reputation as one of North Dakota's leading sportsmen was exemplified by the hypermasculine refuge he called home. The walls of his dining room were decorated with two thousand mounted birds, while another room featured his photos of game and birds. Throughout the house, mounted heads of grizzly bears, mountain goats, and other wild game greeted visitors, including Lillian and Rod whenever they took the train from Minneapolis.[14]

The Pecks' lifestyle reflected the excesses of wealth and privilege among America's nouveau riche. Pleasures were bought, flamboyant personalities rewarded, and a reckless sense of invincibility encouraged. During the same years when Horace established himself as a stylish, freewheeling investor in the promising boom town of Kenmare, his sister Alice established herself in Detroit as the socialite wife of the successful and self-satisfied Bingley Fales, who once publicly bragged of stiffing a New York waiter as punishment for his "surly and inattentive" attitude. The successes of the former lawyer, stage actor, and "hero" of the Spanish-American War, now an inventor and business entrepreneur, seemed limitless.[15]

Soon after Bingley and Alice married, Bingley entered the world of utilities, where he led the way in developing a citywide steam-heating plant. In 1903, as assistant manager of Edison Illuminating Company, he founded the Central Heating Company (CHC) with help from none other than Herbert Peck, always ready to invest with younger kinfolk. While Herbert and Horace established themselves as financial brokers in Kenmare, Herbert assisted Bingley in becoming the wonder boy of Detroit. "If the Panama Canal commissioner would pave the zone with asphalt," quipped the *Detroit Free Press,* "it could get Bingley Fales to do the rest!"[16]

Corporate consolidation of banks, businesses, and privately funded public utilities swept the United States in the first decade of the twentieth century, transforming physical and financial landscapes in and around Detroit and other cities. Investment capitalists like Herbert, Horace, and Bingley were lifted to new heights of wealth. By March 1905, Detroit and several other American cities had awarded franchises to Bingley's CHC. In 1906, the company's entire $120,000 stock was sold to the Edison Illuminating Company. Edison's spokesman, Alex Dow, shamelessly "dreamed" that the company would extend its "chain of electric power and light" throughout the "whole of the Huron Valley reaching to Lake Huron and possibly to Toledo." At the center of the valley's transformation stood Bingley Fales, a "man of marked ability," whose CHC investors stood to gain substantial returns on their investment.[17]

The following year, Bingley commissioned the building of a 2,724-square-foot neo-Georgian mansion for his growing family, which already included five-year-old Georgianna and three-year-old Herbert. Designed by Chittenden & Kotting and located in Detroit's posh new Indian Village subdivision, the Bingley Fales House, as it is still known today, was erected at 375 Seminole Street, just four minutes from downtown Detroit. Renowned architects designed the homes in Indian Village, the first of which was built in 1895. By the 1920s, seventeen different architectural styles were represented.[18]

I doubt that Mary knew much about the Fales branch of the Peck family. They lived in far-off Detroit, and she likely saw them only at weddings and holiday gatherings. By contrast, she was deeply enmeshed in the lives of her sister Lillian and Horace, who frequently employed her as a nursemaid for Rod. Lillian treated Mary with sisterly condescension while exploiting her services, paying her a mere quarter a week during the summer, although she slept at the Pecks' home to tend Rod in the middle of the night. Still, Mary "loved it because I loved Roderick."[19]

Working for Horace and Lillian changed her feelings for them, however. One night while Rod was asleep in bed, she accidentally locked herself out of the house and was forced to wait on the porch until they returned home. When they did so, they berated Mary endlessly for her carelessness, with Lillian declaring that someone so stupid was surely headed toward a disastrous future. She soon began escaping by taking hours-long bicycle rides, enjoying "the sense of freedom and power that bike gave me."[20]

Mary found her classroom experiences both exciting and at times difficult. She had to repeat algebra and German, but she excelled in medieval history, civics, and English. History was "like reading a stirring, continuing true story," she wrote. In civics class, her intellectual abilities shone so brightly that her (male) teacher commented that "for a girl, I showed a remarkable grasp of the subject." Mary accepted this "very doubtful compliment" but found her true calling in her English class. "I could think with a pen better than I could orally, so I wrote compositions and read Dickens on the long streetcar rides to and from school." "In time," she wrote, "I began to fancy myself as a budding authoress and filled whole pencil tablets with novels about things of which I had no firsthand knowledge." Just for pure fun, she added a drawing class to her busy schedule.[21]

School events enabled Mary to form close friendships that further countered her alienation from her siblings. In 1902, her high school German class hosted a Christmas party that featured food, singing, and good cheer. Afterward, she recalled, "I could hardly sleep. . . . I don't believe I've ever had such a completely jolly and unspoiled evening of fun in all my life since that night." She developed a mild crush on Gordon Bohmbach, a fellow student who shared her love of drawing, but as a working-class boy with neither time nor money for extracurricular activities, and so the two never socialized beyond the noon hour between classes. Still their friendship "lent a sort of glamour to that year in school," and Gordon appears to have shared many traits—among them class background and German ancestry—with Mary's future husband, William B. Huckenpoehler.[22]

During these years, Roderick Daniel's declining health allowed him and his youngest daughter to grow closer to each other. Around 1902, Roderick suffered the first of several strokes, collapsing on the street and being taken to the hospital in an ambulance. As his health deteriorated, Mary accompanied him on long walks during which he talked about his Civil War experiences and his courtship of Mary Ellen Lewis. These conversations enabled Mary to feel a connection to the mother she had never known.[23] But Roderick's illness "changed his personality so much" that the family "couldn't have any social life at all" from the time Mary was fifteen until she was twenty-one. He died on 17 October 1908.[24]

Roderick suffered from high blood pressure and congested arteries, an early victim of the dramatic increase in heart-related deaths in modern America. He survived his father, Evan, by only thirteen years and Margaret Lewis, the mother of his first wife, by a mere five. Sometime between 1897 and 1902, Roderick lost the mortgage on Kenwood, and the Daniels became renters of the house. If Mary knew why the family's circumstances had become so reduced, she never wrote about it.[25]

Roderick's death instantly raised questions about the future of Kenwood's household. In addition to Jeannette and her unmarried brother, Dr. Herbert W. Jones, its members included Mary and her half-brother Donald (Doddy), now sixteen, who planned to enter medical school at the University of Minnesota after graduating from high school. Marge, who had recently returned from Madison, Wisconsin, to teach at the Johnson School of Music, was also back living at Kenwood. Should they continue to live there as renters? That problem was solved when Herb proposed marriage to Marge, and she accepted. Herb immediately purchased the home, and they and their family continued living at Kenwood. Though the marriage resolved one issue, it created some awkwardness. Because Jeannette was now Marge's sister-in-law as well as her stepmother, Marge objected when Mary called Jeannette "Mama" in front of guests.[26]

Now a widow with grown stepchildren and her son about to enter college, Jeannette considered moving to her own apartment and accepting an offer of what Mary remembered as "a good management job." Herb and Marge convinced Jeannette to stay on at Kenwood as the family's household manager, which Mary interpreted as a glorified housekeeping and future child-care position, and Mary surmised that Jeannette would have been happier with a salaried position and her own apartment.[27]

The family then gathered to address the future of twenty-one-year-old Mary, whose dreams of one day becoming a professional artist or a novelist who lived in a book-filled loft were quickly dashed. Her siblings dismissed drawing and writing as impractical careers, particularly for women, though they agreed she needed a profession, especially since she had no discernable prospects for marriage. And so began the process of elimination. Voice lessons had already been ruled out, and working as a "beauty operator" (beautician) or in one of the burgeoning department stores was out of the question because such positions were too much like being a servant. Mary realized that she was being pushed toward a career as an educator, and before the year ended, she was enrolled at Minnesota's Winona Normal School to receive training as a kindergarten teacher. Horace and Lillian assumed the costs of her education in return for her continued care of Rod during summer breaks.[28]

Mary enjoyed her time at Winona Normal and later appreciated that attending college away from home stimulated her intellect and enabled her to develop the confidence and social skills that she had lacked throughout her childhood and to make friends outside her Minneapolis family circle. Nevertheless, for a young woman brimming with artistic talent and a desire to learn creative writing, teachers college seemed like a curse. Unlike her brother-in-law Horace, the talents with which Mary had been gifted would remain mere hobbies. She would never forgive society—or her family—for dictating her options, and she viewed that family meeting as the "funeral" for her "feeling of belonging to the family."[29]

Ironically, two years later, when Mary was graduating from Winona Normal, a professor advised her that teaching was not really her calling and suggested that she take some advanced drawing classes and pursue a career in commercial art. Though the holders of the purse strings had given her

Mary Daniel at the time of her graduation from Winona Normal School, 1911.

no choice in the matter, Mary blamed her situation on herself as much as anyone. If she had been a "genius," she would have "gone office-scrubbing at night and spent four hours a day studying art and writing 'pot boilers' in the days till I popped up famous one day. But what I had was just a talent, not backed up by the depth of intelligence nor the boundless vitality that accompanies true genius."[30]

Immediately after her June 1910 graduation, Mary spent a week with the family of one of her new friends, Lucy Clark, who lived about two hundred miles west of Winona in Lamberton, Minnesota. Mary adored the small-town, middle-class normalcy of the Clarks, labeling them "one of the finest families in America." Lucy's dad was a hardworking "hardware man" whose family enjoyed the simple pleasures of fixing breakfast together and picking berries on a cousin's farm. Laughter came easily and often. Mary spent the final day of her visit making ice cream with the family for the local Presbyterian ice cream social. Then it was back to Lillian and Horace's home for what proved to be another long summer during which, as usual, she felt that she was in the way.[31]

In the fall of 1911, Mary began her first teaching job in Morgan, Minnesota. Teaching provided her with another growth experience, but it was not a positive one. The contrast between attending college in Winona and teaching grade-school children in the grim town of Morgan, where "spiritually small" and "spiteful" townsfolk gossiped endlessly about the young schoolteachers, was all too stark. Combined with unsatisfying visits to Minneapolis, the experience left Mary feeling even more hopeless about her future. To make things worse, she began 1912 strapped for money after buying new clothes for a round of Minneapolis soirees she felt obliged to attend over the holidays.[32]

Nearly a year later, she remained dispirited. As usual, she traveled to Minneapolis to spend the holidays with her Daniel, Jones, and Peck relatives, celebrating Christmas Day at the Hawthorn Avenue mansion, which Herbert Peck had reclaimed from renters. Mary, who reverentially called Herbert Father Peck, described the evening as her "first formal dinner," though meal-times at Kenwood could hardly have been considered informal. The "splen-dor" of the Peck home and the "multitude of silver pieces" that adorned the table overwhelmed her. She felt like "a poor small town school ma'am with a very small purse and few presentable clothes and no poise to speak of and no conversational ability."[33]

As Rod's caretaker, Mary had not expected to join the adults in the big din-ing room, but Father Peck insisted. Forced to sit among her stately and proper relatives, Mary found the occasion particularly excruciating and resolved to avoid Minneapolis altogether during future holiday seasons.[34]

Mary's alienation from her family and her distance from the Faleses in Detroit may explain the fact that her memoir includes no mention of Bingley Fales's illness beginning in February 1909, when he suffered a nervous break-down. The incident was reported prominently in the *Detroit Free Press*, which cited overwork as the cause and noted that his health had been failing for "weeks" and that his family had committed him to the Oak Grove Sanitarium near Flint, Michigan, "one of the classiest mental hospitals around."[35] But if Bingley's health was a topic of whispers or open discussion at one of the Minneapolis Christmas dinners, Mary chose not to write about it.

Bingley's mental state may have been declining for more than a year prior to his breakdown. For the first eight years of their marriage, Bingley and Alice Fales were prominent in the Detroit newspapers, which reported on their expensive vacations (including a 1907 visit to the eastern resort town of Atlantic City, New Jersey, with Julius and Frances Burrows and Frederick and Luella Wadsworth) and other social doings. But Bingley had only two public engagements in 1808 (an "informal talk" before the Detroit newsboys' weekly meeting at Association Hall and a speech before the Sons of the American Revolution), and the society pages featured no gala Christmas events at the Faleses' grand new mansion.[36]

Economic problems and public embarrassment may have played a major role in Bingley's mental breakdown. He and Alice had contracted to build their mansion in 1907, during one of the nation's worst economic panics, and at around the same time that newspapers began to report on the Edison Company's economic shenanigans. On 7 April 1908, the Detroit City Council confronted Bingley over the CHC's failure to lower the city's heating costs, citing an increase of $179.35 in the public library's heating bill. When alderman Otto C. Goeschel, a fierce critic of the power and profits enjoyed by Detroit's business class at the expense of ordinary people, ridiculed Bingley's attempt to account for the increase by using terms such as *thermesthesiometer* and *thermic conductivity*, he responded with uncharacteristic meekness, pledging his "willingness to reduce" heating costs "in keeping with what is right."[37]

There is no way to know whether Bingley's ailments resulted from stress and pressure, from genetic factors, from early onset dementia or Alzheimer's disease, or from a combination of some or all of those causes. He spent twenty-eight months at Oak Grove, but his condition continued to decline despite the luxurious surroundings and the care of his personal doctor, and on 20 October 1911 he was transferred to Kalamazoo State Hospital, Michigan's largest mental institution, where he remained until his death on 11 February 1913. His death certificate merely gave "organic brain disease" as the cause.[38]

In November 1909, less than a year after Bingley's collapse, his father, Loren Fales, suffered a fatal stroke. In light of Loren's death and Bingley's institutionalization, Herbert Peck moved quickly to protect his daughter and grandchildren's future by putting the Faleses' Indian Village mansion on the market, where it sold for $35,000 (equivalent to more than $1 million today). A few years later, Herbert also sold the Hawthorn Avenue mansion in Minneapolis.[39]

Mary's memoir noted Bingley's death but not its details. During this period, she was far more interested in Horace Peck's Kenmare adventure and her efforts to find a teaching position in the wake of the news that she and her Morgan colleagues would not be rehired for the fall of 1912, a development that made her feel both insulted as well as relieved to escape such an unsatisfying position in a provincial town. Horace, Lillian, and Rod spent the summer shuttling between Minneapolis and Kenmare, and Rod invited her to accompany him and his mother by train to Kenmare, where Horace awaited their arrival. She was delighted to take an unexpected trip to a new place.[40]

She was not impressed. "Kenmare," Mary wrote, "was set in rolling prairie country where, when the wind blew—and the wind always blew—the tall grass looked just like green billowy waves perpetually rolling eastward." There were but few amusements. A nearby creamery that sold jugs of buttermilk and the sounds of laughter in the night emanating from a house of prostitution "up on the horizon" provided the main entertainment. One afternoon, Horace piled everyone into his Apperson Jackrabbit and away they went, deep down into the prairie's "billowing waves," where Horace demonstrated his prowess by killing a few prairie chickens and roasting them on a long fork over a campfire made from buffalo chips and sagebrush—roughing it in the wilderness with the Millionaire of Kenmare.[41]

The sojourn in Kenmare was likely the last time Mary spent extended time with the Peck family. When she returned to Minneapolis, she learned of a teaching position in nearby Waconia, a rural community made up largely of second- and third-generation German, Bohemian, Swedish, and Swiss immigrants. Located thirty-five miles west of Minneapolis, the summer resort town featured beautiful Lake Waconia for rest and recreation. Here, female teachers attended dances and were expected to be "lively and sociable"—and of course to avoid the numerous saloons that served fun-loving tourists. Waconia seemed pretty appealing to Mary after a year in Morgan and among her Minneapolis relatives. She applied for the position, was hired, and moved there in the fall of 1913. Suddenly, life was once again interesting.[42]

In Mary's absence, the Peck family continued to experience drama. In March 1912, Horace had made the North Dakota newspapers for opposing a law that devoted a portion of the state's real estate taxes to furnishing seed grain for needy farmers. Horace believed the law unconstitutional and threatened to challenge it in court. He did not follow through on the threat, but the following year he sued Albert Gardner, an indigent farmer who defaulted on a land loan from Horace's bank.[43]

Horace was furious that Gardner had declined the opportunity to lease the land back from the bank. Instead, he attempted to haul his "shack" back to his wife's land, where the structure had originally stood. Horace then sued Gardner for grand larceny in the amount of $150, even though the house was assessed at only $20. Gardner entered onto the property to reclaim his house, and each time, Horace had him arrested for trespassing. Even after Ward County jurors ruled in Gardner's favor, Horace denied the man his home yet again.[44]

Gardner then countersued Horace for $20,000 for "malicious prosecution." Horace then bolted with a friend to Canada to hunt mountain sheep and goats. When he returned, the "prominent banker" and "sportsman" soon settled back into his usual lifestyle of work and pleasure. But the press was no longer so enamored of him, and regarding the eight head of game, suitable for mounting, that he and his friend had bagged in Canada, the *Bowbells Tribune* noted sarcastically that game was "now so scarce, travelers are forced to visit the very highest points in mountains for a shot."[45]

The battle between the millionaire banker and the lowly farmer symbolized North Dakota's long-standing political split over its economic future, and Horace must have been further angered in 1915 when North Dakota Socialists founded the Nonpartisan League (NPL) to unite Progressives, reformers, and radicals around cooperative, anticapitalist commonwealth principles. "If the 'local' businessman is to have the hearty cooperation of the farmer," editorialized the *Fargo Nonpartisan Leader* on 2 December 1915, "he must get on common grounds with him. He must sympathize with him in his fights for better marketing conditions, cleaner politics, and more just treatment." Between 1916 and 1918, the NPL dominated the state's Republican Party, which passed bills expanding public education and health care programs while regulating corporations. By 1921, however, North Dakota's engine of progressivism had sputtered thanks to attacks on its loyalty to the United States in World War I.[46]

Horace witnessed little of the NPL's rise and fall before his death on a hot August day in 1916. Although he had not felt well while camping with friends at Lake Metigoshe in the Turtle Mountains, he volunteered to drive a group of women back to Kenmare in his Packard Six touring car. While cruising west, Horace suddenly turned the steering wheel over to the woman seated next to him and keeled over, dead of a heart attack at age forty-three.[47]

Lillian had been visiting family in Michigan and rushed back to Minneapolis and then on to North Dakota. The intrepid paternalist Herbert N. Peck was soon at her side, accompanying her to court to settle Horace's estate and arranging to have Horace's body transported by train to Minneapolis for burial. For a third time, Herbert had invested in business ventures with young family members only to preside over their deaths. The members of the Peck family might be fabulously wealthy, but their riches did not insulate them from personal tragedy. Mary, busy with her new life in Waconia, learned of her uncle's death in a letter from Jeannette, who reported that Herbert had assured Lillian that Rod "was to go right on with his present education." Father Peck would look out for Lillian and Rod, just as he did for his Fales grandchildren.[48]

Shortly after Bingley's death, Alice took Georgianna and Herbert and moved to Pasadena, California, where in April 1918 she married Charles Lovel Wright, an officer of the National Security Bank who was "well known in the banking world of Southern California." Herbert Peck stood alongside his daughter and beamed, no doubt delighted to know that a rich stepfather would provide for his grandchildren. With that worry removed from his mind, he died at age seventy-two on 7 February 1920.[49]

Alice's move to California was not the first time the state had beckoned Mary's kinfolk. Beginning around 1870, the state's southern half became a magnet for the wealthy as palatial homes and expensive resorts sprang up amid a mania of building and advertising. The climate attracted those suffering from a variety of maladies, among them arthritis, tuberculosis, nervous disorders, and plain old age, and around 1906, Dr. Thomas Willett Bishop began operating the Pasadena Sanitarium for Nervous and Mental Diseases in the Oneonta Park area of South Pasadena. According to a 1909 advertisement, the "beautifully located" Bishop Sanitarium offered a "home like private retreat" that housed patients in small cottages on a thirty-acre spread. [50]

Mary's aunt Libby Ullmann was also a regular visitor to Pasadena. If, as Mary contended, Libby's daughter Bessie had suffered a nervous breakdown, at least some of these trips may have involved treatment for her. In the winter of 1927, Libby, Bessie, and another daughter, Daisy, were vacationing at a hotel near the new theater in the Playhouse Village District, when fifty-one-year-old Bessie collapsed and died of heart failure.[51]

Fifteen years later, Libby's son Fred also died suddenly while on vacation in California, one of a number of Mary's well-to-do relatives—most of them men—who succumbed to heart attacks and strokes at relatively young ages. The benefits of wealth, including restful trips to exotic locations, apparently were not enough to counteract the stress of their personal and professional lives and their rich, heart-clogging diets.[52] The women of the family, however, generally fared much better. Lillian Daniel Peck lived to age 78; Anna Lewis Kimball to 80; Libby Lewis Ullmann and Jeannette Jones Daniel to 82; Esther Martindale Daniel (wife of Lewis Daniel) to 89; Marge Daniel Jones to 91; Agnes Lewis Bennett to 95; and Daisy Grimes Daniel to 105. Mary herself lived to be 91.

Among the men in Mary's family, Tom Daniel, the only sibling and long-time business partner of her father, was an exception. Perhaps prompted by Roderick's health issues, Tom moved to Southern California in 1908, trading the rat race of insurance work for retirement with his wife, Mary, in Pasadena until his death in 1926.[53]

In the four years after Uncle Tom's passing, Mary's two longest-living aunts followed him—Anna Kimball in Fond du Lac, Wisconsin, in 1929 and Libby Ullmann in Winnetka, Illinois, less than a year later. A decade after she had removed herself from the nexus of her Daniel-Lewis kinfolk, Mary seemed barely to notice that her parents' generation was gone. Although only thirty-five miles separated Waconia and Minneapolis, the unfolding of Mary's life, first as a small-town schoolteacher, then as a wife and mother in a small German American community, made the distance seem more like a thousand miles. In 1912, young Mary Daniel eagerly began the process of changing her address, religion, social circle, and name. Her 1918 marriage to William B. Huckenpoehler completed the transformation.

PART II

Mary and Harrigan

5

Mary's Great Rebellion

The whole family took turns telling me how wrong it was, that he
just wouldn't fit into the family circle. But I had never fit into the
family circle myself so I couldn't feel the force of that argument.
—MARY DANIEL HUCKENPOEHLER, "Notes on My Life"

In September 1913, at a dance held at the Carver County Fair in Waconia, Mary
Daniel caught the eye a man who introduced himself as Bill Harrigan. He asked
Mary to dance, she accepted, and he twirled her on the floor all evening long.
Naive and unused to male attention, Mary was flattered by the attentions of this
"smooth," popular dancer whose nickname led her to assume that he was Irish.[1]

As Mary had been promised, the townsfolk of Waconia expected their
young female teachers to be lively and sociable. She was happy about the
prospects of a vibrant social life though initially less-than-impressed by her
surroundings: the county fair seemed wanting in comparison to the Barnum
and Bailey circuses of her urban childhood. The dance was another story
entirely, and although she was a bit overwhelmed by Harrigan's attentions, she
welcomed the excitement and the flattery. She soon came to love Waconia.[2]

In addition to her new social life, Mary enjoyed the intellectual compan-
ionship of Alice, Lydia, and Amanda Tester, sisters who managed the North
Star Hotel where she boarded. Expressing the sort of admiration she normally

reserved for her stepmother, Jeannette, and a few college roommates, she praised the sisters for placing intellect and curiosity over beauty and decorum: "They all had the good looks that spring from that look of aliveness and intelligent interest in the world around them, a sort of outgoing spirit in contrast to the self-centered expression so often seen in the face of a woman who thinks she is beautiful or is striving to be popular."[3]

Like Mary, the Tester sisters represented an exuberant middle-class version of the twentieth century's New Woman. In the years preceding World War I, *Ladies' Home Journal* portrayed these modern young women as educated, adventurous, and athletic—or "foot loose and fancy free," as Mary described herself in 1913. When not developing lesson plans, teaching Sunday school, or singing in the Moravian choir, Mary attended dances, skated with friends, and organized school events. "And sometimes I played circle games on the street corner with the primary-aged youngsters in the evening," she remembered. "I was bubbling over with energy and without a care in the world."[4]

Though Mary continued to attend special family gatherings, she was proud that she occasionally spent Saturdays in Minneapolis, shopping, lunching, or attending a show, without visiting the Daniel family. Yet she could not resist mentioning "Mr. Harrigan" in letters to the ever-protective Jeannette, who shared Mary's words with her older siblings. Lewis was so concerned that he ventured to Waconia to have a look at Harrigan—and was not impressed. When Mary attended Thanksgiving dinner at Kenwood, Jeannette took the lead in asking her about the "gentleman" whose name had entered her letters. Mary deflected their attention, describing Harrigan as "kind of an ordinary looking guy, with kind of a flat broad face and mousey brown hair . . . but, a 'very good dancer.'" She was not yet completely smitten but was privately intrigued by his attention.[5]

In January 1914, Mary learned from her colleague and roommate, Harriet Van Rhee, that Bill Harrigan's real name was William Bernard Huckenpoehler and that he was German, not Irish. Called Willie—at least by his mother—he had allegedly received the nickname Harrigan because he loved the rollicking lifestyle of his Irish neighbors and the George M. Cohan song, "Harrigan," a paean to the Irish heritage. The nickname may also have softened the effects of anti-German sentiment during World War I. Whatever the case, he was Harrigan for the rest of his life. The twenty-five-year-old Welsh American schoolteacher and the thirty-four-year-old German American bartender made an unlikely couple.

Meeting the man with the Irish nickname began Mary's foray into the German immigrant cultures of America's Great Northwest. Harrigan's paternal grandparents, innkeeper Heinrich F. Huckenpoehler and his second wife, Christina Wasmuth Huckenpoehler, had immigrated to the United States in 1858 from Brenken, Prussia (now in North Rhine-Westphalia in western Germany). Sailing aboard the *Herzogen Von Brabant* from Bremen to New York City with the couple were their four small children, Christina, Bernard Wilhelm, Mary, and Heinrich Jr.[6]

By 1858, the Huckenpoehler family had moved to the new state of Minnesota, where Waconia became their new home. Platted in 1857, Waconia attracted Swedish, Swiss, and German immigrants eager to homestead on fertile lands formerly occupied by Dakota (Sioux) and Ojibwa (Chippewa) Native Americans. The lands, transferred through treaties that specified reciprocal rights and duties for the US government and Minnesota's tribal nations, proved easily and quickly abused by government agents. As the Dakota and Ojibwa watched Congress whittle away their land base and way of life, the treaties became empty words on paper. Between 1858 and 1870, Christina and Heinrich had six more children: Elizabeth, August, Joseph, Herman, Lena, and Anna.[7]

Joining the Huckenpoehlers in Waconia were Harrigan's maternal forebears, the Claesgenses. His grandfather Anton Claesgens migrated to New York from what is now southwestern Germany with his father and four siblings in 1842, when he was twenty-six. In 1854, Anton married Josepha Maier, a young newly arrived Prussian immigrant. Anton and Josepha first settled in Utica, New York, where they had two children—Mary (born 11 November 1855) and Josephine (born 10 May 1857). Sometime between Josephine's birth and 1860, the family migrated to Waconia and began farming.[8]

Though the Huckenpoehlers and Claesgens were in the United States prior to the Civil War, neither the members of the immigrant generation nor their sons served in the Union Army. However, they were present if not actively involved in fighting much closer to their Minnesota home during the Dakota War (Sioux Uprising), which raged from 18 August to 26 December 1862. The Lower Sioux (or Redwood) Agency was located about one hundred miles northeast of Waconia, and tensions there rose over the issue of whether the US government, its coffers strained by the demands of fighting the insurrectionist southern states, would pay the Natives their full annuity. As hunger mounted, a small group of Dakota argued one night about whether to steal eggs from a white settler family. The argument turned violent and escalated into an attack on the settlers, and by morning, five whites lay dead. The Dakota then launched a full-scale attack on agents and settlers, killing twenty people on 18 August. Local officials organized militia groups and called the 3rd Minnesota Volunteer Infantry Regiment back from the South to battle the Dakota. Settlers scrambled to hide, fled across the river by ferry, or fought to their deaths, although friendly Dakotas saved some settlers and took others, mostly women and children, captive. Preparing for the worst, many Waconia settlers buried their belongings and fled to an island in what later became known as Lake Waconia, though the fighting never reached Carver County.[9]

On 26 December 1862, a hasty military trial resulted in the conviction of more than three hundred Dakota all of whom would have hanged if President Abraham Lincoln had not intervened and commuted the sentences of all but thirty-nine of the men. Next, the US government exiled the entire Dakota Nation to Nebraska and North Dakota.[10]

Even in peacetime after 1865, life on the northwestern frontier remained a struggle. For Josepha Maier Claesgens and other immigrant women there, life consisted mostly of farmwork, housework, and caring for children. Josepha was almost constantly pregnant during this era, giving birth to eight children between 1860 and 1871. According to Josepha's granddaughter, Elizabeth Bleichner Bahr, on a cold winter's day that year, Josepha was working outdoors near the end of yet another pregnancy when she noticed that one of the family's cows had escaped the farm. She scrambled under a fence but became entangled in barbed wire, panicked, and went into premature labor. Neither she nor the twins she was carrying survived. In the aftermath, the burden of running the household and caring for six younger children fell to Josepha and Anton's two oldest daughters, Mary, age sixteen, and Josephine, age fourteen. Two years later, on 15 October 1873, Mary married Moritz Wagner, leaving Josephine with sole responsibility for the household.[11]

In 1876, Josephine became engaged to Bernard William Huckenpoehler. Late that summer, before they were married, Josephine discovered that she was pregnant. To her horror, Bernard then balked at getting married, leaving her facing the threat of humiliation and the possibility that she would never marry.[12]

When Anton Claesgens learned of his daughter's predicament, the Old World patriarch rose up to make right the wrong done to her—and to him. Now "damaged goods," Josephine and her bastard child threatened to become her father's financial burden as well as his shame. An outraged Anton filed

Josephine Claesgens, ca. 1875.

charges of "seduction under false promises of marriage" against Bernard Huckenpoehler, and on 14 April 1877, he was convicted and sentenced to two years in prison. There he sat one month later as Josephine gave birth to their daughter Anna Marie (Annie). Minnesota governor John S. Pillsbury finally intervened when the child was a year old, offering to free Bernard if he married Josephine and pledged to treat her with all the kindness due a wife. Bernard accepted the deal, and they married on 23 May 1878, inside the prison's walls. Almost exactly ten months later, on 27 March 1879, their son William Bernard was born.[13]

It is doubtful that Willie, aka Harrigan, was aware of his parents' scandalous past. Mary Daniel certainly knew nothing of Harrigan's personal family history and little about the German community in which he lived. When she learned from Harriet Van Rhee that Harrigan and Michael Zahler, who had married Harrigan's older sister, were joint proprietors of the Sherman House saloon and beer garden, she despaired of the relationship. The next time Harrigan invited her on a date, she virtuously turned him down, explaining that she could not teach temperance in the schools and date someone who operated a drinking establishment.[14]

Nevertheless, she continued to flirt with Harrigan and dance with him when they encountered each other at social events. She warded off his sexual advances while her own sexual feelings grew. In February 1914, Mary revealed a daring side of herself at Waconia's annual masquerade ball, sewing and then wearing a striking red-and-black gypsy outfit that barely covered her knees. For sparkle, she donned "all the jewelry I could find or borrow," including "several yards of brass chain" that she draped across the dress.[15]

I love imagining my grandmother in masquerade. And her memory that when "some big, tall fellow got fresh, I clipped him with my tambourine." At the same time, she was guardedly delighted at Harrigan's interest at what must have been her sexiest moment ever. Not only did he ask her to dance several times that evening, but "some of the things he said made me afraid to go to any more dances."[16]

Mary was ecstatic to learn that Harrigan and Mike had sold their beer garden—until she learned that he had taken a job bartending at Waconia's North Star Hotel. Then came the good news that Harrigan and another friend, Walter Kusserow, had decided to start an oil delivery business. Harrigan purchased a couple of horses and quit bartending, and the romance was back on. She rewarded his turn to respectability by agreeing to a double date with Harriet and her new beau. Summer picnics, dances, movies, and hayrides followed, and Mary and Harrigan were in love by the Fourth of July.[17]

Despite their ethnic, religious, and class differences, the Huckenpoehler and Claesgens clans were only a decade behind the Daniels and Lewises in migrating to America. Both Mary's and Harrigan's mothers had been born in Utica, New York, and both of their families pioneered in settling ethnic American communities. Both sets of immigrants obtained American educations for their children, and all adopted English as their first language.

Like many immigrant farm children, however, Harrigan's education had ended after the sixth grade. His rural world centered on work, church, men's beer halls, and dance hall celebrations that replicated his parents' Old World culture, and although he was born in the United States, he maintained a strong German accent throughout his life. Circumstances frequently forced him to work outside Waconia, but he always returned to his hometown. Harrigan knew little about the California vacations, restaurant dining, and elegant weddings so familiar to Mary's family, but she didn't care. In spite of his presumably sexual remarks to her, she was charmed by his otherwise gentle, courteous ways. Even his slight stutter endeared her (and apparently other women) to him. Harrigan was equally enamored of Mary and was likely intrigued by her education, moral certainty, and social consciousness. To show his love, in December he loaned her his sister's diamond ring to wear it until he could afford to buy her an engagement ring.[18]

In addition to loving Harrigan, Mary enjoyed the fact that the Daniel family thought he was unsuitable for her and deliberately wore her engagement ring to dinner at Kenwood. "The whole family took turns telling me how wrong it was," she remembered, arguing that "he just wouldn't fit into the family circle. But I had never fit into the family circle myself so I couldn't feel the force of that argument." If anything, the Daniel family's objections fueled her attraction.[19]

During the couple's engagement, Mary made the second religious conversion of her life, becoming a Catholic at a crucial crossroads in her life. Mary was not just going along to please others. She initially felt that she could not in good conscience make the required promises to the Catholic Church and broke off the engagement in 1915, a decision that not surprisingly left her family "overjoyed." Mary believed that the Daniels saw her single status as the "cross they had to bear" yet also viewed themselves as "martyrs to the cause of keeping me unmarried." But she and Harrigan were miserable.[20]

Harrigan urged Mary to speak with his old sweetheart Norah Fallon, who was now married to someone else, before cutting all ties with him. When Mary poured her heart out to Norah, she gently prodded Mary to reconsider the marriage and her conversion to Catholicism. Mary next had a long talk with the kindly parish priest of Rosedale kindergarten in Minneapolis, where she was now teaching. Without applying pressure, he, too, encouraged her to examine the Catholic faith in more depth. The genuine concern for her shown by two Catholics had a profound effect on Mary, who saw a sharp contrast with her family's emphasis on social conventions. When she lost her job at Rosedale and was forced to return to Kenwood, where she felt like the "roving old maid member of the family, always under foot," her sense of the

Catholic Church as a refuge intensified. "I was at home, idle, and miserable," she wrote. "I had a rosary which I secretly used although I had not yet made up my mind about becoming a member of the Catholic Church."[21]

Norah became "a great comfort" to Mary, "sweet, warm hearted, and thoroughly good." And like Harrigan, from Mary's perspective, Norah offered the added benefit of being "a great thorn in" the flesh of Marge Daniel Jones, who "was and still is a rabid anti-Catholic." In the fall of 1916, Mary accepted a teaching offer at the public grade school in Onamia, Minnesota, where her good friend Harriet, now married to Martin Moe, taught. Mary enjoyed Onamia's more northerly, wooded location, especially on nights when the howling of timber wolves blended with the steady drumbeat of a Blackfoot Native American rice festival. She was equally pleased to find "a little Indian Princess" in her first-grade class.[22]

Occasional trips to Minneapolis allowed Mary and Harrigan to continue seeing each other, with Norah as an intermediary. Mary's widening circle of connections made her even more critical of the Daniels. When stuck in their world, she felt "apologetic," "subdued," and "inwardly resentful." When away, she felt like a "warm and normal human" instead of a depressed, burdensome charge. On one Kenwood visit, she observed that family members shamelessly slandered one another and used her as a conduit for back-and-forth gossip. "I decided that one more year of this life would drive me crazy. . . . I felt that I must remove myself from these influences for the preservation of my own soul."[23]

With the engagement still on hold in early 1917, Mary began taking instruction in the Catholic faith to prove to herself that she was not doing so merely for Harrigan. Her instructor was a helpful priest whose earnest, humble personality touched her heart, and after three months, she felt certain she "could never be satisfied with any other church . . . even if I never married." If Harrigan no longer wanted her, she now believed, "I would have to find another Catholic man or never marry anyone." When word got out that she was studying to become Catholic, her family members were not the only people who objected. Her Onamia landlords compelled her to find a new rooming house, and her teaching contract was rescinded. Although religious-based discrimination was against the law in Minnesota, every school to which Mary applied asked for her "church preference" and refused to hire her. Finally, a "Bishop's special committee" won her a contract in nearby Park Rapids, "where the principal was a Jew and there was no religious discrimination."[24]

On her next visit to Kenwood, Mary left her rosary lying on her bedroom dresser, where Marge's young son, Herbie, found it. His mother, Mary wrote, "nearly threw me out of the house." In August 1917, she learned that Harrigan indeed wanted her back but was disappointed at his suggestion that they wait to marry until after World War I ended so they could "live right" economically. Mary initially agreed but later, at her priest's suggestion, refused to see Harrigan until "he felt ready for marriage." While enduring yet another Christmas at Kenwood, Harrigan called and invited her to have dinner with him in the city. Mary accepted but afterward felt confused and depressed. All she wanted at that point was to return to Park Rapids, where she had been reappointed for the spring term.[25]

For his part, Harrigan moved from small-town service jobs to the nation's burgeoning industrial workforce. After the failure of his business venture with Walter Kusserow, Harrigan worked as a locomotive fireman with the Oliver Iron Mining Company in nearby Hibbing. Moving from Waconia, the only community he had ever known, Harrigan was now a mine worker who lived in a boardinghouse with other men. Founded by Henry E. Oliver, a wealthy manufacturer of farm machinery, in the early 1890s, the company was emblematic of the corporate conglomerates that dominated the extractive industries of Minnesota's Mesabi Range during this era.[26]

A huge wave of emigration from Southern and Eastern Europe (especially Italy, Hungary, and the Slavic nations) and Asia after the 1880s provided a bonanza of cheap labor for the rapidly industrializing United States. These second-wave immigrants were generally less assimilated than the Northern Europeans—Harrigan and Mary's forebears among them—who comprised the country's first wave of immigration. In the 1890s, social scientists, businessmen, and white supremacists posited a theory of Social Darwinism that seized on differences in skin shade, culture, and levels of assimilation to rank Asians and Eastern and Southern Europeans lower on the evolutionary scale than Northern Europeans but above Native Americans, Mexicans, and Africans. Although the industrial jobs performed by Harrigan were dangerous, underpaid, and insecure, his status as a second-generation German American gave him a distinct advantage over darker-skinned immigrants, who were restricted to unskilled, low-wage jobs.[27]

In December 1917, Mary spent her last Christmas as a single woman at Kenwood. When Jeannette asked if she was "still satisfied" to be a Catholic, Mary replied that she had never been "so satisfied and sure of my decision in anything before." In the morning, before the family began its exchange of gifts, she left to attend mass at a nearby Catholic church. As her faith in Catholicism deepened, Mary found Christmas at the Daniels' home "just a great big spectacle and sort of glorified grab bag. . . . All the rest of the day I never heard the name Jesus mentioned."[28]

A fiercely cold January 1918 forced Mary to move from her Park Rapids hotel room to a small house much closer to the Park Rapids School, where she had an attic bedroom to herself. She took her meals with her landlady, Mrs. Petrie, with wartime shortages of meat and wheat flour resulting in an unsatisfying and fattening diet that featured cornmeal mush and molasses for breakfast, rice pudding at lunch, and cornbread for supper. Mary "was often hungry even when I felt stuffed with food."[29]

In March, she "caught a bad cold, and it kept getting worse." With no substitute teacher available, she soldiered on, though to protect the children from her germs, she "drew a line around the deck and told the children to stay outside that line and I would stay inside it." By spring break, she had pneumonia; her landlady called in a doctor, who ordered her to bed for the entire spring break. Looking back, Mary credited her survival to the intervention of Easter vacation and her landlady.[30]

Mary's "bad cold" might in fact have been the flu, the first cases of which were reported in Kansas in January 1918 and which went on to become a worldwide pandemic. On 9 April, the *Minneapolis Star Tribune* reported that nine Fort Snelling soldiers had died as a result of an "epidemic in influenza occasioned by weather conditions." Nine days later, the newspaper noted that "the city's mortality rate for the past week has been one of the highest known in recent years" and that the epidemic had spread "country wide."[31]

Mary coughed throughout the summer but gradually regained her health. Harrigan continued to hesitate about getting married, likely concerned about their economic situation. Would Mary give up her Park Rapids job? Could she find a position in Hibbing? Would they be forced to continue living apart? In April, Harrigan suggested to Mary that they "get together for some good times once in a while and forget the idea of getting married." Mary answered neither this letter nor the ones that followed and supposed that their relationship was over.[32]

In July, as Mary summered with her brother Lewis and his wife, Esther, in Minneapolis, Harrigan telephoned. "In spite of myself," Mary remembered, she was "thrilled" to hear his voice. They spent a whirlwind day and evening together, eating both lunch and dinner and attending a band concert, and the engagement was back on. Harrigan wanted to obtain a civil license and seal the deal right then, but Mary insisted that they contact Father John Stelmes in Waconia and follow church rules. The wedding was set for 17 August. Mary wrote to the principal of the Park Rapids School to ask whether she would be permitted to continue at the school: not only were married women often barred from teaching positions, but she feared the consequences of marrying a German Catholic. But the principal assured her "that no matter what my name was they wanted me back for the coming school year. He added that he thought the name Huckenpoehler had a very distinguished sound." With that matter settled, she insisted the wedding take place in Onamia, where her conversion had taken place.[33]

On the morning of 12 August, Jeannette accompanied Mary to the Minneapolis train station to catch the train to Onamia. As they awaited its arrival, Jeannette asked if Mary was certain she wanted to "take this step." Wasn't she just a little afraid that the marriage wouldn't work out as she hoped? "Well, if you mean maybe it won't be all roses," Mary replied, "Sure, I know that. I've lived around enough married couples to know there's bound to be hard feelings and misunderstandings."[34]

When Jeannette persisted in warning about the difficulties of marriage, Mary dismissed such concerns: "We may fight, but at least we are both Catholics, so we are going to stay married." "But that's just it," responded Jeannette. "It's an awfully serious step and you ought to be very sure. . . . It isn't too late to change your mind!" Mary remained adamant, and Jeannette began to sob, "I don't know what your mother would say about this." Mary confidently responded that her mother now knew the true (Catholic) Word of God, just as Jeannette someday would. Looking back, Mary "supposed" she had been "a bit of a fanatic" in dismissing her stepmother's genuine concerns: "I must have been quite a trial, carrying my adolescent forthrightness into my twenties so far." Mary "kissed Jeannette goodbye and was on my fatal way."[35]

After a small, traditional ceremony and a two-week traveling honeymoon, Mary reported to work at the Park Rapids School while Harrigan returned to his job in Hibbing. Three months later, with all but six of Mary's forty students felled by the second wave of the flu pandemic, the Park Rapids School closed. The school's shutdown allowed her a much-desired visit with her new husband in Hibbing, but their time together was ruined by a heated argument that erupted after Harrigan "scolded" Mary. When she meekly

Harrigan Huckenpoehler and Mary Daniel Huckenpoehler on their wedding day,
17 August 1918.

deferred to his criticism, he admitted, "I often wonder how you would look mad," and she realized that he was manipulating her emotions. Feeling like a "curiosity" rather than a person, Mary unleashed her ferocious temper on Harrigan for the first—but certainly not the last—time. She then slammed out of the room, hurried to the train station, and bought a return ticket to Park Rapids.[36]

Mary's angry departure may have prompted Harrigan to cancel their plans to spend Christmas with his parents. On 1 December, Josephine Huckenpoehler wrote that she was upset to learn that they were not coming: she and "Dada" had "planned on having a kind of Christmas & wedding dinner together." She not only urged him to reconsider but implored him to tell Mary that she was welcome to come even if he could not. The couple ultimately decided to spend the holidays with the Huckenpoehlers, with the visit including a wonderful day of making candy at the home of Harrigan's sister and brother-in-law, Annie and Mike Zahler. Mary also spent a day at

Kenwood during the holiday break, mainly to show the Daniel family "how well married life agreed with me."[37]

Despite the confident front Mary put on at Kenwood, she had only begun to get to know the man that she had married. Her religious conversion had rendered her a far more devout Catholic than Harrigan. She honored all church doctrines, while he ignored those that threatened his love of fun and "good times." In the years of marriage that followed, Harrigan struggled with work on the Mesabi Iron Range while Mary adjusted to being a wife and mother in small-town Waconia, and the Great Depression later threatened to overwhelm them. Drafting her memoir years later, she concluded that "the only hopeful healthy thing in my life was my love of Jesus Christ and my absolute faith in His love for me." But she also admitted, "I did not have a matured personality. I was not emotionally stable or ready for a healthy marriage or any kind of successful living."[38]

6

Schooled by Life

This place is simply awful. Life consists of nothing but
housework, backache, sleepless nights and tired days,
and silly, useless, vicious, prying, nosey gossip.
—MARY DANIEL HUCKENPOEHLER, "Notes on My Life"

By Christmas 1918, Mary and Harrigan had been married for more than
four months but still did not live together. After celebrating New Year's Day
in Waconia, she returned to the Park Rapids School and he went back to
Hibbing. The separation was tough. The nation remained in the grip of the
flu epidemic, and national events outside their control compounded their
economic problems. Harrigan faced an uncertain future in Minnesota's mining and railroad industry, and Mary soon traded the status of a professional
woman for that of a working-class wife and mother. Her new life brought
responsibilities well beyond the range of her privileged upbringing.

As World War I ended, the country's labor issues began to heat up. Workers
sought decent wages and humane workplace conditions through labor
unions, while corporate bosses used police forces, strikebreakers, and even
the Ku Klux Klan in an effort to protect profits. Harrigan's employer, the
Oliver Mining Company, now a subsidiary of US Steel, short-circuited strikes
and destroyed unions by exploiting ethnic conflicts among workers on the

Mesabi Iron Range. The company hired Southern Europeans, Mexicans, and African Americans as strikebreakers, deliberately driving a wedge between them and "whiter," more assimilated Swedes and German Americans.

Between 1917 and 1920, "Americanization" campaigns and anticommunist propaganda merged with white supremacist campaigns of terror against Black citizens. The Ku Klux Klan, revitalized in 1915 by the silent movie *The Birth of a Nation*, planted Klaverns in many steel towns rocked by labor and political unrest. Throughout the Midwest and Northwest, whites who had rarely if ever seen a Black American before World War I accepted the film's message as one of patriotism. My grandmother, the proud daughter of a Civil War soldier from the Abolitionist Regiment, was among them. During the era in which Mary grew up, pro-Confederate "Lost Cause" writers rewrote the Civil War as a dispute over constitutional principles, not slavery, and Reconstruction as a "tragic era" of Black misrule. *Birth of a Nation* did not create those myths but brought them to the big screen. The movie's racist message about Black brutality and inferiority was easily folded into the rising tensions of an industrial society, where Black strikebreakers were pitted against native-born and immigrant laborers struggling to earn a living wage.[1]

Powerful political and social organizations supported big business in suppressing worker agitation. Congress's support for big business in turn encouraged class-conscious workers, particularly Finns, Swedes, and Germans, to embrace socialism and to a lesser extent communism. Both the Democratic and Republican Parties responded by labeling labor unions and immigrants, many of whom had also opposed US entry into World War I, as disloyal to the United States. Many dissidents had been fined or imprisoned under the Espionage (1917) and Sedition (1918) Acts. Minnesota's Commission for Public Safety, organized in 1917 to mobilize wartime resources, used its broad powers to suppress unions and immigrant dissent in the name of national loyalty. The Ku Klux Klan became a terroristic arm of corporate America's antilabor, antiradical forces.[2]

At the same time, World War I stirred a boiling cauldron of hate and anti-Semitism. Russia's Bolshevik Revolution promised a socialist workers' state, but it spurred a backlash of vicious pogroms against Jews in Europe and anticommunist hysteria in America. International anti-Semitism rapidly escalated, especially in Germany but also in the United States. Violent attacks on workers, especially immigrants and Blacks, flourished in such an atmosphere.[3]

In 1919, Mary's thoughts and fears centered on the nation's labor unrest, Harrigan's well-being, and the raging pandemic. Mostly, she focused on Harrigan's work situation in Hibbing: "Trouble was beginning in the mines. There was enough skilled labor there now that the boys were getting separated from the armed services. There was union trouble and Harrigan expected to be fired any day." He was right. In April 1919, shortly after he visited Mary in Park Rapids, the Oliver Mining Company laid him off. When the Nineteenth Amendment gave women the right to vote two months later, Mary barely mentioned it.[4]

Mary also was undoubtedly distracted by the fact that she was pregnant. Although she and Harrigan were excited by the news, the timing was terrible. They sighed with relief when Harrigan quickly found a new job with the Duluth, Missabe, and Northern Railway, which hauled ore from the Vermilion and Mesabi Iron Range mines to Duluth and Two Harbors, Minnesota. The railroad too was owned by US Steel, meaning that the Huckenpoehlers remained enmeshed in labor unrest, but Harrigan gratefully moved to Duluth.[5]

As soon as Mary's school year ended in June, she joined Harrigan at the railway's company hotel and they began hunting for a place to live. Those efforts soon revealed the dismal living conditions for working families in Duluth: they could afford nothing better than a third-story apartment with only a two-burner gas hot plate for cooking. Running water was limited to the bathroom, which, like the hot plate, was shared among three households. "Pigs," Mary labeled the landlords under her breath. Neither she nor Harrigan had ever lived under such conditions, and they decided to continue living apart. Mary moved in with his parents in Waconia, while he lived and worked in Duluth.[6]

Mary's Minneapolis connections continued to provide her with comforts that were not available to most working-class wives. She depended on her sister Marge's husband, Dr. Herbert W. Jones, for prenatal care, taking advantage of her visits to the city to tool around with Jeannette in her car as well as enjoy restaurant meals and afternoons at the movie theater. By mid-August, however, her advancing pregnancy ended such pleasant sojourns. Although Mary had found Waconia delightful and welcoming when she was an unmarried teacher, as a pregnant woman whose husband lived and worked elsewhere, she was an outsider in the close-knit German American community, living with in-laws whom she barely knew. Even the

Catholic church offered little comfort, since sermons and prayers took place in German. It was a lonely life.[7]

Moreover, Mary had few household skills other than sewing items for the baby. "Mother Josephine," raised in a vastly different world from that of her new daughter-in-law, was kind, but she was a domestic powerhouse who preferred that Mary follow simple directives or stay out of the way. Throughout the summer of 1919, Mary helped Josephine with endless loads of laundry and snapped mountains of green beans. Mary was particularly dazzled by Josephine's culinary skills, pronouncing her "a genius at fixing appetizing Friday meals with egg, milk, and cheese. . . . She made a dilly of a baked custard pie." On one occasion, Josephine spent a weekend in the nearby town of Watkins and left Mary to handle the household chores. "Poor Dada," Mary remembered. "I wasn't the fine cook that Mother was and was shy about using up things in her carefully managed house." Mary gamely served up meals of bacon, wieners, potatoes, and green beans but felt the sting of her father-in-law's disappointment.[8]

Matters were further complicated by Harrigan's seeming inattention. Weeks passed between letters from him, and one evening, while she was crocheting a jacket for the baby, she lapsed into a "blue" funk. To raise her spirits, she returned to taking long walks, a practice that became a lifelong habit, and the arrival of a newsy letter from Harrigan accompanied by $25 for the purchase of baby supplies cheered her up, at least temporarily.[9]

Mary also used the time to study the world around her with a writer's eye for detail. She noted in her diary that Mother Josephine had "a long hard life with Dada" and his domineering and demanding ways, which Mary described as "the old German attitude toward all women." She sympathized with the older woman's lot in life: "I think mother had been worn down with caring for all of us when it was a job too heavy for a woman of her age, and she had lost courage. . . . She had no enthusiasm for anything." Mary noted that Josephine worked hard and demanded little: "No one could help her. She just wouldn't have it." Mary worried that if she were ever away while Josephine was "sick abed," the "menfolk" might give her no attention at all.[10]

In addition to Annie and Harrigan, Mother Josephine and Dada had a third child, Josephine (Josie), born in April 1882, who led a troubled life. According to my aunt Mary Jo, Josie began having psychological problems after she fell in the snow and almost froze to death. But although hypothermia can indeed cause temporary derangement, it seems an unlikely cause

Josephine Claesgens Huckenpoehler and Dada Huckenpoehler, ca. 1890.

for Josie's lifelong issues. Mary Jo, my aunt Jeanne, and my mother remembered hearing that Josie suffered fits of rage during her menstrual periods (a condition now labeled premenstrual dysphoric disorder) that rendered her impossible to live with, and Jeanne heard that Josie once attacked her mother with a knife. Whatever the circumstances, on 11 July 1911, Sheriff G. A. Gatz took twenty-nine-year-old Josie into custody and transported her to St. Peter State Hospital. According to her admittance records, she was "depressed, suspicious, and introspective"; had "brooded over her health" in the previous year; and suffered from insomnia, digestive problems, and impaired nutrition and vitality. At five foot, two inches tall, Josie weighed less than ninety pounds.[11]

Josie was "paroled" from St. Peter in September 1911 but returned one month later and remained there for nearly three decades. She was released briefly on 19 August 1940 and on 9 June 1947, likely to the care of her older

Josie Huckenpoehler, ca. 1910.

sister Annie since both Josephine and Bernard were dead. On 7 June 1951, Josie was transferred to Anoka State Hospital, where she remained until her death on 12 February 1959. My mother and her sister Jeanne were told that Josie recovered from her illness after passing through menopause but chose to remain at Anoka State Hospital because after her decades of confinement there, it was home.[12]

When Mary and Harrigan married, Josie had already been institutionalized for seven years. But Mary's memories leave little doubt that Josephine Huckenpoehler was deeply affected by her daughter's mental illness and commitment to a psychiatric ward and that these events sapped her enthusiasm for life. And Mary went on to encounter other mental disorders among members of her family.

In August 1919, the tedium of Mary's life with the elder Huckenpoehlers was relieved by a visit from Harrigan. Home for just one week, he visited family and friends and took his pregnant wife to a ball game and dinner. Then he left her at home while he attended the state fair in Minneapolis, bringing her a *Ladies' Home Journal* as a "conscience offering." Back in Duluth, Harrigan was promoted to supervisor at the railroad yards in nearby Proctor. Three days later, on 22 September 1919, the Great Steel Strike erupted as workers, led by the American Federation of Labor, pushed back against employers' antiunion efforts.[13]

Mary was initially reassured about Harrigan's continued employment after he sent her a newspaper article about the strike: "From all I could get from a thorough reading of it," she recalled, "the steel strike ought not to cause Harrigan to lose his job on the railroad very soon." But in October, dock-workers joined the walkout: "All the ore boats that load from the northern Minnesota mines at Duluth Harbor have reached the Pittsburgh docks full of ore and as long as no one would unload them, they just have to sit there and wait." Further, she noted, "No more ore can leave the Duluth docks because there are no more boats. No more ore could be brought down from Hibbing because there was no place to put it. So there was no more work for trainmen and they were laid off." Harrigan was among the victims.[14]

Mary shared Harrigan's anger at a system that "tossed him aside when he had a wife and expected to have a baby to support," but she became alarmed when he subscribed to a Socialist paper "just to get that side of the story" and because "he felt the Socialist paper was telling the truth." In the context of the Red Scare hysteria and her strict Catholicism, Mary had no tolerance for what she called "blood-red Socialism." Like many mainstream Americans, she believed that Socialists sought the "downfall of all government, all author-ity, including the authority of the Church." She comforted herself with the thought that "Harrigan was not really indoctrinated with the Socialist slant. His chief interest in the steel strike was because of his own job."[15]

After losing his job, Harrigan returned to Waconia and sought work there. Mary was delighted to be reunited with her husband, even if they were liv-ing with his parents. The winter of 1919 was frightfully cold, and the family purchased a stove for the couple's upstairs sleeping quarters. But they had to carefully ration their use of coal, with Mary noting in early November that "even with an early settlement of the coal strikes we wouldn't be able to get another carload in Waconia until January." She occupied herself by keeping the couple's room neat and by taking her daily walks. She and the other members of the household regularly came down with colds.[16]

Mary discovered that although Harrigan worked hard both inside and outside their home, he had no desire to socialize there—understandably, in her view. The Huckenpoehlers' home life centered almost entirely on work and meals; outside of an occasional game of cards, Josephine and Dada had little time or space for leisure and entertainment. Harrigan had long since established the habit of heading downtown in the evenings for a few beers with his buddies. Maybe, Mary hoped, "when we got into our own home, I could make more of an effort to keep him home. I dreamed of getting a Victrola before anything else, and some records that would be lively and full of drumming, and polkas, and such things so he would enjoy playing it." But for the rest of his life, Harrigan's social life revolved around downtown taverns, card rooms, and flirtatious women. According to Mary, even when he was ninety-six and confined to a nursing home, he occasionally played his violin for his companions and still enjoyed playing the bachelor for the ladies.[17]

In January 1920, the Great Steel Strike collapsed, and the Oliver Iron Mining Company called Harrigan back to work. He returned to Duluth and rented a room at the La France Hotel. It is therefore possible that he was in Duluth in the early summer of 1920 when the racial tensions that had been mounting there over the preceding three years exploded.[18]

On 15 June, police arrested six Black circus workers and charged them with raping a white woman. A mob attacked police headquarters, seized three of the men (Elias Clayton, Elmer Jackson, and Isaac McGhie), and then lynched them in full view of thousands of townspeople. Photographs of the murdered men soon appeared on postcards.[19]

Duluth's workers had not joined the strike, which meant that Black men had not been used as strikebreakers. But US Steel had brought Black field hands directly from southern plantations to defuse the threat of a strike, and many whites in the ethnically and economically divided city believed that Blacks were getting hired at the expense of Great War veterans. In the wake of the rape charge, whites began to cry, "They're taking our jobs; now they're raping our women!," and the lynching resulted. On 19 June, the *Duluth Labor World* decried the hangings as "anarchy and murder" and called for an end to hatred, whether generated by race, nationality, politics, religion, class, sectionalism, or neighborhood. One week later, in "Not the First Lynching," the paper reminded readers that Olli Kinkkonen, a Finnish dockworker who had opposed the US entry into World War I, had been lynched during the conflict.[20]

By that time, Mary and Harrigan had a six-month-old daughter. Named for her grandmothers, Mary Josephine Huckenpoehler had entered the world on 1 December 1919. Mary believed that the new baby would fill the void in her life, jubilantly embracing Mary Jo as her "life's work," her "hope," and her "happiness." But Mary's joy had an ominous undertone: for her daughter, she could "slave and plan and endure the deadly monotony of life in that deadly, miserable little one-horse, gossipy, dead Deutch village."[21]

Mary's disgust did not wane in the months that followed. Though she had loved Waconia when she was a "foot loose and fancy free" single woman, she now pronounced it "awful." "Life consists of nothing but housework, back-ache, sleepless nights, and tired days," she wrote, "and silly, useless, vicious, prying, nosey gossip." Months of misery had exhausted my grandmother's sympathy for her in-laws, and she now blamed their German working-class culture for her predicament. In truth, the fault lay with marriage, mother-hood, and the predatory postwar economy.[22]

What came next has long perplexed me. As winter began to thaw, my grandparents moved to their own apartment above a tire shop, leaving four-month-old Mary Jo with Dada and Josephine. And Mary Jo remained with her grandparents until she was three years old—until after Mary and Harrigan's second child, William Bernard Huckenpoehler Jr., was born on 17 July 1921. I suspect that the answer to the question of why Mary and Harrigan allowed their daughter to live with his parents lies with Dada and Josephine. From the moment that Josephine's pregnancy forced their marriage, their relationship centered on their duties to each other. For both good and ill, their children and then grandchildren brought tears, laughter, and meaning to the life they built together.

Just in time for Christmas 1922, Mary and Harrigan reclaimed Mary Jo, finally uniting the entire family under the same roof. At long last, my grand-mother faced the world as mistress of her own family and household. But the daughter she had welcomed as her "salvation," "hope," and "happiness" proved to be her greatest torment.[23]

7

Motherhood Gone Awry

[Mary Jo] was sick and foot-sore and I never guessed that she was
in trouble, but her father knew and sent her away lest she ruin the
other girls' right to a place in the good esteem of the town.
—MARY DANIEL HUCKENPOEHLER, Memoir, 1920–42

As Mary and Harrigan's firstborn child, Mary Jo was the most indulged by
parents and grandparents who competed for her affection. Mary's "biggest
nightmare" was that "the very ones who are now amusing themselves spoiling
her, will dislike to have her around and will go around telling everyone what
a fresh, spoiled disagreeable little girl Mary Jo is." Even the standoffish members of the Daniel family got in on the action. After showering the newborn
with gifts, step-grandmother Jeannette, aunt Lillian, uncles Llewellyn and
Lewis, and Lewis's wife, Esther, drove to Waconia on a beautiful Memorial
Day weekend to meet five-month-old Mary Jo in person. They brought a
picnic lunch of "gigantic proportions" and gathered Mary and the baby into
the car and headed to the Lakeside Park picnic grounds. It was a "merry"
afternoon, with all the relatives taking turns holding Mary Jo, commenting
on how beautiful she was, and snapping photos. Mary relished showing off
her new baby and the fact that she and Harrigan now had their own apartment, but she made no mention of her husband joining the outing, and he

and the Daniels apparently maintained a distant relationship for the rest of their lives. According to my mother, Marge Daniel Jones never addressed him as anything other than "Mr. Huckenpoehler." Despite the participants' evident enjoyment of the day, such visits rarely if ever recurred. Mary and Harrigan's children hardly knew her side of the family, although they consistently sent gifts over the years.[1]

When Mary Jo came to live with her parents in December 1922, the transition was not an easy one. In addition to being deprived of the daily presence of her grandparents and of what still felt like her true home, she also had to share the limelight with seventeen-month-old Billy, who himself was accustomed to being the center of their parents' attention. Mary Jo also chafed under her mother's authority while honing her skills at eliciting praise from others. On Mary Jo's fourth birthday, Mary observed, "she may be naughty at home but she behaves beautifully in company, sharing things with Billy in a way that makes me very proud and draws remarks of wonderment from our hostess." Mary felt trapped and manipulated by her toddler.[2]

In 1922, Harrigan became Waconia's chief of police, succeeding his brother-in-law Mike Zahler in the position and likely obtaining it via family connections. On 18 April 1924, Mary gave birth to the couple's third child, Margaret Ann, dubbed Mungi because her older brother could not pronounce her name. Mary's harried days were exacerbated by the new baby's fussy, "peevish" temperament and constant demands for attention. As the children grew older, they remained close to their Huckenpoehler grandparents, who lived just minutes away, with Mary Jo in particular frequently dining and sleeping at their house. Harrigan was an affectionate parent and, like his father, a traditional patriarch who worked hard to provide for his family, though his employment status remained shaky. Fun-loving and never particularly religious, he often socialized with friends rather than attending Sunday mass. Apparently, no more socialist talk disturbed Mary's peace of mind.[3]

In April 1925, Harrigan began working as a salesman of petroleum products for William Lipp, a "wholesale jobber" in Carver County. The salary, Mary happily reported in her diary, was $100 a month (equivalent to about $1,700 today).[4]

Mary's 1925 diary is one of the few that remains extant: after destroying a few entries that she considered too nasty in tone, she saved the volume, perhaps for the express purpose of writing her family's history. It is an unusual journal, written on notebook paper and more like a daybook than a diary.

Almost every day, in nearly hourly detail, she chronicled the minutia of her monotonous days—sweeping floors, washing dishes and clothes, preparing meals, changing diapers, and tending children. On rare occasions, she noted a visitor. She referred to herself and Harrigan in the third person as "Mother" or "Mama" and "Father" or "Papa."[5]

Mary was more than a decade removed from her Minneapolis childhood, college years, and teaching career, and she had lived in Waconia for many years. Nevertheless, she still stood out in the rural community of German American farmers, tradesmen, and frugal housewives. To write was her outlet. Pausing regularly throughout the day to record her activities provided her with fleeting escapes from her mundane domestic responsibilities and perhaps compensated for long days without adult company. A typical entry read: "Papa away at work. Mama beating milk into bought cottage cheese. Mary Jo getting her wraps to go & play in sun. Billy playing with a match box & toy rooster. Mungi crying & wailing & scolding & nearly swearing on the parlor floor near the stove where floor is warm." Some days contained between twenty and seventy numbered snapshots of her doings. On special days such as birthdays, Sundays, and holidays, she interspersed descriptions of household tasks with entries about baking cakes and other treats or trying to clean and dress herself and the children as well as with details about the event itself.[6]

On 27 March, Mary's day began badly as she was suffering from the "Blue Devil," the name she gave to premenstrual syndrome. She spent the day preparing for Harrigan's birthday celebration that evening, but shortly before he arrived home from work, baby Mungi fell while playing and scraped her cheek. Upset by the injury, he harangued Mary all evening, berating her for allowing such a thing to happen as well as for everything else he found amiss. Mary ended the day by writing directly to her husband: "So far as you are concerned," she wrote, "the less we see of you the happier we will be. You are never a whiz at being entertaining and [I] hope you'll be very busy for a few days." The next morning, she added: "We will no longer seriously consider Father's birthday. He has rejected our efforts and he is in a surly mood about everything."[7]

During these years, keeping a diary enabled Mary to nurture her dream of becoming a writer and provided an outlet for an exhausted wife and mother whose romantic dreams of love had turned to ashes. The Huckenpoehlers' mornings generally began with her making coffee, toast, and oatmeal for the family's breakfast. Then, between sweeping floors, making beds, carrying out the slops, or supplying a bored, cranky child with a diversion of bread and butter, she put potatoes on to boil for the noon meal, which often featured bacon or sausage and eggs unless Harrigan brought home a slice of ham, a steak, or pork chops. Mary also prepared bread, cakes, and puddings in abundance, but she rarely mentioned fresh produce as part of these starchy, dairy-rich, and protein-packed meals.[8]

Mary's three children had contrasting temperaments. Five-year-old Mary Jo was extroverted and willful. Billy, age four, was sweet-natured, quiet, and thoughtful but also elusive. Like Mary Jo, he treated their grandparents' house as a second home, often walking there without Mary's permission and, to her great embarrassment, with his hair uncombed and his face unwashed. When not sleeping, one-year-old Mungi clamored for attention and was sometimes tied to her high chair and given a toy or cookie. Barely mobile, she often whined in frustration as her siblings cavorted or "growled" at her mother for attention. One evening, while preparing for Harrigan's return from work, Mary wrote hastily, "Mary Jo scolding Billy for getting inside clothes bar. Billy begging Mary Jo to help him out. Mungi scolding & whining from the bed."[9]

Mary particularly resented the baby when she was wakeful in the evenings and interfered with her mother's reading time. Although Harrigan was usually tired and irritated after work, he enjoyed playing with his tiny girl and occasionally took her off Mary's hands. Still, Mary was sometimes frustrated and used her diary as an outlet for suppressed anger. With more than a tinge of sarcasm, she noted that on one occasion when Harrigan was playing with Mungi, "while father was thus 'resting,' mother did his chore of bringing in the wood and coal. Cheered, and flirting joyously with Mungi, he ate his supper without comment."[10]

Mary was clearly overwhelmed. And rather than sympathizing, her husband was demanding and frequently critical: the house wasn't clean enough; dinner wasn't ready on time; the children were unruly. In late March, she wrote, "He growled, swore, grumbled, criticized & sneered . . . that the house was always a mess, nothing was ever in order," and the children were always "quarreling & misbehaving." And he blamed these shortcomings on the fact that "Mama was always puttering around." In short, in Harrigan's eyes, she failed as both a mother and a homemaker.[11]

Shortly before the year ended, Mary discovered she was pregnant again. Privately, she wished herself and the child dead, but when Roderick Herbert died just three months after his birth on 1 April 1926, she was devastated. Alone as she washed, packed, and disposed of her baby's things, she was overcome by "such a paralyzing spell of grief I could barely move." She remained depressed as the Christmas season approached, and she was grateful that Harrigan took the lead in decorating the family's tree and buying presents. Others pitched in, too. Grandma Josephine made the children gifts of pork cake, cookies, and knitted mittens, while the Minneapolis kinfolk sent the usual Christmas boxes filled with new clothes and toys.[12]

At the insistence of seven-year-old Mary Jo, the family began opening gifts on Christmas Eve rather than the traditional Christmas morning so that she could wear her new clothes to Sunday mass the way her friends did. Mary was irritated but lacked the energy to object to her oldest child's latest demand. She had already delayed Mary Jo's enrollment in first grade by a year because of her ongoing mischief, fights, and tantrums. Her daughter was just too "nervous," Mary feared, to muster the self-discipline required in the classroom. She may also have feared having to respond to a teacher's complaints. She never had much luck governing Mary Jo and increasingly found it easier to just let her have her way.[13]

Perhaps Mary Jo's tantrums reminded Mary of her childhood anxiety and temporary removal from school at age five. In any case, she seemed determined to provide her children with the happy childhood that she had lacked. That goal seemed more in reach than ever in 1927 when the family moved to a new house on Main Street that Harrigan helped to build. The Huckenpoehlers were moving up in the world, and the three children fondly remembered the "brick house" for the rest of their lives.[14]

Reflecting the family's improved status, Mary Jo began taking piano lessons, and birthdays and Christmases became gala events that featured cakes, gifts, and neighborhood children. When Grandpa Dada died three days before Mungi's third birthday, the party nonetheless proceeded, and food left over from his funeral breakfast made a nice "birthday feast" for Mungi and her little friends. In 1929, Mary Jo took over the reins of her tenth birthday party. She prepared a nice lunch and arranged card games complete with prizes for her guests. Mary was a bit dazzled by her oldest child's resourcefulness.[15]

But Mary Jo's assertiveness was also accompanied by a sense of entitlement, and her siblings, like their mother, soon learned that the way to preserve family harmony was to give in to her demands. When five-year-old

Mary Jo Huckenpoehler and Billy Huckenpoehler, ca. 1929.   Mungi Huckenpoehler in front of the brick house, Waconia, Minnesota, ca. 1931.

Mungi donned her new bonnet for mass on Easter Sunday, Mary Jo decided that her straw bonnet was too "plain" and complained, "It's not fair; I never get pretty things!" At Mary Jo's insistence, Mungi reluctantly traded bonnets, an early instance of what became a lifetime of deference to her older sister.

The Great Depression, ushered in by the stock market crash of 29 October 1929, brought the Huckenpoehlers' growing prosperity to a screeching halt. In March 1931, fifty-two-year-old Harrigan lost his sales job. For most of the rest of his life, he labored for wages, often with an out-of-town road crew or sometimes, after Prohibition was repealed, tending bar in downtown Waconia. The Huckenpoehlers initially adjusted by simplifying birthdays and Christmases, although the Daniels continued to send lavish gifts, such as the Shirley Temple doll Mary Jo received as a birthday present from her aunt Lillian. In November 1931, Mary discovered she was again pregnant.

Jeanne Huckenpoehler, 1932.

She became alarmingly sick and traveled to Kenwood, where Dr. Jones diagnosed her with gestational diabetes and provided treatment that quickly restored her health. She then spent an additional few days there, enjoying a visit with Jeannette and Marge. Mary returned home just in time to prepare Thanksgiving dinner for her family. Their Christmas celebration a few weeks later included plenty of homemade candy, cookies, and cakes, but books from the library took the place of gifts from Mary and Harrigan.[16]

With Harrigan's continued unemployment, the Huckenpoehlers could barely pay the mortgage and upkeep costs of the brick house. They closed off several rooms to save on fuel during the winter, and Mary was grateful when their local priest brought them coal. With Harrigan's mother gravely ill with cancer, they did not tell her of Mary's pregnancy, and Josephine died on her seventy-fifth birthday, 10 May 1932. On 9 July, less than two months later, Mary's brother Llew passed away. When Jeanne Patricia Huckenpoehler was born the following day, Mary noted bitterly that "the newcomer was not welcomed by anyone but me."[17]

Desperate for work, Harrigan went on the road, leaving Mary and the four children for months at a time. Mary Jo, Billy, and Mungi helped with the baby and joined Mary in cleaning neighbors' gardens and orchards in return for fruit, vegetables, and canned goods. The nearby Godfrey family—John, Mamie, and their nine children—became the Huckenpoehlers' closest friends and sources of charity. John, a self-employed house painter, found relatively steady work, and the Godfreys' oldest child, Glenn, had a stable job fixing radios.[18]

As fall approached, Mary Jo clamored to leave St. Joseph's Catholic school and attend seventh grade in the public school system. Knowing that she chafed at the family's growing poverty, Mary capitulated. Attending public school gave Mary Jo a new lease on life, but not the sort for which her mother had hoped. On 1 December 1932, Mary Jo's thirteenth birthday as well as Mary's forty-fifth, she described the girl as "wild, and a constant source of worry" and regretted having allowed her to leave St. Joseph's. A few weeks later, Mary described Christmas as "horrible."[19]

Although the family's economic situation deteriorated further in 1933 and they became dependent on relief, the Waconia community rallied to make that year's holiday season more festive for poor families, and Mary took advantage of downtown events, including a visit from Santa Claus, the beautiful municipal Christmas tree, and bags of treats for Jeannie and other toddlers. The Daniels also sent gifts as usual—"clothes, provisions, and one game each for the children," and Aunt Lillian provided a much-appreciated red snowsuit for Jeannie.[20]

The Huckenpoehlers also began to see benefits from several programs initiated as part of President Franklin D. Roosevelt's New Deal. According to Mary, Jeannie attended a nursery operated by the federal Works Progress Administration in 1935, and Billy participated in a program for children two years later. Sometime between 1938 and 1940, Harrigan found a job with a government-funded road project. According to the 1940 census, his income that year totaled $400, one-third of what he had earned in 1925.[21]

Harrigan's government job did not come soon enough to prevent the family's eviction from their beloved brick house. As the family hustled to pack their belongings and vacate their home before the court-ordered deadline of 1 September 1936, Mary's brother Lewis died on 29 August. Consumed by the struggle to find shelter and food, Mary did not even mention his death.[22]

The family briefly moved to a basement apartment they nicknamed the hole in the ground, where they subsisted on government-surplus foodstuffs as well as potatoes, tomatoes, and windfall apples that Mary received in exchange for helping the farmers with their crops. She and the children soon left the basement apartment to live above a local café. The owner, May Burke, charged them $15 per month rent, and Mary, Mary Jo, and Mungi washed towels while Billy mopped the café every morning. During this time, Harrigan roomed at the Northern Hotel in Hibbing, where he found work as a watchman for the W. G. Remington Company.[23]

Living above a café had its advantages. The apartment stayed warm in the winter, and Mary and the children often received leftover food from the kitchen. But they sorely lacked privacy. Burke retained one of the top floor bedrooms for her family, and the Huckenpoehlers had to share their bathroom with the café's female customers. In June 1939, the Burkes sold the building, forcing Mary and her children to make a "hurried and desperate" move to the upper floor of a converted icehouse. Not surprisingly, their new living quarters were difficult to heat in winter. In addition, rats shared the space.[24]

Mary Jo, who loved making a big splash socially and was used to having her way and who knew "what it felt like to be well-off one day and poor practically the next," had a particularly difficult time adjusting to the hardships of the Great Depression. Tall and lanky, with thick dark curly hair and large luminous eyes, she lost interest in academics by the time she entered high school and excelled only in sewing. That skill enabled her to make her own outfits, which she used to attract the interest of older boys.[25]

Both Mary Jo and Mungi suffered social discomfort as a consequence of the visibility of their poverty and of their mother's failure to meet conventional standards of female domesticity. Waconia's close-knit German community judged wives and mothers by how efficiently they kept house and fed and clothed their families despite the hard times, and Mary did not measure up. Mary Jo and Mungi's cousins and friends all seemed to come from orderly homes bathed in the savory smell of German sausages and sweet aroma of baked goods, whereas their distracted mother always had her head in the clouds or a book even when she was bent over a stove or a broom. More than once, Mungi recalled with approval, her father demanded in his German accent that Mary "Trow dat book avay!"

Mamie Godfrey, the mother of Mungi's best friend, Betty, made Mary's deficiencies seem especially apparent. A warm and sympathetic woman who baked three loaves of bread every morning for her large family, Mamie seemed more of a mother to Mungi than did Mary. Mungi hated her family's messy house, especially on laundry day, when Mary would take their clothes to the Godfrey house, use Mamie's washing machine, and then haul the clothes home and pile them on the furniture. On those days, Mungi raced home from school to put the clothes away before her friends could enter. Mary knew she failed to measure up and felt ashamed when visitors caught her with unwashed dishes and unswept floors, but she would not or could not forgo reading, drawing, and writing, the creative interests that made her life bearable.[26]

Sometime during the 1930s, Harrigan began an affair with Marge O'Reilly, whose husband owned his favorite tavern. One fine day, Mary headed downtown in a rage, carrying a brick to hurl through the window of the O'Reilly home. Behind her ran Mungi, crying and begging her mother to turn back. Mary ultimately relented and trudged back home without throwing the brick, but Mungi found the experience harrowing—yet another personal embarrassment that she blamed squarely on her mother.

The lessons my mother learned from her parents' relationship shaped her own choices in life. As a child, Mungi was a daddy's girl. She loved Harrigan's dancing, his droll sense of humor, and his enjoyment of life's pleasures. Her earliest and fondest memory was of jumping up and down on her bed in the early morning while calling out, "Papa, dwess me." By age ten, she was finagling dimes for the picture show by badgering him at his favorite tavern while his drinking buddies looked on. She never tired of her father's fun-loving side, though she and Mary Jo flinched when he bought nylon stockings for Marge O'Reilly's teenaged daughter. In her old age, Mom delighted in imitating my grandpa singing George M. Cohan's "Harrigan" while performing a jig for his family and friends. "He loved the Irish," she remembered with a grin, "and Marge O'Reilly was Irish."

While Mary struggled against poverty and intellectual isolation, her sister, Marge Jones, and stepmother Jeannette continued to live in the original Daniel home. Despite the short distance between Minneapolis and Waconia, life's demands kept their families apart. Marge and Mary's oldest sister, Lillian, might as well have lived a thousand miles away, so different was her life from theirs. She never remarried after Horace Peck's death and lived a life of privilege, sailing to France in 1927 and England in 1930 and frequently visiting Vancouver, British Columbia, where her son, Rod, a lawyer, lived with his socially prominent wife, Rachel Eddy Peck. While Mary scrambled to find adequate housing and put food on the table, Lillian enjoyed grand accommodations at the Woman's Club in Minneapolis's Loring Park, where she and a dozen other well-heeled women without husbands resided. The club's lovely Renaissance Revival–style building provided members and tenants with catered meals, museum-like surroundings, and sponsored events. Lillian's unusual living arrangement was not mentioned in my grandmother's memoir, although she gratefully noted Lillian's gifts to the children.[27]

Jeannette Daniel served for a time as the Woman's Club secretary. At the club's February 1935 meeting, she poured tea for members gathered at tables covered with lace tablecloths and bowls of pastel spring flowers. Jeannette and the other ladies present listened to John Strachey, a British Socialist economist and Labour Party politician, deliver an address on "The Coming Struggle for Power," in which he discussed the shortcomings of capitalism during the Great Depression. As she listened, Jeannette's thoughts must have turned to her impoverished stepdaughter a time or two. Had Mary heeded her stepmother's emotional plea to reconsider marrying Harrigan, she, too, might have attended Strachey's lecture on the world's economic crisis. Instead, she lived it.[28]

There is no way of knowing how often or deeply Mary thought about her Minneapolis relatives during this decade of struggle. In 1937, her list of problems grew longer when seventeen-year-old Mary Jo became pregnant by a man who was ten years her senior. He quickly left her to face the pregnancy alone. When Mary learned of the situation, she consulted the family priest, who helped arrange for Mary Jo to go to the Catholic foundling home in St. Paul. In March 1938, she gave birth to a son she named Michael Dennis and placed him up for adoption. It is not clear whether Mary's extended family knew of Mary Jo's pregnancy.[29]

In the fall of 1938, Mary Jo left Waconia for St. Paul, where she enrolled in business school and took a part-time job doing housework. She returned home for Christmas bearing gifts for the entire family, and all seemed well. Around the same time, Harrigan took a new job with the Atworth and Hutchinson Road Construction Company, and the Huckenpoehlers enjoyed their merriest Christmas in years.[30]

Bill Huckenpoehler at time of his high school graduation, 1939.

In 1939, quiet, studious Billy Huckenpoehler graduated from high school, and he and Mary visited Kenwood to ask for help in financing his college education. Mary did not record which specific members of her family they spoke with, but whoever it was declined to help because they lacked the "liquid assets" to do so. Eighteen-year-old Billy then went straight to the US Navy's recruiting office and enlisted. Mary never again mentioned Kenwood in her memoir, failing to note Herbert Jones's death on 9 July 1940, less than a year later, when he suffered a heart attack while driving alone in his car.[31]

When Mary Jo returned home looking tired and down, Harrigan suspected—correctly—that she was again pregnant and banished her from the household. An old-school patriarch like his grandfather almost sixty years earlier, Harrigan was outraged that his daughter ruined the family's standing. In shame, Mary Jo returned to St. Paul, while the Huckenpoehlers observed a glum Christmas in their shabby apartment, graced with a small, decorated tree for the sake of young Jeannie. Mary Jo began living under a false name and gave birth to a daughter on 26 March 1940, apparently with the child's father nowhere in sight. This time, Mary Jo decided to keep the baby and raise her alone. But working, living in a rented room, and caring for an infant proved more than Mary Jo could manage: when the tiny girl became sick, her mother panicked and placed her in an infant home, promising to return and pay for her upkeep. But she didn't.[32]

The baby's caretakers launched a search for her mother and somehow found Mary. She was home alone when the agents arrived, and after they learned that she had no idea where her daughter was, they pressed her to relinquish Mary Jo's parental rights. Doing so, they pointed out, would mean that the child would be raised in a good Catholic home rather than grow up as a ward of the state. Forced to make a decision on the spot and convinced that she was acting in her granddaughter's best interests, Mary signed the necessary papers. When the agency put the girl up for adoption, Rudolph G. Baetz and Mary Welter Baetz, a devoutly Catholic childless couple from St. Paul whose parents had immigrated from Germany, eagerly stepped up, excited to find a child whose ethnic and religious background matched theirs. By this time, the girl was close to eighteen months old, and she was named Jane Frances Baetz.[33]

In August 1940, Mary found much-needed seasonal employment at the corn cannery in nearby Watertown, where the schedule required her to work for six hours and then have six hours off and she felt lucky if she got four hours sleep in a twenty-four-hour period. For the remainder of the summer, Mungi was charged with caring for seven-year-old Jeanne and assisting with housekeeping, a situation that left the sixteen-year old feeling lonely and put upon and itching for fun. Mary, too, was lonely, with Mary Jo and Billy gone and Harrigan again on the road. She complained that Mungi "sometimes didn't even see to it that there was any food in the house to make a meal and wasn't around to send to the grocer."[34]

After a decade of poverty and strife, the Huckenpoehler family had splintered. Mary Jo resurfaced sometime in 1940 or 1941 and was furious at her mother for relinquishing the baby. Soon, however, she met Wayne Drumm, a soldier stationed at Fort Snelling in Minneapolis–St. Paul, and they married in 1941 and moved to Macon, Georgia, where he was stationed at Cochran Army Airfield and Wellston Air Depot (renamed Warner Robins Army Air Depot the following year). Billy, now known as Bill, was admitted to the US Naval Academy in Annapolis. While home for Christmas in 1941, he took special notice of Mungi, perhaps recognizing her restlessness, and promised her that if she finished high school, he would pay her graduation expenses and bring her to Annapolis for his graduation. But Mungi had another offer. Mary Jo was pregnant again and invited her younger sister to come to Macon. So in the early spring of 1942, my mother quit high school and headed to live with Mary Jo and Wayne. In April, with the baby due any day, Mary Jo asked her mother to come and help. Mary jumped at the chance, packed a couple of suitcases, and got herself and Jeannie onto a bus bound for Georgia. For Mary, the trip marked the beginning of three decades of crisscrossing the country to visit her children. Sometimes Harrigan accompanied her, but often she traveled alone.

8

"A Lonesome Mother's Futile Hobby"

> Jeanne and I alone don't make a Round Robin fly, so I will just
> answer whatever letters I get. And let them write each other as
> they wish. I shall not relay news to one about the other.
> —MARY DANIEL HUCKENPOEHLER, 1957

World War II drew Mary and Harrigan's children into a wider world in which they sought adventure and an escape from poverty. Ranging in age from nine to twenty-two at the time the United States entered the conflict, the Huckenpoehlers were transformed by geographic mobility, cultural mixing, and a sexual revolution. By the time the 1940s ended, all were married with families of their own. Throughout the following decade, whether seeking their livelihood in the vastly expanded military, buying a home in the new suburbs, or enjoying the freedom of expanded highways and roadside attractions, they all chased the American Dream and embraced the mass consumption touted by leaders as the reward for the nation's new economic and military prowess.

Mary and Jeannie arrived in Macon shortly before Wayne Drumm Jr.'s birth on 13 April 1942. With "Ma" on hand to watch the baby and manage the household, Mary Jo was able to return to her job as a carhop at a drive-in, where Mungi, who now went by Margaret, also worked. The sisters worked for tips, which didn't

(*left to right*) Jeanne Huckenpoehler, Mary Jo Huckenpoehler Drumm, and Mary Daniel Huckenpoehler, Macon, Georgia, 1942.

(*left to right*) Mary Jo Drumm, Wayne Drumm, and Margaret Huckenpoehler, Macon, Georgia, 1942.

amount to much, but they supplemented Wayne's meager army pay. Shoehorned into the Drumm apartment were four adults, a nine-year-old, and a baby.[1]

Mary Jo and Margaret enjoyed the excitement of wartime Macon, where they could go to the theaters and watch movie musicals and listen to the sounds of big bands blaring forth from nightclubs. In 1942, Frank Sinatra and the Tommy Dorsey Band excited adoring fans with their big hit, "Night and Day," while Bing Crosby soothed them with "White Christmas." The blockbuster film *Casablanca*, released in November, dramatized the uncertainty of love during wartime, giving America two new romantic idols, Humphrey Bogart and Ingrid Bergman. The booming entertainment industry implicitly challenged racial segregation. In search of carefree fun, the Huckenpoehler children belonged to a generation that increasingly crossed the color line to find it. As mobility, music, and movies encouraged interracial contact, Black artists like Billie Holiday, Duke Ellington, Lena Horne, and Fats Waller contributed to the civil rights movement's efforts to chip away at Jim Crow policies and racial prejudices.

The year 1942 was perhaps the most exciting of Margaret's life. Wearing her wavy blond hair long, often with a flower tucked behind one ear, and her

Margaret Huckenpoehler, 1942.

skirts short to show off her slim legs, she now spent evenings with Mary Jo and Wayne at their favorite hangout, the Khaki Club. There, young people drank and jitterbugged away whatever worries they had about what tomorrow might bring. One night, Margaret impulsively danced with a young Black soldier, shocking many at the club and effectively clearing the dance floor. Equally disconcerting to some folks was her new soldier boyfriend, Ben Marshall, an Oglala Lakota Sioux born and raised on South Dakota's Pine Ridge Reservation. Her children's behavior might have prompted Mary to reflect on her own rebellious actions thirty years earlier, when she shocked her proper Kenwood relatives by pursuing her romance with a German Catholic bartender. Perhaps the apples hadn't fallen far from the tree.[2]

The money earned by Wayne, Mary Jo, and Margaret was not enough to support six people, so after a few months in Macon, Mary and Jeannie returned to Waconia, taking Wayne Jr. with them. They arrived back to Minnesota just in time for the Fourth of July. Mary had never laid eyes on Mary Jo's first two babies and was completely charmed by her first publicly acknowledged grandchild. Doting on Junior, whom she nicknamed "Dooner," she lovingly photographed him at ages three, four, and five months. But after he returned to his parents later in the year, she rarely saw him again.[3] Mary was delighted by the normalcy Mary Jo seemed to have achieved through marriage and motherhood. But "normalcy" did not mean that life for the Macon branch of the Huckenpoehler family was dull. A little more than a month after Mary returned to Waconia, she learned that Margaret had married Stanley Bynum, a soldier from Mississippi about whom Mary had heard virtually nothing and whom she had never met. Plus Mary Jo was pregnant yet again. On the day before Junior's first birthday, his younger brothers, Patrick Arthur and Michael Victor Drumm, entered the world.[4]

Sixteen months later, Mary gained yet another grandson when Margaret and Stan welcomed James Stanley Bynum on 18 August 1944. Then came Mary Jo and Wayne's fourth child, William Allen Drumm, on 26 May 1945. That summer, Mary, Harrigan, and Jeannie traveled to Macon to help with the babies, moving into the Drumms' apartment, where Margaret and Jimmy were already living after Stan's deployment to the Pacific in late March. By this time, all the adults, including Mary and Harrigan, had found jobs at a defense plant. When not at work, the grandparents babysat while Margaret, Mary Jo, and Wayne refreshed themselves at the Khaki Club, where they had become regulars and good friends with the owner, Judy.[5]

Jeannie sometimes accompanied her sisters and brother-in-law to the Khaki Club, where she caught the eye of Judy's nineteen-year-old son, Joe. Though she looked older, Jeannie was just twelve years old when they became sexually involved and she became pregnant. Her sisters and parents were horrified. Mary, Harrigan, and Jeannie hastened back to Minnesota to place Jeannie in an unwed mothers' home, where Jeannie, bewildered and frightened, learned about childbirth from the older residents. Her son, whom she named John Gregory, was born in March 1946 and immediately put up for adoption. She then returned to teenage life, working at a roller rink and becoming an excellent skater.[6]

Bill Huckenpoehler Jr. graduated from Annapolis in June 1944 and began his career in the US Navy. On 4 August 1945, just two days before the United States dropped the first atomic bomb on Hiroshima, he married Constance Batcheller, who came from a distinguished Minneapolis family and had recently graduated from the University of Minnesota. He was subsequently stationed on Bikini Atoll in the Marshall Islands, where he participated in Joint Task Force One (atomic bomb testing) from 13 March 1946 to 30 September 1946. Mary and Harrigan apparently did not attend

Bill and Connie's wedding but took great pride in his accomplishments and welcomed his new wife into their lives.[7]

After the war ended in August 1945, Stan Bynum returned to the States and was stationed at Muroc Army Airfield in California's Mojave Desert, where Margaret joined him. When Margaret again became pregnant, Stan sent Mary a postcard imploring her to come help with his growing family. After six months in Georgia and another six in Minnesota, Mary gamely boarded a bus to California. Arriving in September 1946, less than two weeks after William Oran Bynum's birth, she remained for six months. Though California had been a mecca for so many of her rich relatives in the early twentieth century, she found it a terrible disappointment. Beneath a photo of a Joshua tree in the Mojave Desert, Mary wrote that she wondered if "some previous civilization in this part of the world didn't invent an atom bomb & wipe itself out thousands of years ago & these 'mutations' & this ugly dead looking desert resulted."[8]

Never an attraction for the rich, who flocked to Pasadena, the Mojave Desert attracted railroads, a few hearty homesteaders, and drifters heading West. My grandmother's dismal view of the desert is echoed in an outdated video in which the narrator grimly describes how Muroc Army Airfield was built on "barren" lands where "incessant sun, wind, and land" signaled "the bankrupt end of Nature's bounty." In fact, during the 1930s the Army Air Corps had built a gunnery range in the desert, and the destruction caused by the repeated bombing of the natural environment, along with the use of the flat beds of dry lakes as runways for testing new fighter jets, likely contributed to the "ugly dead looking" environment that greeted Mary when she arrived at Muroc Air Base.[9]

I was born in this militarized desert on 21 November 1947, the same year that the US Air Force became a full-fledged branch of the military. Although we lived in the small desert town of Rosamond, the gateway to Muroc Army Airfield, my mother preferred to say I was born in Lancaster, ten miles away. Billy and I were baptized there at the Sacred Heart Catholic Church on 11 January 1948. Mary returned to the California desert she so hated for the occasion and took photographs for her album, proudly noting that "Victoria Lee Bynum and William Oran Bynum" had been baptized as Catholics.[10]

For the rest of her visit, Mary dutifully helped care for me and my older brothers. A photograph from that period shows the children looking healthy but Margaret looking tired. By then, Stan had a serious drinking problem,

The Bynum family: (*left to right*) Vikki, Margaret, Jimmy, Stan, and Billy, Rosamond, California, 1948.

though he was sweet and attentive as long as he was sober. Mary especially loved that Stan had taken "instructions" in Catholicism before marrying her daughter. However, on 11 October 1948, while Mary was in California, sixteen-year-old Jeanne married Andrew Jackson Van Sise, a friend of a family for whom she babysat. Not only was Jack thirty-two years old, but he did not believe in God, and Mary did not approve, to say the least. She later wrote, "My faith in God was all that kept me from doing away with myself when Jeanne ran away & 'married' a man twice her age and an atheist." More than once in her writings, Mary put quotation marks around the word *married* when referring to her three children who had not had Catholic weddings, and fifteen years later, she was "still praying hard" for them. She did concede, however, that Jack had turned out to be "a good man."[11]

Jeanne Huckenpoehler, ca. 1948.

The 1950s brought divorces and more marriages, moves, and babies for the Huckenpoehlers. Our family was briefly stationed at Hunter Air Force Base in Savannah, Georgia, where Mom gave birth to a fourth child, Charles Aden, on 7 June 1951. He died less than three months later, and the following year, we moved to Tampa, Florida, where Dad was assigned to MacDill Air Force Base. Around 1951, Wayne and Mary Jo moved from Macon to Glendale, Arizona, where Wayne's parents and siblings now lived. Three years later, the couple separated. Bill and Connie divorced in 1954, and in January 1955, he married Elizabeth Charlotte Slabe, an art teacher and dancer who had appeared in movie musicals during the 1940s. Later that year, they moved to Guayaquil, Ecuador, where Bill was assigned to the US naval mission.[12]

In 1954, with her children scattered, my grandmother devised a family letter system, the Round Robin. One family would compile a letter and photographs and send it on to the next family; they in turn would add a letter and photographs and forward the packet to another family, which would do the same. Mary did all the organizing, gathering addresses and assigning the order in the packets would circulate. After every family had added their information, the packet returned to her, and she painstakingly copied each letter by hand and added drawings and magazine images as illustrations.

The Round Robin stalled in December 1954 when Grandma slipped on an icy Waconia sidewalk, broke her hip, and was hospitalized for a month. She reorganized the letter system the following October while preparing for a healing winter visit to our home in sunny Florida. For the latter half of the 1950s, the Round Robin kept her and my grandfather informed about their children's and grandchildren's lives.

Those lives, like the lives of other Americans, were increasingly filled with interstate highways, suburban tract homes, television sets, and an ever-expanding array of other consumer goods. The American Dream of upward mobility became a staple of Cold War–era explanations for the superiority of capitalism to communism. In July 1959, Vice President Richard Nixon bragged to Soviet premier Nikita Khrushchev that free markets made America a land of opportunity where families and particularly housewives enjoyed modern high-tech conveniences and appliances. This image of middle-class equality of course overlooked racial segregation, gender inequities, and class divisions.[13]

Bill and Betty came closest to embodying the economic and social ideals of American capitalism. Considered wealthy by his siblings, Bill built a successful naval career before retiring from active duty in 1957 and joining the faculty at the US Naval Academy. Bill remained in the Naval Reserve until 1982, when he retired with the rank of commander. Throughout much of their lives, Bill and Betty taught dance and were active in Annapolis's community theater group. They owned a lovely home that included a large dance studio, and they frequently hosted parties for friends, colleagues, and civic and business groups.[14]

But Mary and Harrigan's daughters struggled to achieve middle-class status. Thanks to Dad's reenlistment in the Air Force and the post–World War II GI bill, my parents bought a modest three-bedroom home in the sprawling new Gandy Gardens subdivision of Tampa, Florida. In October 1955, he was assigned temporary duty in Africa and not scheduled to return until the following January, leaving Mom to run our household alone. In her first Round Robin letter, she drew the floor plan of our new home, penciling in all the furniture; the appliances, including the electric stove and refrigerator; and the bathtub, shower, and toilet. She even included the outdoor clotheslines. She also proudly described the gladiolas and bushes she planted. Though she barely knew how to sew, Mom told her parents and siblings that she had "bought traverse rods and drapery material and made my own draw drapes for the living room." She was clearly delighted that she and Dad had left behind the cramped living spaces and outhouses of the Depression and post–World War II years.[15]

Mom displayed little interest in bragging about my brothers and me. The urgency of having "gifted" children had not yet permeated 1950s America, likely because middle-class status appeared attainable without a college education. Thanks to vigorous efforts by labor unions in the 1930s and 1940s, wages and work conditions had improved for the working class, and many families, including ours, felt little need to send their children to college. So, while my mother noted that I was doing "wonderfully well" in third grade, she showed little concern that sixth-grader Jimmy was "an average student" or that Billy "dreams and plays too much" in fourth grade.[16]

Jeanne and Jack sought economic prosperity through the time-honored methods of hard work, frugality, and patience. While in the navy, Jack was briefly stationed in Millington, Tennessee, where he worked as a radio instructor and where their daughter Jill was born in 1951. The family next moved to Salem, Virginia, where son Jackie was born, so that Jack could attend trade school in Danville. In late 1955, he obtained his radio operator's license and sought work at local stations while the family lived in a tar-paper cabin next to a small trailer. As Jeanne explained in her first Round Robin letter, they were saving money and hoped someday to build a home in the countryside."[17]

Mary Jo remained mired in personal conflicts. After Wayne left her for another woman, she worked at various restaurant jobs in the Phoenix area. Twenty-five years after organizing her own birthday party and changing the rules of Christmas to suit herself, she had moved on to openly flouting society's rules and flaunting her unconventional lifestyle.

Mary Jo was the first contributor to the revived Round Robin and started the ball rolling in October 1955 by announcing that she and Wayne had divorced, Wayne had married his girlfriend in Las Vegas, and that marriage, too, had ended. Wayne and Mary Jo were now moving back and forth between each other's and their friends' homes, with their four boys living wherever the environment proved most amenable. At one point, Wayne and the kids had been living with yet another woman, but now all six Drumms were back under the same roof, with Mary Jo writing that he had finally realized "there are worse women in the world than me" and that she thought "he is about ready to settle down now." They were getting along well "most of the time," she said, and lived in a large two-bedroom house with a "nice yard with trees and a big front porch." The boys were happy, too, she wrote. Always proudest of the twins, Mary Jo bragged that Pat and Mike were "about the smartest kids in their grade," though Junior had been kept back a grade. He and Willie were just "average" students.[18]

On 30 November, my grandmother opened her response to her daughters' letters by writing that "Pa and I are both walking on air" at the news of Mary Jo and Wayne's apparent reconciliation. She had been "storming heaven for help for *that branch* of our family" and would now make a "thanks offering for a mass because I promised that" to God. After describing how she and Grandpa had spent Thanksgiving and reflecting on her impending visit to us in Florida, Grandma got to the heart of her letter: a discussion of the "newsy" pre-Thanksgiving letter they had received from Bill, which she included for his sisters in the new Round Robin. He and Betty had recently arrived in Guayaquil, and Grandma thought he sounded "a little lonesome for news, don't you think?"[19]

Bill's letter opened with salutations in Spanish, followed by a light-hearted, "Dig that Espanol, will you?" There was "always something" to do in Guayaquil, and he and Betty had received invitations to Thanksgiving and Christmas Eve gatherings from the US consul general. They had also recently attended a cocktail party and buffet hosted by the Ecuadorian navy, a reception thrown by the British consul, and a US Marine birthday ball in Quito, where they had flown in an airplane. Bill was especially pleased with their lodgings because Betty had suffered a miscarriage before leaving the States and still tired easily. The navy supplied them with a home that included a "modern kitchen," four bedrooms, two bathrooms, a garage, a patio, and a maid and a "houseboy" who served their meals, mixed their drinks, and was a "good cook." According to Bill, the maid was a "hard worker" who spoke English fairly well. He concluded by describing all the "nice things" they planned to buy during their stay: "silver and silverplate . . . crystal, rugs, clothes, furniture, etc." He was looking forward to hearing about the family's doings and reminded his mother to join whatever book clubs she liked and to "be sure to send the bills down here." After Grandma arrived at our house for Christmas, she and my mother received colorful Christmas gifts from Bill and Betty—"wood carvings of a peasant praying, and one of Our Lady of Perpetual Help, and a serape of violent red, yellow and green, and a leather cigarette case, and a nice handmade straw and wood wastebasket"—but Bill contributed no more letters and Betty only one to the Round Robin.[20]

Like Bill's proud parents, Mary Jo, Jeanne, and my mother were no doubt impressed by the life he led, but Jeanne seemed not to know what to say to someone whose lifestyle was so vastly different from hers: her next letter mainly described the Christmas gifts Jill and Jackie had received. Mom's response is not extant, but true to form, Mary Jo seemed unfazed. She greeted Bill with "Muy bien, Gracias," declaring that she was learning to speak "Mexican": "I say Mexican instead of Espanol because it's as different as American is from English." She knew this because she now had a Mexican boyfriend who was a "good dancer, tall, dark and so-so." She was delighted to report that at twenty-nine, he was six years younger than she was and that he bought her expensive gifts like an Elgin cigarette lighter. According to Mary Jo, she and Wayne had never intended to remarry and their relationship was strictly utilitarian: "He pays the bills and I take care of kids & do the housework." Wayne had found yet another new girlfriend whom Mary Jo described as "young & dumb" and "not too good looking." After adding a few lines about Thanksgiving dinner with Wayne, his girlfriend, and the kids, she signed off with "Merry Christmas to all and to all a 'Buenos Noches.'"[21]

My grandfather, alone in Waconia since Grandma had joined us in Florida, seemed unimpressed by his children's aspirations or their problems. In a brief mid-January 1956 letter to what he called the "Red Robin," he expounded on what he wagered was "the best soup in Carver County." The downstairs landlords furnished the soup bones, while he supplied the vegetables, and "when it's ready, I take the kettle with the soup downstairs for dinner *and how they enjoy it!* We live like kings." Retired at long last, Harrigan took more pride than ever in his cooking and dancing skills. Reminding his children that he would turn seventy-seven on 27 March, he noted that "people say that I am the best dancer in town, and you know it keeps me in good shape." Weather permitting, Harrigan walked downtown to his favorite taverns daily. He found peace in the familiar world of his younger days. In contrast to his children's generation, he sought nothing more and settled for nothing less.[22]

Mary Jo, Mom, and Jeanne took great delight in their father's rare and quaint letters, joking about his reference to the "Red Robin." Mary Jo's letter quickly turned to sadder news, however: Wayne had a car accident while driving drunk on New Year's Eve, and she was "tired of Arizona" and needed a job. She was thinking about moving somewhere else, but a persistent cough made her feel lazy and unmotivated. She speculated about taking "hormone shots," "Geritol," or maybe "ionized yeast" to pep herself up and joked about quitting smoking.[23]

My grandmother could not resist scolding Mary Jo for feeling lazy and "over the hill" at such a young age, exclaiming that she and Grandpa were "spryer now then we were around 40!" She urged her daughter to get a chest X-ray but also suspected that spiritual lassitude accounted for much of Mary Jo's listlessness. Still hoping to resuscitate her marriage to Wayne and perhaps even to bring her back to the church, Grandma cryptically warned that "a house divided against itself shall not stand." The daughter who had always ignored her mother's advice continued to do so.[24]

Mom added a brief letter to the Round Robin three days later. Her news centered again on our family's new suburban life. She and Dad had purchased a new Amana freezer, and she had begun attending home parties where wives got together to buy housewares, cosmetics, and the like. Although my dad had returned from Africa, as a flight boom operator, he was often away from home on missions. Jeanne's letter followed with news about Jack's new job with General Electric in Waynesboro, Virginia, where they continued their spartan life by temporarily renting a four-room house with no hot water or bathroom: they were still saving money to buy land and build a home. Problems soon emerged with the quality of their water, and they were forced to buy a coal stove because their oil stove was inadequate, leaving the family "shiver[ing] from the cold" in the sparsely furnished house. Still, they were excited about building their own home and loved living in the country. Whereas Mom described a freezer filled with vegetables, Jeanne described a garden flourishing with kohlrabi, radishes, beets, tomatoes, corn, and melons.[25]

Grandma remained with us in Florida until the spring, helping my brothers and me with our school lessons and taking us on outings by bus. When she left, she headed to Virginia to visit Jeanne and her family. In May, Mom wrote that Dad was home from overseas duty, this time in England, and followed with joyful descriptions of visits from friends and relatives, weekend fish fries, and swimming excursions. Billy and I had made our First Communions, and the family had a new cocker spaniel, Sparky. In

November, Jeanne reported that she was again pregnant and that she and Jack had bought a used car, were paying off debts, and were still saving for the future. By 1957, the Van Sises lived in Crimora, Virginia, where they would finally build their dream home.[26]

Shortly after Grandma returned to Waconia in August, she and Grandpa realized that they needed to bolster their "sagging backlog of funds." At age seventy, she found a live-in position doing housework and caring "for a very sick lady" in St. Paul. In return, she received room, board, laundry privileges, and $100 a month. The work was hard and did not become easier after she invited Mary Jo, who was having dental problems, to make an extended visit to Waconia.[27]

The situation improved after Mary Jo found work as a companion and housekeeper for a family and Grandpa found a "good, steady job in Schwalbe's Bowling Alley bar" that paid enough that Grandma could quit her job and move back home. Once Mary Jo's teeth were fixed, she made plans to visit us in Florida. This pattern lasted for the rest of her life: when her health suffered and job prospects sagged, she headed to stay with her parents or with one of her siblings—usually my mom.[28]

By 1957, the Round Robin appeared to be losing steam. Only Jeanne, always the best correspondent, could be counted on to write. Bill and Betty were busy in Ecuador, and Mom and Mary Jo were together in Florida. Disgusted, Grandma announced that from now on, she would only answer letters written directly to her and that she would "not relay news" about her children to each other. And with that, Grandma declared the "end of a lonesome mother's futile hobby."[29]

In truth, the Huckenpoehler children were not particularly close to each other. Jeanne had been only nine when her last sibling left home, and she rarely saw any of them after she married Jack and they focused on their rural family life and on building a home. None of the sisters saw much of Bill, and Mom did not see him at all between 1942 and 1961. Distance was an obvious barrier, and the cost of travel and long-distance phone calls discouraged contact. Moreover, Bill and Betty's upwardly mobile, professional lives intimidated and somewhat alienated his sisters. And so, with each passing year, the families grew further apart. Only Mom and Mary Jo, who decided to settle in Florida, maintained an ongoing relationship. They had been close as young women in Macon, where they bonded over their mutual love of music, men, and dancing—and of alcohol.

In June 1961, the extended Huckenpoehler family finally reunited in Waconia. All four of Mary and Harrigan's children attended along with their spouses and children, except for Mary Jo, who came by herself. The highlight of the reunion was an all-day picnic on Lake Waconia when all three generations came together. Grandma and Grandpa were there. Bill and Betty brought John, age four, and Inga, sixteen months. In addition to Jeanne and Jack, the Van Sise children—ten-year-old Jill, nine-year-old Jackie, and four-year-old Clark—were all in attendance, as were my parents and my brothers Jim, sixteen, and Bill, fourteen. I was thirteen. Jim and Bill mostly hung out together, while I tagged along with my mom and Mary Jo everywhere I could, especially to the lakeside tavern.

It was an enjoyable day, and when we said our goodbyes, Mom and her siblings resolved to stay in better touch. But despite their good intentions and a brief flurry of letters, by 1962, Grandma was doing exactly what she had vowed not to do five years earlier: summarizing each family's news in a skeletal version of the Round Robin. Over the next two decades, various siblings occasionally visited each other, but the four of them never again gathered.

PART III

The Eyes and Ears of a Child

9

My Mother's Secrets

Oh, what a tangled web we weave,
when first we practice to deceive.
—SIR WALTER SCOTT

Reading Grandma's memoir and letters gave me valuable insights into the childhood of my mother and her siblings. Now I understood my mother's distant relationship with Uncle Bill and her closeness late in life to Aunt Jeanne and why both of those relationships differed so much from Mom's relationship to Aunt Mary Jo. Although Grandma knew a great deal about Mary Jo's descent into alcoholism and mental disorder, she knew comparatively little about my own family's troubled history and Mary Jo's connections to it. Mom's 1955 Round Robin letters described her proudest domestic accomplishments but concealed the dark side of life with my father, a troubled and violent alcoholic. From the vantage point of a young girl growing up in the 1950s and early 1960s, I observed her and Dad's twisted relationship with each other and with Mary Jo, who frequently visited our family.

My memories reach back to early 1950, the year I turned three, but I grew up hearing Mom's stories about her youthful days in the exciting 1940s. She and Dad regaled my brothers and me with tales of how they had danced the night away to the big band sounds of Glenn Miller and Benny Goodman, how they loved popular performers such as Louis Armstrong, Frank Sinatra, and Ella Fitzgerald. We understood that the 1940s, despite wartime dislocations, were good times, preserved forever in our parents' music collections and carefully tended photograph albums. With flowers in her hair, Mom reminded me of Lana Turner or Rita Hayworth, and Dad, with his Montgomery Clift eyes, was more handsome in his dress blues than I could ever have imagined. It was as though they had walked right off a movie set to go build a family together. But things changed quickly! By 1952, Mom had traded her flowers for a sensible Toni perm, and Dad's dress uniform mostly hung in the back closet. She succeeded at homemaking where her mother had failed, while he struggled to become the loving father he had never had.

Mom confided certain stories to me only when Dad wasn't around. One of her favorites was about her first Macon boyfriend, Ben Marshall, the Oglala Lakota Sioux from South Dakota's Pine Ridge Reservation. When she told him that she was leaving him for Dad, Ben became distraught, beating his head in anguish against a wall right in front of her. You could tell she felt sorry for him but flattered that he cared so much about her. Soon after their breakup, Mom claimed, Ben was shipped overseas into combat and killed in action. Much later, after I had grown up, she added a shocking detail—no doubt over drinks. Ben was my brother Billy's father. Old photos of Ben now took on a whole new meaning as I searched to see Bill's face in his. Later, Mom replaced that story of my brother's origins with another one, only to return to the original bombshell much later.

Who was Ben Marshall? Years later, I found out that he had been born Benjamin Yellow Hair in 1910. His mother died when he was very young. Despite the fact that his father was still alive, in 1923, he and his seventeen-year-old sister, Esther, were adopted by seventy-year-old Elizabeth Marshall, a mixed-ethnic Lakota Sioux from Pine Ridge who was kin to their mother. He completed four years of high school and in 1935 was living and working on a farm in Pennington, South Dakota. In 1939, he joined the US Army. That's how he met Wayne Drumm Sr., Aunt Mary Jo, and later Mom. Ben saw combat in France, earning a Purple Heart for wounds sustained there, and died in Minneapolis of unspecified causes on 22 June 1948—not during World War II, as Mom claimed.[1]

When Mom threw Ben over for Dad, Mary Jo joined the chorus of friends who advised her not to marry a man she barely knew. Stan was anything but husband material—a "rum pot," Mary Jo called him. And Mary Jo would

Ben Marshall, Macon, Georgia, 1942.

have known—she had been messing around with him behind Wayne's back. But although some friends predicted that the marriage would not last a year, Mary Jo gave it five years "because Margaret has a lot of guts." In telling me that story again and again, Mom seemed almost proud that she had stayed married to an alcoholic.[2]

During a whirlwind affair that began in July 1942, Mom and Dad made a hasty trip to Mississippi to meet his family. When they returned, they drove to the courthouse in Houston County, Georgia, and tied the knot on 19 August. With liquor flowing and probably big band music in the background, they celebrated their daringly foolish marriage. Their early years together were frequently interrupted by Dad's temporary duty orders as well as by World War II, which is probably why Mom did not become pregnant for more than a year after their marriage. In late 1942, he attended gunnery school in Fort Myers, Florida, in preparation for service overseas with the 345th Bombardment Group. While Dad was away, Mom kept busy by taking a property accounting course at the Wellston Air Depot.[3]

Dad was none too sure he trusted his pretty wife, who was more than six years his junior: two beers at the Khaki Club, and she was laughing and joking with all the other guys. He likely was not present on the occasion when she danced with a Black soldier, but that behavior would have embarrassed the hell out of him. More and more, he seethed when she had too much fun, and jealousy and alcohol brought out his violent side. More than once, Mom told me, he lost his temper after a night of drinking and knocked her around when they got home. In November 1943, Mom became pregnant, and the tensions between them worsened as Dad contemplated not only the burdens of supporting a wife and child but also the prospect of being sent overseas and into combat.

In addition to not knowing each other very well, my parents had a sort of "mixed marriage" common in post-Depression World War II America. Both were white, but her whiteness emanated from northern Catholic immigrants of the post–Civil War era, while his traced back to early Southern Baptists, farmers, and small enslavers. She came from a community filled with kinfolk with whom she grew up dancing and sipping beer in brightly lit German dance halls. He lacked an extended family and found his fun chugging moonshine behind barns and drinking whiskey in dives no respectable woman would enter. Their second trip to Dad's home state of Mississippi highlighted their religious differences. When Dad took Mom to meet his late mother's family in Jones County, they were met at the door by his cousin, Curtis Shows. Curtis was a fundamentalist hard-shell Baptist preacher who was not about to let a Catholic woman enter his home. Dad went inside but left Mom sitting on the porch.

On another Mississippi visit, Dad later told me, Curtis asked if he was still married to "that woman." By now enraged at hearing how Mom was treated, I asked Dad how he responded to this second round of insults, and he replied, "I told him, yes, I was still married to 'that woman,' and I was gonna stay married to her!" That was the answer I wanted to hear, but I've never quite been sure it was the one Dad actually gave.

On the surface, the shy, sweet Mungi from Waconia, Minnesota, had become independent, fun-loving Margaret or Marge, holding down a job, drinking, and smoking. Yet despite her love of fun and her rebellious streak, especially when fueled by a few drinks, Mom generally relied on those with bolder, more reckless personalities to stir things up. When she frequented taverns with Mary Jo, she appeared somewhat quiet, even demure, in comparison. Yet it was Mom who spitefully bent down the antenna of a car that belonged to some fellow who had offended the sisters in the bar. When the guy caught her, she claimed that someone else had done it and that she was merely trying to fix his antenna. Mom's first rule of mischief was Don't get caught, and the second was If caught, deny, deny, deny.

Dad was deployed to the Pacific Theater on 29 March 1945, several months after Jimmy's birth on 18 August 1944. After the war ended, the 345th Bombardment Group was deactivated at Iejima, an island in Japan's Okinawa Prefecture, on 10 December 1945. He and the unit's other men, smiling and happy to be alive, snapped photographs of themselves, including one in front of the Ernie Pyle Monument and two in front of their camp tents. In one photo, Dad, sporting a beard, smiles broadly as he kneels with six of his buddies; in another, he stands alone, grinning at the cameraman. He was eager by then to put the war behind him, find a good job, and build a stable family life. On 14 January 1946, he was honorably discharged from the Army Air Corps at Camp Shelby in Mississippi. He planned to make a home for his wife and son near his hometown, and after a brief stay with his sister Merle and her family, he rented two furnished rooms in an otherwise empty house managed by his adoptive father in Millard. Dad set out to sell insurance, but he did not own a car, which made it difficult to find customers. He began drinking heavily. Desperate to find a better job or at least sell more policies, one night he stole a car, got caught, and landed in jail down in Bay St. Louis.[4]

Mom had no idea where he was. She lay awake for two nights, listening to noises in the cavernous house, hugging Jimmy, and trying to sleep. On the second night, she heard someone fooling with the front door. Trembling and scared out of her mind, she grabbed the gun Dad kept in the corner of the bedroom and crept to the doorway, only to discover no one was there. It was just a train chugging up the nearby hill.

The next day, she walked with Jimmy to the post office and burst into tears when the kindly postmistress politely asked how she was doing. Hearing Mom's story, the postmistress brought them to her home and called the police station, where they learned what had happened to Dad. Throughout the ordeal, Mom stuck by his side. Truth be known, his reckless ways thrilled her. Plus, she had a two-year-old child and, unknown to Dad, another on the way. Many single mothers were poor, and she never wanted to be poor again. Having failed miserably in the civilian world, Dad rejoined the military on 12 April 1946, enlisting in the US Air Force for five years. He was immediately assigned to Muroc Army Airfield in Mojave, California. Mom then told him that she was pregnant again.[5]

Billy was born on 23 August 1946, less than eight months after Dad returned from the war, leading him to wonder how a "premature" baby could be so large and robust. But having risked his life in combat, he was not ready to risk his marriage, too, and he played the proud papa. In later years, however, Dad would get drunk and occasionally rail that Billy was not his son. Around 1967, Mom told a friend—again, over drinks—that Bill was not Dad's son, and the friend repeated the remark to my brother. But Mom never told either Dad or Grandma the story of Billy's origins.

When Mom told me that Ben Marshall was Billy's biological father, I understood why my brother was dark-skinned and resembled neither her nor Dad. But years later, around 1998, Mom told me and my husband, Gregg, yet another, much more disturbing version of the story. In November 1945, she, Mary Jo, and Wayne were nightclubbing in Macon. At some point, a handsome, "Indian-looking" soldier whose drinking buddies called him Chief caught her eye. She never caught his real name, just that he was from Texas and perhaps Mexican as well as Native American. Soon, the two were bantering and flirting. I suspect Chief reminded her of happier times with Ben.

With a new baby at home, Mary Jo and Wayne left the bar a bit earlier than usual that night. "Better come on, Margaret, you can't stay here by yourself," Wayne called out. Mom just laughed and said, "I can get myself home. You go on—I'm staying here." After more drinks and flirting, Chief offered to drive her home, and Mom accepted. As she told me the rest of the story, she cried: Chief raped her before dropping her at the home she shared with Wayne and Mary Jo. She was too ashamed and emotionally devastated to tell them what happened. And then a few weeks later, she realized she was pregnant.

In October 2010, I was present when Mom told the rape story to her psychiatrist. She cried then, just as she cried when she told me of the pregnancy that resulted. But whatever the truth was regarding Bill's paternity, she never shared it with Dad, and I imagine that the question tormented him, though he never spoke about it in front of me. Was Billy's father someone he knew? Did Mary Jo and Wayne know who it was? One of Mom's favorite sayings was, "Oh, what a tangled web we weave, when first we practice to deceive."

Major geographical changes soon absorbed my parents' time and thoughts. During the next five years, we lived in Mississippi, California, Georgia, and Mississippi again. Then it was back to Georgia, followed by an extended stay in Minnesota before we settled in Tampa, Florida, where we arrived early in 1952 and spent the next six years. On our way from California to Georgia in the spring or summer of 1950, we were cruising along Route 66 somewhere in the Texas Panhandle when five-year-old Jimmy fell out of our moving car. Though not yet three, I remember the whoosh of air as the back door flew open and he disappeared out onto the barren landscape. Nearly four, Billy gaped at the open door for a moment before crying out to Mom and Dad. Dad immediately turned the car around, and soon we saw Jimmy running along the highway in his underwear, shaken but miraculously unhurt.

Disaster averted, we drove on to Macon, where Dad deposited Mom and us kids at the home of Mary Jo, Wayne, and their unruly tribe of four boys before continuing on to Hunter Air Force Base in Savannah, where he was stationed. In Macon, Mom found a job waitressing a few miles down the road from the Drumm home. Mary Jo became the designated babysitter for my brothers and me as well as her own boys. Jimmy was unhappy with our new life. In addition to having been uprooted yet again, he now faced a male pecking order of four rambunctious cousins. One day while at work, Mom was taking a cigarette break at the café when she spotted Jimmy trudging up the highway toward her. Frustrated with her life and astonished that her five-year-old son had walked two miles in the blazing heat, she began to cry. Her boss drove them home, where she discovered that Mary Jo had not noticed that Jimmy was gone.

It is not surprising that one kid escaped Mary Jo's scrutiny, such as it was, or that Jimmy was that one kid. The Drumm boys were relentless pranksters. One day, they coaxed him into drinking pee disguised as lemonade. On another occasion, they gleefully urged me, though not yet three, to jump from the top bunk bed onto a thin brown army blanket on the floor. I can still hear them goading me: "Come on, jump! It won't hurt; there's a blanket here for you to land on!" Ever eager to please, I screwed up my courage, looked down, and took the plunge. Bam! I hit the floor so hard that the room spun. And the Drumm boys laughed.

Every day after work, Mom returned to general bedlam: noisy kids, furniture flecked with food crumbs, tables sticky with spilled soda pop, poorly prepared suppers—or no supper. Mary Jo was an even worse homemaker than Grandma. She and Wayne turned ever more to booze to calm their nerves, and their marriage deteriorated as they blamed each other for their miserable lives. One day amid the mayhem of boys on the run, I watched as Wayne, just home from work, pulled off his leather belt and began lashing at the six boys. Standing too close, I felt the sting of his belt as it nicked my bare legs.

Front row: (*left to right*) Willie Drumm and Billy and Jimmy Bynum; back row: (*left to right*) Mike, Junior, and Pat Drumm, Macon, Georgia, 1950.

Mom longed to have her own home again, a place where beds were made, floors swept, and tables wiped. A place where she could prepare her favorite meals. A place where she could raise her children in a less chaotic atmosphere. She loved to cook, and over the years her specialty became a slow-roasted chuck roast smothered in onions, rutabaga, and carrots and served with mashed potatoes and gravy. She already had mastered a mile-high apple pie with the flakiest crust imaginable.

At the same time, my emotionally and financially unstable father was worrying—and with good reason—that he was losing the love of the woman he adored. To save his marriage, Dad committed himself to being a military lifer and went to work putting their finances in order. While temporarily living in quarters at Hunter Air Force Base, he completed a will in which he left all his worldly goods to Mom and secondarily to my brothers and me. He designated Mom as his executrix and her mother as the alternative executrix and "guardian and trustee of the person and property of my children." Dad's choice of Grandma over any of his Mississippi kinfolk as well as over Grandpa demonstrated not only his lack of close family but also the affection and trust he felt for his mother-in-law.[6]

Dad was promoted to staff sergeant in August 1950, another important step toward establishing an economically stable future for his family. Soon after, he was off on another temporary duty assignment. Around the same time, the Drumms talked of moving to Glendale, Arizona, where Wayne had family and hopes for a better job. Since we could not move to Arizona with them, Dad moved Mom and us kids temporarily to Jones County, Mississippi, back to his sister's home. That was fine with Mom, who was weary of living with her hard-drinking, domestically challenged sister.

Our new living arrangement at Aunt Merle and Uncle Grover's tenant farmer's house was decidedly better, though sparser in its accommodations. A hazy visual snapshot of Merle and Grover's house remains in my head. As I peered into one of its rooms, I saw a double bed and not much more. In fact, the entire house was largely devoid of furniture. There were no rugs on the floor, no colors anywhere that I remember. And once again, I was the only girl in a house full of rowdy boys. Uncle Grover was as much of a drinker as Wayne and Mary Jo, but at least I felt welcome. Unlike Aunt Mary Jo, Aunt Merle was sober, hardworking, and motherly. She seemed happy to help Mom take care of my brothers and me. I remember one dark night when she took me to the outhouse. I was scared that a snake might slither up on the stinky two-seater and bite me in the butt, and I worried that my cousins, who I could hear yelling and chasing each other outside, would see me with my pants down. "Aunt Merle, don't let those boys see me," I begged. "Them boys ain't gonna see you, Honey," she said as she stood guard.

The move to Jones County was number five for Jimmy, who turned six in August and entered first grade at Sweetwater Elementary School. Already schooled in the pranks of his Drumm cousins, he more easily adjusted to his Breazeale cousins—Sonny (who was not Grover's son), Buddy, Conrad, and the twins, Royce and Richard. They were older, less competitive with

Jimmy, and even somewhat protective of him. As an adult, Jimmy remembered that Merle and Grover frequently exchanged blows. Brawling couples were nothing new for us, but Sonny was not fond of his gruff stepfather and defended his mother. Jimmy recalled watching in awe one night as Merle raged at Grover for spending what little money they had on liquor. She came up behind him and jerked his pockets inside-out and then grabbed the loose change that tumbled out and threw it into the yard. The cousins immediately began diving for the money, as though they had witnessed this scene before, so Jimmy dove right in with them.

Royce Breazeale remembered that he and his twin, Richard, were a bit dazzled by Mom and her "tailor made" (store-bought) cigarettes and tight capri pants. To get her attention, one or both of them sneaked chicken shit into her bed one night—as smitten country boys will do, I suppose. Merle became great friends with Mom and marveled at her beautifully sculpted apple pies. They did their best to make life fun, sometimes resorting to games of strip poker with Grover and Dad's brother Cliff. Mom claimed that she and Merle always managed to win, forcing the men to face threats of a "pater pullin." As much as that memory amused Mom in later years, nothing tickled her more than remembering Merle's canned farts. If someone broke wind in the women's presence, Merle would jump up, run fetch a can, wave it in the air, and then snap it shut in time to "can" the fart. Telling that story, Mom laughed until she had tears in her eyes.

Baking pies, playing poker, and canning farts may have helped pass the time but did not cure Mom's boredom. Eventually, she ventured out to make friends, and at some point, she met and began an affair with a guy named Earl. Our Mississippi kin began to gossip that my parents might split up. And in rural Jones County, folks likely knew exactly why. A few years later, I overheard a lively family conversation about this time: initially unaware that I was within earshot, Aunt Merle described discussions about which family members might take my brothers and me in that case. But when she noticed me standing nearby with a quizzical look on my face, Merle said that she had told her brothers to stop that kind of talk; "besides, ain't no one gonna take Vikki away from me." I rewarded my aunt with a grateful smile, while silently noting the existence of mysteries about my parents' past.

Vikki Bynum (*left*) and Margaret Huckenpoehler Bynum, 1984.

Much of what I learned about my parents' history, I learned in my thirties over a few bourbons with Mom. Dad retired from the Air Force in 1962, and by 1967 they had moved to Monterey, California, where he operated the city's street sweeper. After Burt and I split up in 1975, the kids and I regularly caught buses or trains to Monterey during summers and holiday breaks to spend time with my parents. My brothers and their families generally joined us. By 1982, Dad was fully retired, his health ravaged by years of heavy drinking and smoking. Taking care of him limited Mom's social life to occasional gatherings with women friends and a love affair here and there. Mostly, her days were filled with housework, cooking, gardening, and TV soap operas. Visits from her children and grandchildren helped keep life interesting.

During those visits, Mom and I always found time for a trip to Segovia's on Lighthouse Avenue or to Bosso's across the street. We would relax, laugh, and talk privately. After a drink or two had warmed our insides, she would punch up Bob Dylan on the jukebox and become the feisty, outspoken woman who had crossed the color line—at least on the dance floor—back in 1942. Now a fierce critic of the Vietnam War and the New Right backlash against the 1960s protests, she loved to argue about politics. Once, she was ordered out of Bosso's for blasting Nixon, condemning the war, and advocating amnesty for deserters. But as much as she relished being a firebrand, her rebellious spirit always melted away in the sobering light of morning.

Mom's intellectual bent came from Grandma and a good Catholic school education, but she had no reverence for higher education or religious doctrine. After all, neither had prepared Grandma to feed four children and maintain a household in the Depression-ridden 1930s when Mom was a child. Her passion for politics and Dylan came from Billy, who was also the first of Mom's kids to attend college. Although she never joined political groups or sought to expand her formal education, she read voraciously. In addition to expounding on current music and politics, she relived her younger days by telling me stories from the past. When I went off to college, I affectionately referred to her as my "armchair radical" mom.

At the same time, I began to understand my mother's frequent affairs in the context of a marriage in which she felt trapped by economic need and my father's emotional dependence. Merle had given her a firsthand look at the effects of alcoholism on a husband's ability to support his family, while Mary Jo had demonstrated the economic and social degradation of divorce. Mom had an alcoholic husband, but she had no way to earn a good living without him, and his military career provided financial stability. Her solution was to stay married and look elsewhere for romance and excitement.

10

Lifting the Curtain of Guilt and Shame

On a hot August day in 1951, I squatted on the sidewalk near our yard to gaze at my baby brother, who was lying motionless in a tub of shallow water. My mother stood nearby, crying as a middle-aged female nurse leaned over Chuckie and attempted to breathe life into his mouth. In the background I heard the word *dead*. I silently wondered why the nurse kept breathing into his mouth.

Memories of two-and-a-half-month-old Chuckie mark the dawning of my consciousness as I approached my fourth birthday. My only memory of him alive is that of my mother breast-feeding and cooing to him while she sat in a kitchen chair. Today, his death speaks to perplexing family mysteries at the root of her later emotional detachment, my father's frightening rage, and the divided paths to maturity taken by my older brothers and me. Almost preternaturally, the life and death of our youngest brother connected the heady World War II era when Mom and Dad met, fell in love, and married with the troubled decade of booze, secret affairs, and family upheavals that followed. Much later, she confided to me that Chuckie had been the child of a man named Earl with whom she had an affair and that as with my brother Billy, she and Dad had silently pretended the baby was his. What else was Dad to do?

(*left to right*) Billy, Vikki, and Jimmy Bynum, 1951.

Charles Aden Bynum was born on 7 June 1951, not long after Dad moved us from Aunt Merle's home near Ellisville, Mississippi, to Hunter Air Force Base in Savannah, Georgia. Initially, we moved to the modest Nelson Apartments, newly built to accommodate Savannah's population boom and conveniently located near the air base and schools. Shortly after Chuckie's birth, we moved to a larger apartment in Savannah's South Gardens neighborhood. Then, Dad was off on another temporary duty assignment, this time to England.

On 28 August 1951, the day Chuckie died, Jimmy was outside on the porch attaching pinochle cards to his bicycle spokes with clothespins to achieve the clacking sound that was all the rage among kids. Suddenly, Mom's scream pierced the air. The gathering of family and neighbors around the nurse who labored to revive my unconscious brother followed. The next day, a local newspaper reported that the infant son of Sergeant and Mrs. O. S. Bynum had died of suffocation. Details were brief but gruesomely clear. Just before eleven o'clock in the morning, the infant's mother had found him "with his head between the head of the bed and the mattress at their home." Sergeant Bynum was away "on maneuvers in England" at the time.[1] The newspaper's account fit the story I heard growing up, one that I recounted over and over in my head and occasionally to others. Mom had gone outside to hang laundry, leaving a sleeping Chuckie on her double bed, with pillows surrounding him in case he woke up. She returned to find him lying motionless with his head beneath the bed's headboard. That's when she screamed.

After Dad returned from England, whenever the family drove past the cemetery where Chuckie was buried, Jimmy, Billy, and I (or maybe just I alone) would chirp, as we had been told, that our baby brother had "flown to heaven." Mom and Dad said little or nothing in those moments. The fact that Chuckie was not Dad's child must have made it difficult, even impossible, to comfort each other after the baby died. As years passed, Mom refashioned his death into a crib death, a topic that received an increasing amount of public attention in the 1960s. The inexplicable nature of crib deaths helped quiet her mind and ease her feelings of guilt. But never for long. She grieved for Chuckie all her life, more openly than ever as she approached her own death at age ninety-three.

We soon left Georgia, leaving behind forever the "baby lot" of the Savannah Catholic cemetery where Chuckie is buried. In the fall, Dad was transferred to MacDill Air Force Base in Tampa, Florida, but first he had to complete a course in flight engineering at Kelly Air Force Base in San Antonio, Texas, from December 1951 to January 1952. Rather than leave us in Georgia, he drove us to Waconia, where we wintered with Grandma and Grandpa Huckenpoehler. After attending grade schools in Mississippi and Georgia, Jimmy now entered second grade at Waconia's St. Joseph Catholic School. Judging by several beautifully scripted *F*s on his report card, he did not adjust well to his third school in two years.[2]

My earliest memories of Grandma are from this winter. I have no memories of Grandpa during this time, but Grandma, who read to us children nightly, quickly became a comforting figure in my world. She turned sixty-four during our stay, but she seemed older. At my young age, I assumed she had always been old. A hairnet held her wavy white hair behind her head. Her body was heavy and shapeless. She wore only dresses, never slacks, with sturdy black lace-up shoes. I never had the sense that my grandmother cared to be young again. In this era, only rich women and actresses had "face work," but it was more than that. The first time I saw a photo of her taken when she was my age, I blinked. It didn't seem possible that she had ever been a child. I was shocked to see a little of myself in her face.

Like most children, my earliest surviving memories are of times when I felt confused, scared, or surprised. In Waconia, I experienced all three sensations when Cathy Stenger, the eleven-year-old daughter of one of Grandma's friends, Cathy's sister, and I went to Waconia's park and playground. Cathy, a cheerful girl with ruddy cheeks, had an infectious way of smiling and shrugging her shoulders when talking to people. As the three of us walked toward the park swings, Cathy stopped to banter with some friends, one of whom called out from high in her swing to ask who Cathy had with her. "This is my sister," Cathy replied, adding, "This is my partner." I liked that Cathy called me her partner; it made me feel like I belonged in this new town.

That sunny sense of camaraderie was quickly destroyed. The girl in the swing reminded Cathy of an upcoming social event and then looked directly at me and said, "But *you* can't come because *you're* not invited!" I was cut to the quick. I had never before been treated with open contempt. I told myself, "Well, anyway I don't care because I don't even know what 'invited' means." But I did care! Without saying a word, I turned and walked away alone. When I reached the end of the park and faced the intersection of streets on either side, I felt small and lost. Somehow, I found my courage and made my way back to the safety of Grandma's house.

Minnesota introduced us kids from the South to our first real winter. Playing in the snow for the first time was exciting, especially in my new red hooded snowsuit. One day, all buttoned up and wearing mittens, I repeatedly ran in and out of the house, unable to stand the cold for more than a few minutes at a time before laughing and returning to my grandma's side. Curiously, my memories of my mother during our stay in Waconia are few. Once, I encountered her on the sidewalk outside my grandparents' home, walking toward town to watch a movie alone. I asked her if I could come along, but she smiled gently and said no. Only a few months after losing Chuckie, she must still have sought solitude for her grief.

In the spring of 1952, we prepared to move to Florida. MacDill was an important new Strategic Air Command base, and Dad, attached to the 306th Bombardment Wing, was already there, earning extra flight pay as a boom operator for the new B-47A Stratojet. Mom, Jimmy, Billy, and I excitedly boarded a train to Tampa to join him. In the middle of the night, I woke up to find Mom missing, and I eventually tracked her down primping in the train's large washroom. We were about to arrive. Dad soon greeted us in the darkness outside the Tampa train station. I have a blurry memory of being tired and excited and of us taking a ferry to reach our destination.

We kids were now true Air Force brats. The military helped us move into the fading Gadsden Homes, a concrete housing project built during World War II for MacDill families. Mom and Dad soon made friends with another military couple, Denver and Betty, and my brothers and I became friends with their kids. Patsy, just my age, became my first best friend. Likewise, her brother Mike became Billy's. Summers were typical childhood fare. We played in the sprinkler, spent our allowances on black cherry colas and ice cream sandwiches, and sat with other kids in circles on the lawn, eating popsicles from the ice cream truck that jingled by every day. Gadsden Homes was scheduled for "rehabilitation" in December 1953 to prevent "further depreciation through vandalism, termites, and weather," so in early 1954, we moved to a house on Gabrielle Street, only five blocks from the air base. It was a medium-sized bungalow with two bedrooms and one bathroom. Rather than share a bedroom with my brothers as before, I now slept on a rollaway army cot in the hallway. The best part was our nice yard and screened-in breezeway and garage, none of which we had at Gadsden Homes. The empty lot between our house and the street became a popular place for softball games and general play as we made new friends in the neighborhood.[3]

In February, we had a surprising visit from Grandpa Huckenpoehler, who had hitched a ride with some Waconia buddies heading to South Florida. During his stay, he, Mom, and I enjoyed a wonderful day on the Tampa Bay Causeway. The weather was beautiful. Walking along the bridge, we smelled the salty air and listened to seagulls screeching overhead. Grandpa loved playing tourist and posed for picture after picture in typical Florida settings—holding a handful of sand on the beach, in front of a bait-and-tackle shop or a huge sign advertising a frosted mug of draft beer, in the center of a long line of palm trees. For a man who rarely left Minnesota, visiting the Sunshine State was quite a treat, especially in February.

By the summer of 1954, Mom and Dad had lots of Air Force friends, and beach cookouts were common. A highlight was the joyful week we spent at Bradenton Beach with several other families. The swimming was nonstop, the sunburns fierce. Back home, we kids welcomed the arrival of television. We watched the usual stuff—Jimmy loved *Howdy Doody*, and Billy doted on

Saturday morning cartoons. We all enjoyed *Superman, Sky King*, and especially reruns of old werewolf and Frankenstein horror movies

Music remained important to my parents, although their dancing years
were behind them. Their album collection grew to include white mainstream performers such as Gogi Grant, Kay Starr, Rosemary Clooney, and
the Weavers, a folk quartet that included Pete Seeger and that was black-
listed in 1952 because of the members' left-wing political views. Mom and
Dad continued to listen to Black crossover artists, especially the Ink Spots,
Mills Brothers, Nat King Cole, and Nina Simone. On weekend nights, they
occasionally attended MacDill's "squadron parties," where they drank heavily. However, they generally did not drink during the day unless they were
attending a beach party or special celebration.

At age six, I belonged to what seemed to me an average American family.
Most days were calm and predictable. Mom was a dedicated homemaker who
cleaned our clothes in a wringer washer, scrubbed floors with a string mop,
and cooked tasty dinners almost every night. After dinner, we turned to our
favorite TV shows. On a typical Sunday morning, we kids might pile into
bed with our parents, where Dad would pin us down and call on Mom to
"Shoot these crows!" Mom would run and grab the broom and "shoot" each
of us with it. We would all laugh and begin the day happy and energized.
Sometimes we took the fun to the backyard, where Dad wrestled with the
boys while Mom and I did calisthenics. Mom had superb natural flexibility
and coordination: her splits and backbends amazed me. We both delighted
in walking on our knees with our legs folded up under us, yoga-style. And
of course we had a dog—a cocker spaniel puppy named Poopsie. My saddest
memory of those early days in Florida is of Poopsie contracting distemper.
Dad got us through the crisis by sitting quietly with my brothers and me
in front of an electric heater where we comforted and petted our beloved
puppy until he drew his last breath. Dad was a family man, gentle and fun-
loving—except when he had too much to drink.

Only a year separated Billy and me in age, and we frequently played
together. For a while, we enjoyed cutting out cartoons of the Campbell Soup
kids from magazine advertisements, then searching Penney's and Sears'
catalogs to supply our chubby-cheeked tots with beds and other household
supplies. Our paper doll families entertained us on many afternoons before
Billy moved on to more boyish pursuits. I soon turned to store-bought
paper doll sets that featured famous celebrities and to Katy Keene comic

Margaret Huckenpoehler Bynum and Vikki Bynum, Tampa, Florida, 1955.

books that contained cutout sections and advertised deluxe paper doll books to send away for.

Reading was by far my favorite activity, even before I began school. I did not attend kindergarten, but just before beginning first grade at age five, I cracked the code of reading as I walked around the yard with a book and pencil, circling all the words I recognized. From there, I moved on to devour the six-volume *Child's World* series that mom bought from a traveling salesman. The nursery rhymes in the first volume fascinated me by providing the historical contexts in which the rhymes were created. Other volumes focused on people's great deeds, plants and animals, the wonders of the world, and children of other countries. I especially enjoyed anecdotal histories from around the globe, like how the Chinese developed goldfish by carefully selecting and breeding gold-mottled fishes. My lifelong and even obsessive habit of reading took hold during these years.

Temperamentally, I shared Dad's emotional nature. We both were anxious nail-biters who regularly teared up at sad TV or movie scenes—even corny commercials. Unlike Dad, I blinked my tears back in hopes no one saw and snickered at me the way we did at him for being a bawl baby. Perhaps that's why I preferred playing with paper dolls and reading alone to watching TV with the family. The fact that I had only brothers contributed to my lone pursuit of hobbies. Soon, I discovered drawing. For the longest time, the boys and I drew the same stick figure: a girl or boy with a round head, a triangle dress or square suit, and single lines for arms and legs that ended in circles for feet and hands. Sometimes I got Mom to draw me a pretty young woman (who always resembled World War II pinup Betty Grable): I then cut her out and drew clothes for her. Inspired by Mom's sketching talent, I began to draw more realistic human faces and bodies at around age six. This, too, became a favorite solitary activity.

Billy was the family's only true introvert. He watched so much TV that Dad nicknamed him Television Eyes. He collected Superman comics and baseball cards and invented an elaborate baseball card game that he played alone. Stimulated by movies and television, he played out war scenes with his tiny green plastic soldiers, tanks, and such. Like me, Billy liked to draw, but his drawings were epic scenes of war that began with two rival airplanes poised to attack each other. They always ended with a huge black blur of scribbled bombing campaigns of mutual annihilation ripping through paper.

Jimmy was the most outgoing—extroverted, socially adept, and handsome. To make a splash, he often stretched the truth or told outright lies. Once at the dinner table he told Billy and me that in India they put a plate piled ten inches high with salt in front of you and make you eat it all. Just to imagine being forced to eat even the first spoonful of a pyramid of salt made me feel sick. Jimmy was like Mom. Once, when I asked her about the surgery scar behind her ear, she told me without batting an eye that it was the opening through which she delivered her babies. A few years later, memories of their stories made me furious, and I felt stupid for believing them.

As we kids got older, Mom and Dad's unhappiness grew increasingly apparent. So did Mom's detachment from us. One day I ran in from outside to tell her something oh-so-important. She had been cleaning, upending chairs and mopping the floors, and was taking a break. As she sat on the living room hassock, smoking a cigarette and humming, I began excitedly telling her my concern. She did not so much as bat an eyelash, so I repeated myself. Still no response. Frustrated with all her la-de-da humming, I turned and ran back outside. Looking back, I see that this was when she and Dad began to drink more heavily and when Dad became more violent. I learned not to trust the joyful beginnings of their nights on the town. I loved seeing my parents—especially Mom—all dressed up. When she finally emerged from the bedroom, her lips painted red and her hair carefully waved, wearing a full-skirted, low-cut shiny dress accented by sparkly rhinestone earrings and necklaces, Dad would give her a rousing wolf whistle, and off they'd go. But then in the middle of the night, we kids would awaken to sounds of them shoving and screaming at each other.

Their fights invariably centered on accusations and denials of cheating, with Dad accusing Mom of some flirtation, imagined or real. Mom would deny his charges and swear she was going to leave him before morning: "When you wake up, I'll be gone! And if I come back, it'll only be to get the kids!" More shoving and yelling would follow. Finally, my brothers and I would jump from our beds and run to the living room. Jimmy would bravely bark, "Don't you hit my mother,"—just as Sonny had yelled at Grover—and Dad would turn on Jimmy. I would jump into the fray and start yelling at Dad to stop. One time I yelled so hard that the hairs above my lip stood out straight. Billy was cowering in a corner, terrified, as he later told me, that "he's going to kill her someday."

Come morning, I would creep into the bedroom to see if Mom had really left us. She hadn't. Instead, she'd be lying in bed, smelling sour and imploring me to fetch a Coca-Cola from the fridge for her "hot pipes." Dad would be equally hung over and penitent. "I think he's learned his lesson," Mom would say, signaling that she was giving him another chance. After a while, I no longer feared that Mom would make good on her threats to leave. Instead, I grew to resent her for not doing so—and for not taking us with her.

The tissue of lies that underlay my parents' relationship continued to grow. Mom lied about her affairs, which continued. Much later, she told me of "falling in love" with a tavern friend named Scotty and of the resulting pregnancy. This time, she turned to abortion instead of deception. Mary Jo had self-aborted more than once with knitting needles, but Mom's fears prevented her from taking that route. Instead, she obtained a back-alley abortion. The resulting bleeding terrified her, but the woman who performed the procedure comforted her and stopped the bleeding.

Dad lied about his drinking, both to others and to himself. Typical was the time he took me for a ride to the store on his little red scooter. After purchasing a bottle of liquor that he tucked away in a brown paper bag, he told me, "You don't need to say anything to your mother about this." And I didn't—Why cause another fight? When my parents got into it and neighbors called the police, he affected an amazingly calm mask of innocence: "No officer, we're not fighting; just had a little party here. Sorry if things got noisy." Mom would stand mute in the background as the police left.

When not absurdly denying that he had ever laid a hand on Mom, Dad would admit that sometimes he drank too much and went too far. But it was her fault: "You kids don't know your mother; she drives me to drink!" He was vague about exactly how this worked, but at least once Billy heard him yell at her that he was not Billy's father. If I had heard that comment, I would have dismissed it as outrageous. To me, the idea that Mom cheated on Dad was nuts. In our eyes, she was strictly Dad's victim, entirely innocent.

Jimmy had two other brushes with death. One late summer day around 1953 or '54, when we still lived in the Gadsden Homes, he and Billy walked to the store to buy cokes and snacks. To get there, the boys had to cross a busy thoroughfare during rush hour. As they waited for a green light, Jimmy assumed an older brother's authoritative stance, sticking his leg out at the street's edge like he'd seen grown men do. Suddenly, a car struck him. The driver panicked, slammed on the brakes, and stopped the car on top of Jimmy's lower leg. She jumped out of the car, saw with horror what she had done, and got back in and moved the car. A man pulled Jimmy off the road and ripped the jeans off his leg from the thigh down. Amazed by the man's strength, Jimmy felt helpless and grateful.

Billy ran home, hollering that Jimmy had been "run over" by a car. Mom and Betty jumped up from the lawn chairs where they had been lounging, and since Mom didn't drive, Betty drove them to the scene of the accident. An ambulance had come and taken Jimmy to the hospital, and the woman who had hit him drove Mom there as well. Amazingly, he had no broken bones. Nevertheless, medical personnel wrapped his injured leg in bandages, and gangrene set in. As doctors were debating whether to amputate his leg at the knee, they noticed that hair was growing just below his knee, meaning that Jimmy got to keep it. Skin was grafted from his thighs to replace the gangrenous flesh of the injured leg. Mom and Dad used the $1,200 medical malpractice settlement they received to buy a 1954 Ford sedan, which our family badly needed.

Soon after Jimmy was discharged from the hospital—so soon that I have trouble separating the two stays—he was back there again. He developed a stiff neck, which Mom knew was a warning sign of polio. She took him to the doctor, who diagnosed not polio but spinal meningitis. For weeks, Billy and I played on the maze of wooden ramps outside Jimmy's hospital room, and I can still see the building's lush green grounds and smell the pungent summer air. Best of all were the outdoor vending machines, which seemed to dispense a never-ending stream of eight-ounce Coca-Colas. Sometimes the young orderlies would bring Jimmy outside with us and roll him up and down the ramps at breakneck speed.

After a stay at the base hospital, Jimmy was transferred to Tampa General Hospital at Davis Islands, and about two weeks later, he was discharged. When Dad went to pick him up, Jimmy was so weak from lying in bed for so long that Dad practically had to carry him to the car. On their way home, Dad took a detour down a road shrouded with bushes and vines, and Jimmy was curious about where they were going. The answer: a tavern close to a river, with a monkey tethered to a nearby tree. The monkey jumped and screeched at them as Dad helped Jimmy inside. Dad bought himself a beer and Jimmy a Roy Rogers (cola and grenadine). Jimmy ate the cherry on top as he stared at a gigantic dead rattlesnake hanging behind the bar. The Roy Rogers did wonders for his ability to walk, and he limped outside and played with the monkey while Dad finished his drink. Jimmy was pretty sure that most dads did not stop at bars on the way home from picking up their kids from the hospital, and he was relieved when he finally arrived home. Later, when he mentioned to one of his teachers that he had been hospitalized with meningitis, she told him he had to be mistaken—he would not have survived the disease.

More and more, Dad's drinking intruded on our family life. On the way home from work, he routinely stopped at the NCO Club, where he ran a liquor tab. One day, Mom exploded in anger after discovering his NCO bill was equal to our home's monthly rent. The Air Force facilitated Dad's alcoholism in other ways as well. Military personnel looked the other way when he showed up for roll call on work mornings and then returned home to sleep off a hangover. I hated seeing him asleep on our couch when he should have been at work. The only thing worse was when he was arrested for driving drunk, but an upper-level military official fixed at least one of his drunk-driving tickets.

I was about seven years old when I noticed that Mom and Dad's nights on the town had become more frequent and raucous. Late one night, they brought home some new "friends" from one of their favorite taverns. This was unusual, and my brothers and I were curious and came out to have a look. Mom was passed out in the middle of the living room floor while guests drank and chatted. The sight of her lying there, slim in her satiny tight black skirt and tucked-in white blouse, disturbed me. No one else seemed to notice her. A large, amiable Cuban man greeted us kids from Dad's easy chair. Jimmy and I were taken by his jewelry, particularly his big watch and his turquoise ring. Amid our banter, he allowed Jimmy to wear his watch. The night ended quietly enough, and the next morning I dove into the leftover snacks still sitting out on end tables. Eagerly shoving a handful of pretzels into my mouth, I discovered they were soaked with spilled beer and just as quickly spit them out.

After the most memorable—and horrifying—late-night house "party," we kids woke up to find Mom gone. In the wee hours of the morning, I padded sleepily into the living room and followed a trail of blood droplets that led through the living room to the kitchen, where Dad sat slumped in a chair. He had been beaten up. Looking up at me, his swollen face sadder than I had ever seen it, he mumbled, "Your mother is gone. She won't be back; she's not a good woman." Jimmy, who had been awakened even earlier by sounds of a ruckus, later told me that he saw three men beating up Dad in the bathroom. He yelled out, and they fled. I soon learned that Mom had left with the men and that one of them was a family friend, Sid. As I absorbed what was before me, I felt frightened and confused.

Only later did I learn from Mom what had happened: she and Dad had gotten into a fight at the bar, and he had hit her. Sid then jumped up from his barstool and punched Dad, growling, "This is what I do to men who beat their wives." He and two other men then followed Dad and Mom home, where they worked him over some more before driving off with Mom in tow. She returned home a day or two later. As I quietly sat on a kitchen chair, she brushed my tangled hair and gently asked, "Are you mad at me?" I said no, but I couldn't look at the woman my father had labeled bad. Truth is, I *was* mad! My heart broke for Dad, whose spattered blood and slumped body remained vivid in my mind. At the same time, I badly needed and savored my mother's comforting touch.

At the time, I did not know that Sid was yet another of Mom's lovers and the idea that he was a friend of both my parents was a charade. Months earlier, Billy and I had spent a pleasant afternoon with Mom, Sid, and his two little daughters at Ballast Point Park, playing on swings and climbing on the old bandstand in the center of the park. On another occasion, Mom and Dad drove Sid and his soon-to-be ex-wife to a lawyer's office. From the backseat, I eyed the hard-looking skinny blond sitting in front and thought that must be the way divorced women look.

As alcohol and adultery permeated our parents' lives, Jimmy increasingly engaged in antisocial behavior. He was a magnet for trouble, especially while waiting for the school bus. I became so used to his scrapes that one morning, when I overheard a girl say to another, "Oh, I wouldn't want to be him," my immediate thought was, "Oh, I hope they're not talking about Jimmy." They were. I turned to see him bent over a dirty puddle wiping mud off his arms and his once-clean school clothes. He and another boy, he later explained, had gotten into a slap fight. A more serious scrape occurred after he smarted off to a girl at the same bus stop and she immediately charged home to tell her mother. Next thing I knew, she was running back up the street with her mother running right alongside her. It was a fearsome sight. I had never seen a mother join a fight with her kid against another kid. She persuaded the bus stop monitor to order Jimmy to the principal's office, which he did. He then told Billy and me that we had to go, too. When I protested "But we didn't do anything wrong!" the monitor retorted, "You went into the street to see if the bus was coming." When we arrived at school, he escorted us straight to the principal's office with Jimmy, where we all received a stern lecture about bus stop behavior before being sent to class.

Alcohol-fueled fights between Mom and Dad continued. Dad's beating by Sid et al. was never again mentioned, and in time Sid resumed his status as a family friend. That pretense allowed life to drift along as though all was normal, including the family's participation in a farce about Sid and me getting married when I grew up. I couldn't have been more than seven when it began, because I actually believed that Sid intended to marry me. The idea bothered me more and more. He was clearly too old, and I had no romantic interest in him—or any man—at such a young age. So, one night when he was over for dinner and the usual banter began, I turned and whispered to Billy that I wasn't *really* going to marry Sid when I grew up. To my horror, Billy immediately announced, "Vikki says she's not really going to marry Sid!" I was immediately concerned for Sid's feelings and denied having said what I did. It didn't matter: he wasn't at all bothered by my revelation and continued to treat me as his girl.

Sometime around 1955, the summer before I turned eight, Sid spent the night at our house, as sometimes happened when a visitor was too tired or drunk to drive home. In such cases, my rollaway cot bed would be set up in the living room for the guest and a pallet made for me elsewhere. On this night, however, Mom and Dad allowed me to sleep with Sid on the rollaway cot, a decision that still bewilders and infuriates me. At the time, however, I thought nothing of the arrangement and fell right to sleep.

At some point, I woke up and found my hand wrapped around something very hard. As I lay there, I realized what it was. Had I accidentally placed my hand around Sid's peter while asleep, I wondered in horror? Barely breathing, and without moving another muscle, I slowly removed my hand. Then I lay there, tense and still, hoping I had not awakened him. Without saying a word, Sid slowly took my hand and placed it back around his erect penis. I moved it away again and stuck both my hands under my back, lying on them so he could not reach them. I lay awake there until dawn, frozen in fear. He did not touch me again. I never said anything to him or to Mom and Dad about what had passed in the night. In fact, I don't remember ever again thinking about that night until I was grown. And now I'm not certain whether the sexual assault occurred before or after the night Sid beat up my father.

In August 1955, Dad was approved for a Veterans Administration home loan. What an exciting time it was for the entire family—we were about to own our very first home! We bought into the Gandy Gardens subdivision, which featured street after street of new flat-roofed rectangular homes, all pretty much alike. The development was typical of the sprawl of lower-middle-class housing that soon blanketed much of suburban America, but to us, it meant we had arrived. Our new home included a carport, front and back yards, a sidewalk, and three bedrooms. Our new cocker spaniel, Sparky, completed the portrait of familial bliss. Mom and Dad had reached the high point of their efforts to build a life together. Today, I feel the hopeful joy in the Round Robin letter in which Mom drew each room and piece of furniture and described the curtains she sewed and the flowers she planted.[4] Her comforting image of upward mobility masked the alcoholism, adultery, and violence that had become a regular feature of our lives.

11

Children Unattended

In late August 1955, we moved into our newly built home in Gandy Gardens. Owning a home promised to provide everything we needed to be a happy family. Dad was proud to finance all the new furniture and appliances he could afford on a tech sergeant's credit line. Mom could at last be the domestic paragon her mother never was. My brothers and I played with new friends until dark nearly every day. I loved riding my bike along the endless parade of streets, pretending each one was a different state as I traveled far and wide across border after border.

Mom and Dad particularly enjoyed furnishing our new home. Not only did I have my own bedroom, but I also got a brand-new twin bed—no more rollaway cot in the hallway for me. My parents even bought me an unfinished three-drawer chest that Dad got right to work painting a bright shade of turquoise. Of all our new furniture, I loved the living room set the most. The black-and-gray-flecked sofa and matching chairs were inexpensive and not all that comfortable, but their wrought iron bases with sharp angles and spare lines reflected the modern styles of the rocket-propelled 1950s. Lamps with matching metal cylindrical bases completed the look. The perfect final touch was the living room's beautiful, pleated drapes. It still amazes me that Mom bought traverse rods and reams of flowered cloth and made the drapes with her brand-new Singer sewing machine. She was proud of herself, and so was I. She never sewed anything else with that machine. When I got married and left home, she gave me the sewing machine. Today, her short-circuited attempt at creative homemaking reminds me that for reasons I did not yet understand, achieving the 1950s "good life" did not free my parents from the trap of a troubled one.

Grandma was so impressed with Mom's descriptions of our new home that she came all the way from Minnesota to spend the winter of 1955–56 with us. I was eight years old, excited, and curious to see her again. I still remembered bits and pieces of our time in Waconia when I was four. Dad was away on military assignment in North Africa, and Grandma arrived in time to help decorate our beautiful fir Christmas tree. We hung two strings of lights, including the fancy bubbling kind, and plenty of Shiny Brite ornaments before adding the final touches. I watched in admiration as Grandma created a tree topper by drawing a big star on cardboard, then cutting out the star and wrapping it in aluminum foil, carefully smoothing it to achieve maximum shine. Next came the icicles. Slowly and methodically, she hung them one by one on the tree, explaining that each silver strand should hang perfectly straight, untouched by the others, so that it would look real. Ever since that Christmas, I have hung icicles just the way our grandmother taught us, explaining why to others, just as she did to us.

She was like no one else in my immediate world. An elderly, intellectually vigorous woman, Grandma lived life with a sense of purpose and began each day with a plan. Her visit was in part to prevent her from falling again on the Minnesota ice, and she took long walks each day in the mild Florida weather to strengthen her bones. I soon joined her on walks, and every day we progressed a little further, talking along the way. Once we walked all the way to the highway, past a little souvenir seashell shop that I had previously seen only from my parents' car window. Though I ran and played outside every day, I had never imagined walking such a long distance.

I wasn't used to the sort of attention she gave me. A former teacher but also a nurturer in the old-fashioned sense of a woman's duty, Grandma took it upon herself to tutor me at home when I got sick and had to miss a few days of school. She did the same for Billy when he had the mumps. My fourth-grade teacher, Miss Ebersole, seemed impressed when I proudly told her about my grandmother, which made me want to do things that would impress my teachers. I took note that Grandma kept a journal of her daily thoughts and activities, and not too many more years later, I began keeping my own daily diary. Unlike my grandmother, Mom and Dad rarely did little beyond perusing my school report cards. I didn't mind, though, because school was a place of refuge for me, and I preferred to keep it wholly separate from home. My favorite classroom activity was our silent reading period, which allowed me to retreat into imaginary worlds. Once, I became so absorbed by a Grimms' fairy tale filled with faraway mountains of ice and princesses threatened by death that when the teacher announced it was time to close our books, I felt startled and momentarily disoriented.

Grandma also arranged trips with us kids that seemed more special because they did not include Mom or Dad. In February 1956, she took Jimmy and me to Children's Day at Tampa's annual Gasparilla Festival, though Billy had the mumps and couldn't come. In her usual organized way, she had already visited the fair by herself to learn her way around, and the three of us had a great time watching the reenactment of the exploits of legendary pirate Jose Gaspar and his ship. I loved the bright colors of the fair, its bustling crowds of people, and my new Kewpie doll on a stick. I also discovered that in spite of its pink and wonderful appearance, I hated cotton candy. Later, she took each of us kids separately by bus to a large department store downtown and allowed us to pick out one item as a gift from her. As I struggled to choose my gift from a vast display of children's books, a nun in full habit came walking up the aisle—the first time I ever saw a nun in the regular world. Influenced by Grandma's devout Catholicism, I wanted to talk to the nun, but I was too shy to speak and just stared up at her worshipfully, blocking the aisle and preventing her from moving on. She gestured kindly at me, and I came to my senses and moved aside, embarrassed.

Although Grandma gave me special attention, she frequently retreated into her own books and thoughts the way Mom did. Sometimes I would leave for a minute while we were talking in my bedroom, which was Grandma's room during her visit, and come back to find her still talking, unaware that I had left. At the time, I thought she was just old, but at sixty-eight, she was nowhere near senility or death. My most vivid experience of her "vagueness" (as I called it) occurred on a beautiful spring afternoon. One day, I ran frantically into the house because I had just discovered our neighbors' beautiful long-haired black cat lying dead on their side of the fence that separated our yards, with Dixie, a neighborhood Weimaraner, standing in perfect point position over the cat's body. Grandma was lying on our couch, one hand holding the book she was reading, the other behind her head, and was unmoved by my description of the horrific sight. "I never liked that cat's looks," she offered blandly without looking up from her book. She simply was not in my world at that moment. I stood and stared for a few seconds, struggling to accept that so loving a person could react so casually and without feeling to a cat's violent death. I guess I was seeing the woman from Mom's childhood memories who stirred a pot with one hand while holding a book in the other. The one Grandpa time and again told to "trow dat book avay!"

But in Grandma, I was also seeing my mom, humming and smoking a cigarette, oblivious to her children and surroundings. Retreating to books was an escape from anger and anxiety for both women, and it became that for me, too. Yet while Mom and Grandma shared similar temperaments and habits, they were opposites in many other ways. Grandma's religious faith helped her to control the temper she had displayed as a child and as a young woman. Catholicism gave her rules to live by and faith in God's plan. Mom, however, hated rules as much as she hated open conflict. She preferred sexual adventures to attending church, and she lied rather than prayed about her errant behavior. Secrets and lies helped her avoid confrontations with her mother, her husband, and even her children. At the same time, she carefully hid her true views on religion from Grandma, unlike Uncle Bill and Aunt Jeanne, who openly abandoned the Catholic Church.

Mom kept up a good front, enrolling Jimmy in Catholic school while we lived in Waconia and making sure we kids were baptized and observed important Catholic rituals. In the spring of 1956, shortly after Grandma's departure, Billy and I made our First Communions. I was excited to wear my beautiful white bride-of-Christ dress and veil to confess my sins to the priest. We little confessors were then rushed to the Officers' Club, where bustling waiters in white jackets served up the fluffiest scrambled eggs I'd ever seen. But other than special Catholic events and Christmas and Easter, we rarely attended church.

Like many adult Catholics, Mom privately deplored the church's restrictions on birth control, abortion, and divorce. One day, Grandma told me that Uncle Bill and Aunt Betty were sinners going to hell because they had married outside the Catholic Church. Those harsh words confused me, and I asked Mom about them, causing her to lose her temper and blurt out, "Oh, dammit, that's not true!" She fumed for a good while afterward. Her reaction made me even more confused: Grandma was the most morally upright person I had ever known, but I wanted Mom to be right about Uncle Bill

(*left to right*) Billy, Jimmy, and Vikki Bynum with Sparky, at the time of Billy and Vikki's First Communion, Tampa, Florida, 1956.

and Aunt Betty. To consign people to hell for marrying outside *any* church just seemed wrong. Grandma's words again perplexed me.

Grandma's belief in the sanctity of Catholic marriages was directly challenged after three months of living at our house. When Dad returned home from overseas, he got drunk as a skunk and began raging. Grandma never said anything, but she wrinkled her brow and pursed her lips, nervously watching as the only Catholic marriage among her children was defiled by drunkenness. I wonder today if she was reminded of her own marriage, defiled by Grandpa's adultery, or thought about the eve of her wedding day, when she gave her stepmother, Jeannette, a supremely confident lecture about the infallibility of the Catholic Church. Whatever Grandma's thoughts about my father, her faith in the church's rules on marriage remained intact, at least outwardly. She never once advised Mom to seek safety for herself or her children by filing for divorce. Like most people in the 1950s, including my parents, Grandma considered drinking too much simply a bad habit that led to problems. Men like my dad just needed to learn their lesson and cut back on the hard stuff—maybe stick with beer. Women drunks were lushes, always sexually suspect. Alcoholics Anonymous had been founded in the 1940s, but to belong to it was an admission of having hit rock bottom.

Soon after Dad's drunken tirade, Grandma announced that she was returning to Waconia, explaining, "Vikki needs her room back." I instantly felt guilty for all the times I had whined or complained about anything during her visit. Grandma had become a vital part of my daily life, and I did not want her to leave, especially not earlier than originally planned. But leave she did, and, at age eight, I wrote my first letter to tell her that I missed her. Sometimes, while at school, I imagined her watching over me. Wanting her to be proud of me, I kept my back extra straight as I walked in line with my classmates.

Grandma's visit coincided with the confrontations over racial segregation and second-class citizenship for African Americans that rippled throughout the South in the wake of the US Supreme Court's 1954 and 1955 decisions in *Brown v. Board of Education*. In the most monumental civil rights decision since *Plessy v. Ferguson* in 1896, the high court overturned its concept of "separate but equal" facilities, ruling that racial segregation in education was unconstitutional. I knew none of this at the time, and I have no memory of Grandma or anyone else in my family discussing the racial crisis before the 1960s. Like most white kids in the segregated South, I'm sure that I heard racist remarks while listening to everyday conversations among adults. I'm just as sure, however, that no one ever mentioned the 1957 murder of fourteen-year-old Emmett Till by whites in Mississippi in my presence during this time.

Gandy Gardens had no Black residents, and African Americans appeared in our lives only rarely and fleetingly The man who pulled Jimmy from the road after the car hit him was Black, and so were the cooks and waiters who served Billy and me scrambled eggs following our First Communion. That was about it. I assume that we absorbed the conventional wisdom that Blacks were inferior to whites and that the two races "naturally" lived in separate, unequal worlds. That was the way the world came to us, and most white Americans—especially those in the South—rarely questioned why prior to the civil rights movement of the 1950s and 1960s.

My immediate family said very little to their children about race relations for as long as we lived in the South. None of us, including Dad, identified as a southerner. Insulated by our Air Force connections, we viewed southerners as people who lived around us but not among us. None of us had southern accents—Dad had ditched his soon after he left Mississippi. I sometimes affected a southern accent just for fun, making my parents laugh when I called it my "southern action."

On a summer day around 1953, as I played near a large open field that separated our Gadsden Homes neighborhood from a Black housing project, I connected with some girls from the other side. The darkest-skinned person I had ever seen up close asked in a friendly way to borrow one of my toys. In return, she offered to let me play with her baton. I agreed to the trade, but I had no idea how to twirl a baton. She advised me to just jiggle it back and forth, and so I did. After a short time, we returned each other's property and went our separate ways. The only reason I remember such a pleasantly banal interaction, I'm sure, is because it occurred across the color line in segregated Florida, and likely it was my first personal interaction with a Black girl.

A few years later, probably in 1956, I enrolled in summer school, determined to learn to swim. As I rode the school bus to the municipal pool, I noticed a Black girl about my age sitting by herself. I had never seen a Black student on a school bus before. Just like me, she had her swimsuit wrapped in a towel. She looked straight ahead and never spoke to anyone. Only later did I realize that her presence indicated an early stage of Florida's uneven efforts to integrate its schools. My school, Tinker Elementary, found itself in a dilemma. Tinker was a county school built with federal funds in 1952 to accommodate the children of Air Force personnel. Its administrators had no choice but to abide by federal regulations and to desegregate. At the same time, the Hillsborough County School Board voted to resist integration. Rather than comply with federal policy, Hillsborough County relinquished Tinker Elementary school to the federal government. The principal, secretary, and thirteen teachers elected to remain at Tinker, a decision that forced them to resign from the county school system and be rehired by the federal government.[1]

President Dwight D. Eisenhower took a far more conservative approach to desegregation than did Chief Justice Earl Warren, whom Eisenhower had appointed to the Court in 1953. The president stated that he accepted and would obey the *Brown* decision but failed to endorse its principles and dragged his feet in implementing it. Historians have rightly criticized Eisenhower for taking a legalistic approach to integration that emphasized constitutional duty over human rights. Nevertheless, his actions—and by extension, those of the military—had a tremendous impact on desegregation policies, particularly after he sent the National Guard to Little Rock, Arkansas, to protect the lives of Black students in 1957.[2]

MacDill Air Force Base's approach to integration reflected Eisenhower's adherence to the rule of law even while Florida school boards initially resisted it. I was thus introduced to school integration but shielded from witnessing firsthand the violence committed by white opponents and the resulting terror. Only after 1961, when our family moved to Plattsmouth, Nebraska, a "sundown town" that barred African Americans after dark, did I personally encounter bred-in-the-bones hatred of Blacks. By then, thanks to TV coverage of violent attacks on civil rights activists, I already considered my father's home state of Mississippi the most racist place on earth.[3]

Despite my youthful naivete in 1957, at age ten I got a direct taste of how badly many white Floridians dreaded integration. Jimmy, Billy, and I occasionally played with two brothers and their sister, Darla, in Gandy Gardens. When evening approached after a particularly exhilarating game of hide-and-seek, I asked Darla if I could have a drink of water from her house, and she said sure. In the kitchen, her pretty, friendly mom gave me a glass of water, which I gratefully gulped down. Then her mom asked me, "Vikki, do y'all's parents mind if y'all go to school with coloreds?" "Uh, I don't know," I stammered. I had no idea what she was talking about. "Well, I sure don't want my kids goin' to school with 'em," she stated firmly, staring off toward her living room. I suddenly felt intensely uncomfortable and left immediately. I never told anyone about her comment.

Though ignorant of the civil rights movement, I was quite aware of Cold War anticommunism. Not only were Americans regularly warned about the Soviet Union on the evening TV news, but we kids were informed of the dangers of communism by the *Weekly Reader* magazines distributed in our classrooms and regular tests of the sirens that would warn us of foreign attacks. In college, I learned that the politicians who condemned communism frequently decried the civil rights movement, labor unions, and nascent feminism in the same breath. Smeared as communist fronts by a growing right-wing movement, civil rights organizations and labor unions were labeled as antithetical to the American capitalist way of life. My dad, an Air Force sergeant rather than a wage worker, depended on the military, not industry, for his livelihood. As a result, I heard little or no union talk in our household. At the same time, various racist laws and policies allowed politicians to block most Black veterans from collecting the GI benefits that enabled white veterans like Dad to buy their first homes. Endless movies, television shows, sermons, and magazine articles assured white middle-class wives and mothers that their God-assigned role as homemakers made them the bulwark and beneficiaries of American capitalism.[4]

Air bases were established in distant parts of the world in the name of national security, but they also protected US economic investments. Before college, I knew nothing of the anticolonial and communist-inspired guerrilla movements in the Middle East and Latin America, of the Chinese Communist Revolution of 1949, or of expansionism in Eastern Europe. I knew only what I had been taught in grade school: that military power and anticommunist vigilance were vital to Americans' prosperity and well-being.

Tests of the alert sirens were similar but much scarier than fire drills. During fire drills, we walked outside, lined up, and dutifully waited on the school grounds. We knew that a genuine fire was unlikely to be raging. The sirens, however, were intended to let us know of an impending atomic attack, meaning that the entire nation might be blasted to smithereens at any moment. Dad's service in French Morocco during the height of Cold War deterrent missions likely increased my anxiety. So did the dog tags issued to children by our school so that we could be identified if an atom bomb burned us beyond recognition! Why else would anyone choose to wear a flat oblong steel ID around their neck? In one of my worst nightmares ever, Asian-appearing invaders of the United States forced Americans into hiding, causing me to wake up in a cold sweat.

Even though I read and heard more about communism than about Black civil rights, I stumbled into trouble on that issue, too. During the 1956 presidential election, we kids stayed up late watching the returns on TV. We rooted for our parents' candidate, Democrat Adlai Stevenson, a US senator from Illinois, but in a rerun of the election four years earlier, he lost to Eisenhower. I guess I thought that all smart people agreed with me and my family that Stevenson should have won. Otherwise, I surely would not have carelessly made fun of the president of the United States as I did one day in school.

Sometime soon after Eisenhower's reelection, my teacher assigned our class the task of writing a personal letter to the president. Since he had not been my family's choice, I playfully opened my letter with "Hateful" instead of "Dear" and then giggled as I showed my letter to the girl sitting next to me. Well, she jumped right up and ran to the teacher's desk to report my shocking salutation. Fearing I had committed treason or something, I quickly erased the offending word before the teacher called me forward to answer the charge. Heart beating fast, I lied and denied having written the word. Despite the telltale eraser smudge on my letter, the teacher dropped the matter. As I made my way back to my desk, I heard another student say that what mattered was that *I* knew what I had done, whether or not I admitted it. The teacher nodded her agreement. Shamed, I sat quietly at my desk.

In lighter moments, our family visited the new Britton Plaza Shopping Center, one of many such burgeoning open-air consumer meccas in postwar America. Britton Plaza boasted thirty-eight stores and twenty-two hundred parking spaces on thirty-plus landscaped acres. Housewives were encouraged to drive over as soon as their children left for school and shop to their heart's content, have lunch, and take in a movie at the "modernistic" theater. They could also choose to work off their lunch at the Slenderella weight-loss salon.[5] Our entire family attended Britton Plaza's grand opening on 16 August 1956. I thrilled at the sight of dozens of brightly lit, air-conditioned shops filled with trinkets, toys, clothes, jewelry, and furniture. The larger stores even had sparkling lunch counters. Jimmy, Billy, and I quickly escaped Mom and Dad and ran around as though we were in an amusement park.

While I traipsed wide-eyed among the gaudy displays, the boys pulled off a carnival-like scam. They ordered snacks at one of the lunch counters and walked away without paying their tab. When I met up with them, they invited me to do the same. Taking seats at a different store's crowded lunch counter, we ordered up slices of the most delicious blueberry pie ever and repeated the heist.

In 1957, the year I turned ten, Aunt Mary Jo decided to come stay with us "for a while," just as Grandma had almost two years earlier. I was excited, though I barely remembered Mary Jo from back when our family lived with her and Uncle Wayne in Macon. Right away, I deduced that mom's older sister was fun-loving, liked to tell dirty jokes, and drank lots of beer and vodka. Although Mary Jo was only thirty-eight years old, six babies in twenty years, an active nightlife, and a lack of regard for regular meals had aged her beyond her years. Slim and gangly in her younger days, she still had long legs, but they were now topped by a pear-shaped torso. Her dyed black hair and red lipstick accentuated her aged skin and sagging facial features. With Mary Jo

Mary Jo Huckenpoehler Drumm, Glendale, Arizona, ca. 1955.

around, Mom and Dad sat, drank, and laughed, even in the daytime. I liked the more sociable environment created by her presence.

Once again, my bedroom served as the guest room, but unlike Grandma, Aunt Mary Jo offered no surrogate parenting in return. Still, there *was* a benefit. Entering the room to retrieve my clothes gave me the opportunity to rifle through her suitcase, which lay open on the floor most of the time. I loved touching her scarves, which smelled like perfume and cigarettes and made me think of brightly lit streets at night. One day, I thrilled to discover a small, tattered diary tucked in among her clothes. At first, I assumed it was my aunt's diary, and I dove in. As a divorcée, Mary Jo was not like any woman I knew, and I was eager to learn more about her life. As I read the diary, I quickly realized it was not hers but rather belonged to some man who worked in a garage (as did Wayne) and who chiefly used the diary to record when and where he engaged in sex. The entry "Hell, no pussy today" stands out clearly in my mind. Why Mary Jo had the diary is not clear, but I suspect it figured into her back-and-forth relationship with Wayne. Knowing her as I soon would, it is easy to imagine her laughing at Wayne's discovery that his daily sex log was missing.

Aunt Mary Jo treated us kids much the same way. She always seemed to know what we were up to, and she made sure we knew that she knew it. One day, I was horrified when she remarked to Mom within earshot of me, "I know Vikki's been going through my stuff." That ended my plundering expeditions on the spot. And after pretending to be Jimmy's ally, she immediately double-crossed him by telling Mom—in his presence—that he had been smoking. Whether playing with ex-husbands or with nieces and nephews, gotcha was one of Mary Jo's favorite games.

With Mary Jo in our house, my brothers and I had less parenting and privacy than ever before. Thirteen-year-old Jimmy was running with a fast crowd, heading for trouble. Eleven-year-old Billy turned further inward, absorbed ever more by comics and baseball cards. One day, when we had the house to ourselves, Jimmy pulled Dad's rifle out of my parents' bedroom closet. As he stood in front of their dresser mirror aiming at his reflection, I happened to walk into the room. Seeing me, he whirled around and playfully pointed the gun at me. I got nervous and turned and exited the room. Soon, I heard a loud bang. I ran back to the room to find Jimmy, still holding the rifle, staring in shock at the shattered mirror. He had not known the gun was loaded. For years, the gaping hole and jagged diagonal crack reminded us all—but especially me and Jimmy—of the day he pointed a loaded rifle at my chest just moments before he fired it at his image in the mirror.

The growing chaos in our home not only made me anxious but caused my outward appearance to suffer. I had lost my bedroom as a dressing area, and our only bathroom was now less accessible for personal grooming. My hair was frequently dirty and stringy. When I was younger, mom braided the front part to the side, but now it often hung down over my eyes. One day when I was in fifth grade, as I busily worked on a writing assignment with hair hanging in my face, my teacher, Mrs. Maloni, bent down and whispered in my ear that I needed to do something about my appearance, especially "that hair." "You and that Gail!" she hissed. I couldn't believe Mrs. Maloni would lump me together with "that Gail," a scraggly-haired, ruddy-faced mess of a girl. Surely I didn't look like her!

I went straight to the mirror when I got home that afternoon. I pushed my oily hair around my face a bit, then put on one of Mom's hairnets, which puffed my hair up in a most pleasing manner. Excited by the results, I showed Mom and asked her if I could start wearing a hairnet to school. "Why would you do that?" she asked, and she and Aunt Mary Jo stared at me like I was nuts. Later in the day, I told Mom what Mrs. Maloni had whispered in my ear. Mary Jo overheard and laughed, "Oh, so that's why she wanted to wear that damned hairnet to school!" Completely embarrassed, I dropped the subject.

One afternoon, Dad took me with him to the big new superstore where Mom had recently taken a job as a cashier. The trip was a last-minute decision, so I threw on an old tan corduroy blazer that was missing its buttons. I had no shirt underneath, so I kept my arms folded over the blazer to keep it shut. I was excited to see Mom, and she was chatting with a coworker when we walked up. While we waited for them to finish, I stood at Dad's side with my arms folded, flipping my hair out of my eyes. Mom did not appear happy to see us, and as soon as her coworker left, she scowled at me and scolded Dad for bringing me to the store looking like such a mess. As I looked down at the none-too-clean jacket, my pedal pushers and bare shins, and my flip-flops, a feeling of shame swept over me. As we walked to the car, Dad said sheepishly, "Yeah, you really don't look very nice," or something to that effect.

I also didn't smell very nice. Until about age ten, I was a bed wetter, and with only limited access to our family bathroom, I now sometimes went to school unbathed. One morning on the school bus, I was eavesdropping as a chubby, well-dressed girl whose manner and appearance screamed "officer's kid" gushed to her friend, "Mother promised to buy me that new 'pink pearl' nail polish." Suddenly, the girl gestured toward me and blurted out, "She stinks!" As the other kids around us sat in shocked silence, she repeated her remark. Another girl spoke up and said, "I'm sure you don't smell perfect." But I knew that I and I alone smelled of pee.

With Mary Jo living in our home, drinking and sexual promiscuity were ever more visible. One day, I listened in the background as she and Dad sat at the kitchen table discussing their tavern friends. Dad told Mary Jo about his recent adventure with Mary, a bartender at the Log Cabin: "She took out my peter and I played with her titties, but, nah, she never did much for me," he said in a low voice. Mary Jo listened, nodded, and grinned without comment, both of them unaware of or unconcerned about my presence.

Not surprisingly given their earlier sexual history, Dad and Mary Jo ended up in bed together again. One day, I came home from school to find my bedroom door locked. Figuring Aunt Mary Jo was napping, I went and sat on the living room floor to watch TV with the boys. I hardly noticed when Mom arrived home from work until I heard my bedroom door slam. Mom had forced it open, and I looked up to see her racing down the hall with Dad close behind. For the rest of the afternoon, Dad sat at Mom's knee, repeating over and over again, "Margaret, I did not pump Mary Jo!" Dad insisted that he was struggling with Mary Jo atop my bed to prevent her from taking an overdose of pills. Mom wasn't buying it, and Mary Jo soon confessed to Mom that she had seen exactly what she had thought.

Jimmy and I separately found mischievous ways to express our resentment at Aunt Mary Jo's intrusion into our lives. He paid her back for telling Mom and Dad that he smoked by stealing a pack of her cigarettes and then methodically lighting and taking a puff off each one before throwing it into the toilet. As for me, I got a thrill out of taking Mary Jo's tubes of lipstick, removing the tops, twisting the lipstick all the way up, and then slowly pushing the lid down over the lipstick, savoring the sight of smashed red cream that awaited my aunt. Soon enough, and true to form, Mary Jo casually complained to Mom when I was within earshot that she wished I would quit ruining her lipsticks. I froze but did not cop to anything. I did stop smashing her lipsticks, however, just as I had quit rummaging through her suitcase.

During the months when Mary Jo lived with us, Little League season provided an escape from our crowded, chaotic household. Mary Jo did not attend Jimmy and Billy's ball games, and Mom and Dad neither fought nor drank. Since there were no leagues for girls and I was too restless to sit on bleachers all afternoon, I sometimes wandered across the street to my old school, Tinker Elementary. I roamed the school's pleasantly quiet, empty halls, running my hands along bumpy salmon-colored walls and reminiscing about childhood days that seemed eons ago.

Around this time, my fascination with adult misbehavior led me to the book *I'll Cry Tomorrow*, by actress Lillian Roth, which I stumbled onto while excavating a big box of items Mom stored in our carport utility room. *I'll Cry Tomorrow* helped me to understand alcoholism. Many of Roth's experiences echoed my own, from alcohol-fueled domestic violence to sexual assault by trusted family friends. Though still a child, I was fascinated by the life story of · this famous woman who oscillated between greatness and degradation. I read about her exploitation and sexual assault as a child performer, her knockdown, drag-out marriages, her triumphs and failures so many times that I remember the details today. Likewise, the photographs that cataloged her rise to stardom and descent into alcoholism remain seared in my memory.

I understood from Roth's story that alcoholism runs in families. That scared me. Why did so many children of drunks, as she and I both were, become drunks, too? Was that my destiny? Or was it to marry one, as my mother did? Such fears haunted me for years. At around the same time, my parents took my brothers and me to see *Peyton Place* at the Dale Mabry Drive-In Theater. Normally, adult movies put me to sleep, but not this one. I vividly remember how Selena is raped by her drunken stepfather and then murders him. The movie's trifecta of alcohol, sex, and violence was all too familiar to me.

As my interest in adult misbehavior grew, I began reading the sixth volume of *The Child's World*, the series that had put me on the road to being a lover of books. Although the first five volumes were intended for children, the final volume was the *Mother's Guide*. Though written for parents, it could not have been better timed for my needs. The guide featured illustrated vignettes on how to raise children to accept responsibility for their actions, tell the truth, and be productive citizens. In particular, I took note of its advice to parents not to shame children who wet the bed. I was pretty sure Mom and Dad needed to read volume 6, but it wasn't for me to tell them.

When Mary Jo finally moved out of our house, she didn't go far. She found a job at a nearby bowling alley and rented a cute little place of her own—a bungalow shaded by trees with a nice little carport for her Buick. Then she found a new man. One evening when she and Mom were out on the town, she met Frank King, a good-looking red-haired sergeant stationed at the air base. Frank, who was having a beer with Mom's new boyfriend, Scotty, soon hit it off with Mary Jo. Both drank heavily and hit the taverns regularly. In August 1959, they married. If Mary Jo was seeking economic security in a second marriage, Frank was not the man for the job.

At the end of the 1950s, Jimmy's troubled adolescence came to a head. By age thirteen, he had added nighttime parties and sneaking the family car out in the middle of the night to his roster of misdeeds. Billy and I—junior delinquents in training—began to venture out after dark, too, mostly to spy on Jimmy. One day, Billy told me that he had discovered that our next-door neighbors' house was unlocked and had gone in and looked around. He enlisted me to join him in a second entry. It felt strange to stand uninvited inside someone else's house, plus I was terrified that they might come home and catch us. At the same time, I was fascinated by having breached the private space of people

I barely knew. I quietly crept into their bedroom and spied a woman's ring on top of their dresser. As it sparkled up at me, I considered stealing it. But it occurred to me that I could never wear it around Mom and Dad, much less around our neighbors. Well, then, I thought, maybe I could steal it and just fling it into the nearby woods. That didn't make any sense, either, I reasoned. The danger of being caught and the absurdity of stealing something only to throw it away convinced me to leave without the ring. The outdoor air felt liberating. Never again did I contemplate a life of crime.

I'm not certain when Mom and Dad discovered that Jimmy and his friend George were sneaking our new 1957 Ford station wagon out in the middle of the night and driving it into downtown Tampa. Looking back, Mom laughed at the image of the boys' "little heads" peering up over the car's dashboard in downtown traffic. They were about thirteen years old, and they never once got pulled over by the police. I think she was impressed. It was my turn to be impressed when Jimmy's name and photograph made the local newspaper after he and another friend stole a car. You couldn't really see him in the photo, just an officer on horseback looking down into some weeds where "Jim Bynum" had attempted to hide. The friend had intended to drive the stolen car to his dad's house in Michigan but was dropping Jimmy off at home first when the cops pulled them over.

The whole episode made my pulse race. I felt a strange sort of importance if not quite pride. Like a growing number of teenagers, Jimmy was sentenced to juvie, the juvenile detention center, for car theft, the third-most-popular teen crime of the 1950s. When our family visited him, I took note of how cool he looked in the denim jacket he was issued as a detainee.

Jimmy's waywardness unleashed a level of anger and contempt from Dad that was beyond easy explanation. That Jimmy looked and acted like Glenn Ford's worst nightmare from *Blackboard Jungle* was part of it. "Look at you! Awwh, you suck on cigarettes, and you pull your hair down," Dad railed, imitating Jimmy tugging his hair past his forehead. Whenever Dad came home drunk, he now went after Jimmy, including one afternoon when Dad pushed him back against the kitchen sink and held a butcher knife over him. I don't remember how the confrontation began or ended, only that Jimmy emerged unhurt. In that moment, he became a brave, heroic figure to me, and I knew that from then on, I would tell any lie necessary to shield him from Dad.

In the spring of 1958, we learned that Dad had been transferred to Castle Air Force Base in Atwater, California. The timing was perfect. We were burned out as a family, worn down by Mom and Dad's unhappy marriage and Jimmy's troubles with the law. Here was a chance to start anew. The Golden State promised to be our best fresh start ever. Somewhere, I found a copy of the novel *Peyton Place* and slipped it into my traveling bag. We were on our way!

PART IV

Days of Reckoning

12

Islands of Refuge

"So, what were you doing when you were sixteen?" the doctor jokingly asked his nurse as I lay with my feet suspended in stirrups for my first-ever pelvic exam. "Well, I can tell you that my daughters aren't doing it," she responded with a smirk. Embarrassed, I said nothing as this Air Force doctor and nurse, whom I'd never met before walking into the exam room, casually joked about my sexual history. After all, I was clearly guilty of what the nurse claimed her daughters were *not* doing. The year was 1964, and I, one of the "lucky" pregnant girls, would soon marry my baby's father, Airman Burt Pierce. Though I never intended to become either pregnant or a bride at sixteen, others likely saw it coming. I had been flirting with older boys since I was thirteen. Now, I could only try to be happy about Burt's and my impending wedding day and the child we would raise together.

Six years earlier, Dad had moved our family to California. During our thirty days on the road, we were a happy, all-American family, visiting relatives and tourist attractions across the nation. Billy and I happily ate hamburgers and french fries at every road-stop restaurant along the way. We rented a rambling old farmhouse just outside the small town of Atwater, near Castle Air Force

Base. I had never lived out in the country, and I welcomed the change. Our home had a beautiful, sunny sitting room in addition to a small living room off the kitchen where we watched TV. Stray animals found us. We adopted a smelly little dog who wandered up to our door and named him Shaggy; I fed a feral tabby cat and her kittens that I discovered behind our shed. I enjoyed exploring our property, checking out the outbuildings, walking barefoot on our driveway's hot sand and feeling doodlebugs wiggling under my feet. Billy and I occasionally swam in a nearby irrigation ditch. It felt like we had our own swimming pool.

One day while feeding the cats, I discovered a yellowed stack of newspapers on the shelves of the shed. The front page, dated 1948, featured actress Ida Lupino showing off her legs under the guise of modeling high heels. She was much younger than the actress I recognized from TV. Reading these dusty old newspapers was almost as interesting as viewing Mom and Dad's old photograph albums. My fascination with the past—and with the lives of movie stars—had only just begun.

Life in this bucolic setting lasted only six months. In the fall, Dad found us a three-bedroom tract home near downtown Atwater, similar in size and layout to our Gandy Gardens home back in Tampa. I missed the big farmhouse on Sunset Drive, but I happily traded it for the opportunity to live within walking distance of friends' homes, downtown shops, and my new school. Billy and I attended sixth grade at Shaffer Elementary, while Jimmy, who had missed a lot of school in Tampa during his time in juvie, repeated eighth grade at Mitchell Junior High.

California was far ahead of Florida in integrating schools because Mexican Americans had successfully challenged segregation in a 1947 case, *Mendez v. Westminster*, that helped pave the way for the *Brown* decision. As in Tampa, the presence of the military likely accelerated the process of integration in California. Castle Air Force Base's housing, movie theaters, dance hall, and swimming pools were fully integrated. In Atwater, where most of us Air Force kids attended school, a diverse population of Anglos, Blacks, Mexican and Portuguese Americans, and German American Mennonites also worked and played together in integrated classrooms and school activities, especially sports, despite lingering social segregation.

As the civil rights movement accelerated in the early 1960s, Dr. Martin Luther King Jr. received considerable media attention. At first, Dad solemnly approved of King's message, pointing out that he spoke well because he was "an educated man"—in other words, a "Negro" with more education than Dad had. But as the movement gained momentum, Dad became furious at the sight of King on television, while Mom openly supported Black civil rights. Disgusted with Dad, I attributed his racism to his Mississippi roots.

Rock and roll music had captured our family's attention well before we left Florida. Along with my brothers and me, Mom became enamored of performers such as Fats Domino, Elvis Presley, Jerry Lee Lewis, James Brown, Chuck Berry, and Little Richard, all of whom we eagerly watched on TV shows like Ed Sullivan and Steve Allen. One summer day in the late 1950s, a Tampa radio station held a contest to determine the best rock and roller. Mom and I jumped on the phone and voted over and over for Jerry Lee Lewis, hoping but failing to help him defeat Elvis. Once we settled in California, my tastes shifted toward the Drifters and the Miracles. Sometime in the early 1960s, I noticed that many of the 45 records I bought had "Motown" on their labels.

On 1 January 1961, I began to keep a diary. Just after my thirteenth birthday, I saw beautiful faux leather five-year diaries on sale at our local drugstore and begged Mom to make one appear under our Christmas tree. She did. Owning a private, locked book in which to pour out my feelings brought me unspeakable joy. In addition to recording my thoughts, I became obsessed with my appearance. With my babysitting earnings, I bought mascara, eyebrow pencils, and lipsticks in popular violet shades. My love of purple knew no bounds. Before long, my wardrobe included a lavender skirt, blouse, shorts, and, most spectacularly, spaghetti-strap dress.

I also became obsessed with movie magazines and accompanied Mom to the grocery store for the express goal of wheedling her into buying me one or two of the multitude available. *Modern Screen*, *Photoplay*, and *Motion Picture*—I read all of them. I drew charcoal portraits of my favorite actors, notably Elizabeth Taylor, whom I considered the most beautiful woman in the world. As a result, my drawing skills improved dramatically. Dad was so impressed that one night he came home from a bar, grabbed one of my drawings, and took it back to show to his drinking buddy, who had been drawing sexy women on napkins.

Drawing reinforced my appreciation of being alone. Having the house all to myself was a rare treat that I celebrated one night by making fudge and spending the entire evening drawing portraits. Thanks to Grandma's influence, long walks were my other favorite way to be alone. I often took a less-direct route home from school to avoid walking among a gaggle of giggling, gossiping girlfriends. Sometimes I even rode the school bus and lost myself in its long, circuitous route through unfamiliar neighborhoods. None of my friends rode the bus, so I enjoyed surreptitiously watching kids interact with each other in ways not revealed in the classroom. Outwardly, I longed to be popular and to have a boyfriend. But in the meantime, I sought to understand a larger world of which I was increasingly conscious.

In the summer of 1961, my best friend, Betty, and I tagged along with her older sister and friends to one of the air base swimming pools. There were three to choose from. The officers' pool was beautifully landscaped—and locked. Kids like me whose parents were lowly sergeants could enter only as guests of officers' families. Anyone could use the NCO pool, but most of the people who went there were mothers with their kids. So we headed straight to the airmen's pool, where young men from distant places performed high-dive acrobatics and strutted their stuff in tiny Speedo trunks. I kept my hair blond and my true age to myself. In the summer of '61, I felt flirty and attractive. The awkwardness I felt around high school boys vanished when I was among airmen. They were grown up, and at age thirteen, I fancied that I was, too.

My exciting new social life ended almost before it began. After we moved into town, Dad and Mom quickly discovered Atwater's downtown bars. Within three months, Dad was arrested for drunk driving. As in Florida, they regularly returned home in the middle of the night, fighting. Dad would then commence knocking Mom around. But we kids were now teenagers who intervened forcefully in our parents' fights. Jimmy physically confronted Dad when he got drunk and abusive.[1]

One night when Jimmy was not home, Dad's beating of Mom spurred me to run next door and implore our neighbors to call the police, which they did. A few days later, we were horrified to learn that Dad had retaliated by phoning the neighbors with threats in the middle of the night. They again called the police. At that point, the matter was turned over to military officials, who restricted him to the base and temporarily forbid him from entering our home. Having Dad out of our lives gave me such peace, but it did not last long. He regularly broke the terms of his confinement by entering the house while Mom was at work and we kids were at school. As the first to arrive home, I dreaded turning the corner onto our street. If his car was parked out front, I was sunk—doomed to be alone with him until the others arrived. He would be sitting at the kitchen table, drunk but quiet, sorting through his beloved coin collection, waiting for Mom to return from work so he could beg her to forgive him and let him come home.

Mom did nothing to stop Dad. She didn't lock the door or call the base and report him. Worse yet, she pretended to reach a compromise with him that was absurd on its face. One day she quietly explained to me that he had applied for and received a transfer to Offutt Air Force Base near Omaha, Nebraska, which meant that he would soon be gone from our lives forever. The only catch was that Dad would be allowed to move back home before leaving for Nebraska. I blew up at Mom, denouncing her as "stupid" in my diary. This was bullshit! Dad would never leave alone for Nebraska once he got back into our home. No, we would *all* be going to Nebraska—and surely Mom knew that. But the woman who in 1954 had threatened to take the kids and leave and in 1955 had gloried in her new suburban home had given in to her alcoholic marriage by 1961. Convinced that she could not financially support a family alone, she would just "make the best of things." Taking part-time jobs allowed her to meet new people and supplement the family income. And what did another move matter to her? Wherever we lived, she would cook the same meals, keep a clean home, and find a new lover. Whatever other goals she had once imagined for herself had long since faded.

Dad moved back into the house on 9 June 1961, and, sure enough, the entire family left for Nebraska on 26 June. Our "fresh start" in California, like the one before it in Florida, had begun with such hope and promise. There were no such illusions about Nebraska. Off we headed, driving first to Minnesota for the Huckenpoehler family reunion of 1961, then on to Nebraska, where our new home awaited us. For the first time since 1952, we would not be living in a military town. The closest town to Offutt was Bellevue, but Dad found a large, reasonably priced rental house eleven miles away in Plattsmouth. Suddenly, we were in vintage small-town America—no tract homes, no chain stores, no modern shopping centers, just locally owned businesses and bars on every corner of every block. The town had a quaint red-brick Main Street, with a jail and library right around the corner from its north end. At the south end of Main were Corky's Café and Wimpy's, a raucous burger joint.

Everything in this town, including our new home, made me feel like I had gone back in time. We lived in a nineteenth-century two-story house that, like our farmhouse in Atwater, delighted me. It had a real pantry and a staircase. Upstairs, there were heat registers in the floor that allowed me to spy on the people below. My bedroom window opened onto the roof, where I could go sit and stare out at the night. To an Air Force brat like me, Plattsmouth was a "real" town. It reminded me of Waconia, where multiple generations of the same families lived near each other instead of thousands of miles apart.

By the end of July, I concluded we were in the middle of nowhere. I had become acquainted with my neighbor, Marcie, who was my age and useful for gleaning information about the town and its people. One day when we walked downtown together, I was unimpressed by what I jokingly referred to in my diary as the town's "hoods." "They wear stupid sideburns and are sloppy," I wrote. In a letter to Betty back in Atwater, I exclaimed, "I hate this rotten stinking town." I entertained myself by reading novels, including *Gone with the Wind*, *Raintree County*, and *Marjorie Morningstar*, which had become movies starring Vivien Leigh, Elizabeth Taylor, and Natalie Wood, respectively. In the back pages of my diary, I dutifully recorded the titles of all the books I read.[2]

Jimmy shared my opinion of Plattsmouth. After briefly considering joining the navy, he cut out for Atwater three days before the fall school term began. Billy and I gave him twenty-seven dollars, all the money we had saved, and he used it to buy a bus ticket for as far as it would take him, planning to hitch-hike the rest of the way. Dad realized Jimmy was gone and called the cops, who quickly apprehended him and brought him home. When Jimmy ran away again, Dad gave up. Billy and I made the best of things. A superb athlete, he ran track, won a letter, and later competed in the Ak-Sar-Ben (*Nebraska* spelled backwards) Track and Field Conference.[3] He became friends with Corky Adkins, a star athlete who jogged by our house even on snowy mornings. I took a different route to get recognition. If I could no longer live in the great state of California, I would play up being *from* California. I mean, what could these kids know about the latest music and fashion? Convinced I had a sophisticated edge on them, I prepared for my high school debut.

First, I wrote the names of the school's most popular kids—according to Marcie—in my diary. Later, I added my firsthand observations of them ("cute," "not as cute as I thought," "sharp," "fair," "childish," and in the worst cases "punk" and "very punky"). I carefully prepared for the all-important First Day of High School. I dyed my shoulder-length hair red, set it in curlers, and shined up my black flats. The next morning, I slipped on Mom's sleeveless sheath dress. It was a bit mature for a thirteen-year-old high school freshman, but I liked the way it fit my hips. After styling my flashy new hair, I carefully applied eyebrow pencil and mascara. I felt nervous but ready for judgment day.[4]

The ancient halls of Plattsmouth High were packed with kids as I sashayed to my locker. To my great delight, several boys raised their eyebrows and turned to get a better look as I passed by. This was working out just fine. School let out after just a half day, so when a girl named Maggie invited me to have lunch downtown with her, I eagerly accepted. We headed downtown on foot with hordes of other noisy kids. I soon learned from a carload of boys yelling out the windows that Maggie's bad complexion had won her the nickname *Maggot*. We arrived downtown to see many students streaming into taverns (which far outnumbered restaurants) that advertised tantalizing hot pizzas through plate-glass windows. I wasn't sure what to make of Plattsmouth after so rowdy an introduction to its students, particularly the boys.

My social life truly began when I met Barb one evening at the Plattsmouth Public Library. She was one of the town's few other military kids, and she impressed me right away by telling me that she had previously lived in California, right across the street from Disneyland. Unlike Maggie, she was cute, stylish, and popular—all the things I wanted to be. We immediately became best friends. Barb and her family were from Mississippi, a state I associated with Dad and considered thoroughly backward. Barb, however, was from Meridian, which she assured me was far more sophisticated than backwoods Jones County. On weekends, we walked the downtown streets of Plattsmouth, waving at and sometimes riding with the older boys who cruised Main Street. And then Barb began dating Corky Adkins. We were fourteen-year-old girls obsessed with being pretty and having boyfriends, pretty much in that order.

Barb and I regularly spent nights at each other's houses, hanging out in her family's basement and gossiping or sitting on the roof outside my bedroom window. There was nothing heavy on our minds. The world beyond our social setting was irrelevant. I don't remember us ever talking about racism, for example, or about Black people, period. It was someone else who told me that African Americans were not allowed in Plattsmouth after five o'clock in the evening, which rang true since I only saw one Black person, a construction worker, during the entire year I lived there. Plattsmouth, as far as I could see, was a wholly white town. The townspeople and city fathers celebrated their

Vikki Bynum, Plattsmouth, Nebraska, 1962.

yearly Kass Kounty King Korn Karnival, which they affectionately dubbed the KKK. The racism in 1961 Plattsmouth struck me as far more open and visceral than I had experienced in either Tampa or Atwater. I was older, and this was no Air Force town.

Had I known the history of nearby Omaha, I would have better understood Plattsmouth's racism. At the time, I had no idea that Omaha was the location of one of many race riots in American industrial cities during the Red Summer of 1919. Similar to what Grandpa Huckenpoehler had witnessed on Minnesota's Mesabi Range, labor conflicts and explosive strikes led to fearmongering and organized violence against immigrants, Blacks, and labor unions. Throughout the Northwest and Midwest, Black strikebreakers were accused of taking white men's jobs and raping white women. Nearly one hundred lynchings took place in 1919 alone. Most of the victims were Black men, including several World War I veterans.[5]

South Omaha's meatpacking industry followed the example of US Steel in hiring African Americans from the South as strikebreakers. As Omaha's Black population soared, politicians, criminal mob bosses, and industrial leaders fanned the flames of white racism. Amid such hysteria, Will Brown, a Black packinghouse worker, was tortured and hanged, and then his body was riddled with bullets and set afire. Finally, an angry mob dragged his charred remains through downtown Omaha. Ten years later, in North Platte, about 280 miles to the west, town leaders drove out two hundred Black citizens rather than seek justice for a local Black man lynched by vigilantes.[6]

In researching Nebraska's sordid history of race relations for this book, I wasn't surprised to learn that Plattsmouth had a long history of forbidding African Americans to live within its borders. In 1923, the *Plattsmouth Journal* reported that in 1890, the town's only Black settlement had been "set ablaze" and then flooded. Ever since, locals had made sure that Plattsmouth's "pure Aryan population" remained that way. The story was aimed at twelve Black workers recently brought in by the Burlington Lumber Company, and it had the desired effect: three days later, the paper gleefully reported that the workers had cleared out after the article appeared. In that spirit, Plattsmouth hosted the first of its KKK carnivals in 1932. The festivities opened with a rollicking performance of a popular blackface comedy, "Two Black Crows," with the audience roaring its approval. In a town with not a single Black citizen, blackface buffoonery seemed like good, clean fun. In 1961, old-timers still reminisced about the good old days when "Negroes" were run out of town and "Negro riots" put down with force.[7]

While Mom, Billy, and I scoffed at Plattsmouth's KKK festival, I don't recall that Barb and I ever discussed it. Maybe she and I knew intuitively to stay away from the topic of racism, but we were not so careful in the late 1960s, after I moved back to California and she returned to Mississippi. As we grew older and more politicized by national events, our letters became battlefields for fierce arguments over civil rights and racism. In 1974, I revealed to Barb that I was dating a Black man and never heard from her again. I was stung by her reaction, but it shouldn't have surprised me. Back in our Plattsmouth days, Barb's mom made clear her views on race by playfully needling me with racist gossip about famous people. I remained quiet when she railed about Leslie Uggams on the cover of *TV Guide* magazine, but when she insisted that Dinah Shore had given birth to a Black baby in her younger years, I responded with something like, "Oh, I don't think so." In her sweetest Mississippi drawl, she responded, "It's true, honey." It wasn't.

After about eight months in Plattsmouth, during which time I dated two or three high school boys, I met Earl through his sister, Cathy. Earl was about six feet tall with a face and hairstyle reminiscent of James Dean. Almost twenty years old, he was a devotee of the downtown pool hall, especially when out of work. He and Cathy's parents were divorced. Their dad, a pile driver and lumber company foreman, lived off Main Street in a small trailer. They lived with their more middle-class mom and stepdad. In his boyhood, Earl had been a good Catholic school student and Boy Scout, but now he drank too much, drove too fast, and got into too many fights. On Saturday nights, he typically joined his buddies and headed to Omaha, where they went looking for trouble with African Americans and usually found it.

Bored with high school boys, I gained entree into an older crowd by hanging out with nineteen-year-old Carol, a longtime friend of Earl and Cathy's. My efforts to appear older than fourteen were enhanced by visiting bars with Mom. One night, she and I were at the popular Holman's Beach dance hall when I spied Earl. I made sure to say hello, eager for him to know that I frequented adult joints. I also bowled in a women's league with Mom and Carol where local guys often dropped by to check out the women. My heart skipped a beat whenever Earl was among them.

Jimmy returned to Plattsmouth by Greyhound bus during the Christmas holidays of 1961. Our entire family plus Barb headed to Omaha to pick him up. While awaiting his arrival, I became distracted by two young, well-dressed Black men laughing and talking with two equally well-dressed young white women in the coffee shop. I had never seen an interracial couple before, and I certainly didn't expect to see two such couples enjoying themselves publicly in Omaha, a segregated city filled with racial hatred and conflict. I looked around the bus station but saw no signs of trouble. When Jimmy arrived, we all excitedly hugged him and left for home. No one mentioned the interracial couples. Knowing what I do now, I wonder if they were in some way connected to the Freedom Rides, which had begun challenging segregation on interstate buses and in bus terminals further south in the spring of 1961.

By April I was going steady with Earl, and Jimmy was part of my new group of friends. He and I had not previously hung out with the same people. In Atwater, he told me never to speak to him unless he spoke to me first, so it buoyed me when he dated my friends Carol and Linda. He and Dad continued to fight, however, and before the month of June passed, Jimmy lit out again for Atwater. This time, Mom paid his bus fare. I was too busy running with my new friends, especially Earl, to note exactly when he left.

Jimmy Bynum, Atwater, California, 1961.

Earl's recklessness excited me. I was thrilled that he lusted for me, and the lust was mutual. On a late June night in 1962, we made out in a field behind a late-night young adult house party. I was hot as a pistol and barely managed to keep my pants on. Later, I noted in my diary that Earl and I had exchanged words of love and that "he says I tear him up." Not long after, at a party at Earl's house, I drank a few beers and danced the twist, deliberately taunting him with my moves. Then, rather suddenly, we were all alone in the house and he was removing my shorts and panties. My inhibitions melted. His mother and Cathy arrived home just as my virginity was disappearing. In a haze, I threw on my clothes, sheepishly greeted them, and let myself out. Their knowing smiles were the last thing I remembered about that day.[8]

The next morning, I was devastated by what had happened. The remaining weeks of Earl's and my "relationship" were a series of emotional sessions in which I sought words of love and got none while he sought acts of sex and got none. I cried out my ruination to Barb. I sought forgiveness from God, kneeling and praying in the town's empty Catholic Church. Mom and Dad reacted to my erratic behavior by putting me on restriction, but they were too busy with their own struggles to make it stick.

A few weeks later, I took drugs with two of my friends, Mary and Paul. A popular way to get high in Plattsmouth was to ingest methamphetamine-soaked cotton strips taken from inside Valo nasal inhalers. Paul purchased the inhaler at the local drugstore, opened it, and removed the strip and cut it into three pieces. We each gulped one down with hot coffee. I had never experienced anything like what followed. Mary and I were euphoric and wired all night, talking nonstop into the early hours of the next day. "It gave us a real strange feeling of complete understanding," I wrote in my diary.[9] Fortunately, my family left Plattsmouth and returned to Atwater the following month. Being stationed at Offutt for a year had gotten Dad what he wanted—back into our home. Mission accomplished, he retired from the Air Force and spent the rest of the summer at Offutt, completing his final duties. Mom, Billy, and I headed back to Atwater ahead of him on 3 August 1962.

I have pondered many times what might have become of me if I had remained much longer in Plattsmouth. I remembered the time Carol and I visited a friend of hers who had been married for a few years. The friend lived with her husband and baby in a shabby, cramped upstairs apartment downtown. As impetuous and emotionally immature as I was, I shuddered at her fate. "I'm glad we're leaving," I wrote in my diary that night. Shortly after our return to Atwater, I reminded myself that "I have to think of my future, and I certainly didn't have one there." Yet I grieved the loss of my friends and Earl and missed terribly the excitement of Plattsmouth's small-town dramas.[10]

Less than three months after we left, Mom received a phone call from her Plattsmouth boyfriend, Dutch. Earl and his brother Larry were hospitalized after having been knifed on a Saturday night by "Negroes." Earl's throat had been slashed. A few days later, I received a letter from Barb explaining that Larry's throat, not Earl's, had been slashed, but that Earl did have a cut on the back of his head. The brothers recovered just fine. Many years later, I read a newspaper report of the incident: at least a dozen Plattsmouth youths had attacked thirteen airmen from Offutt Air Force Base who had come into town hoping to date Plattsmouth girls. Race figured into the story, but perhaps only in fevered imaginations—all but one of the airmen were definitely white, though there was some doubt about the other one. But even that possibility was enough to provoke outrage in all-white Plattsmouth.[11]

At the same time Earl was fighting Offutt "flyboys" back in Plattsmouth, I was attending dances at the Castle Air Force Base Airmen's Club with my old friend Betty. Though I was still just fourteen, I was done with Castle's teen club, and I dated neither high school boys nor the small-town guys who gunned their engines on Main Street and hung out in the pool halls. The airmen we flirted and danced with seemed far more worldly and were surprisingly respectful. Feeling ever more confident and ambitious, I announced in my diary future plans to attend art college and "make something *big* of myself. I'm not being a *nobody!*" To prepare, I asked Mom if I might take art lessons in town, as several of my talented classmates did, but she said we couldn't afford it. Nevertheless, making future plans propelled me to attend church the next day and four days later to express relief at having survived "the *wild & mixed-up*" summer of 1962.[12]

From then on, I sporadically took charge of my life, oscillating between my emotional search for cheap thrills and my intellectual desire for enlightenment and a life of purpose. I emulated Grandma by trying to be a good Catholic. I vowed to go to confession during the week, then get up early on Sunday to attend church services and take communion while the family slept. My piety rarely lasted more than a few weeks. As a result, I seldom went to confession, and when I did, I was never sure when to speak after entering one of the dark closets on each side of the priest's listening room. On one occasion, I began to recite my sins nervously into the screened opening only to have the gruff Father O'Shea bang on my screen and hiss, "Would you shut up!" Frozen and utterly humiliated, I dutifully waited my turn.

In late fall 1962, Aunt Mary Jo; her husband, Frank; and eight-month-old Barney visited our family for the holidays and joined us to celebrate both Thanksgiving and Christmas at the ranch of our friend, Tony, a Portuguese dairy farmer. Frank was no longer able to hold down a job and Mary Jo, as was her habit, was seeking help from Mom. By now in my Liz Taylor phase, with dyed black hair, long bangs, and carefully applied black eyeliner with wings at the outer corners of my eyes, I was bored throughout both holidays. Mary Jo accurately assessed my new look as overpowering—and not in a good way—but I figured she wasn't one to talk. As a teenager, I loved bantering and gossiping with her, but I didn't take her advice too seriously.[13]

Much more exciting was an after-Christmas bus trip to San Francisco with Betty. We stayed at the home of her aunt and uncle and visited Sausalito and Chinatown, but best of all was New Year's Eve. We dolled ourselves up in sophisticated outfits (mine was a tight black suit) and high heels, then traversed Market Street while Betty's folks enjoyed their evening in a nearby café. At the stroke of midnight, crowds of celebrants ran through the streets. Betty and I were grabbed and given about a million New Year's kisses, mostly by Asian men from nearby Chinatown. It was delirious fun.

As usual, such spontaneous merriment prompted me to reassert control over my behavior. On 3 January 1963, I visited the Atwater Library and checked out two books on commercial art, plus John Steinbeck's novel *East of Eden*. My latest self-improvement campaign included going on a diet, exercising, and completing several movie star portraits. Though my old Plattsmouth friend Barb and I lived far apart, we considered joining the navy together when we turned eighteen. That plan was forgotten after I made a new friend who shared my first name, though she spelled it *Vicky*. Our mutual dislike of high school society quickly cemented our friendship, and before long, we were planning to attend IBM school in Denver. Vicky knew all about IBM careers.[14]

Mary Jo, Frank, and Barney returned to Atwater in the fall of 1963, further down on their luck than ever. Frank's descent into alcoholism now was punctuated by the worst shakes I have ever seen. Mom's friend Tony took pity and hired them both to work at his dairy ranch, probably as a favor to her. Mary Jo cooked and cleaned for Tony and his crew, while Frank performed whatever odd jobs he could. Occasionally, she paid me to babysit Barney. Predictably, she and Mom enjoyed drinking and laughing together again. And just as predictably, she and Frank didn't last long at Tony's ranch. Before they headed back to Arizona, Mary Jo invited me to come out and finish high school there. Might not be a bad idea, I thought to myself.[15]

I had high hopes when our family returned to Atwater, but I couldn't shake my frequent boredom and intermittent depression. Nothing, it seemed, compared to the excitement of my Plattsmouth gang of friends. My babysitting jobs earned me money but were otherwise a drag. Only the air base offered Vicky and me a respite from the boredom of high school. We swam, attended movies, and enjoyed Friday night dances. We made friends with several airmen, one of whom I dated a few times. But Plattsmouth still called. Barb, Carol, and Mary wrote to me regularly, keeping me connected to the town and filled with the longing to see them and Earl again. "I'd love to take a trip there," I wrote in my diary, "but it's hopeless, I know." Two days later, I complained of being "restless & depressed."[16] In desperation, I wrote to

Grandma and asked if I could come live with her and Grandpa in Waconia. I was overjoyed when she consented. I made plans to leave Atwater the following month, when I turned sixteen. At last, I thought, I would be living again in a "real" (non–Air Force) town. In my diary, I mused that I might also "get to visit Plattsmouth. Oh, I hope so!" The only thing crazier than trying to impose myself on Grandma, age seventy-six, and Grandpa, age eighty-four, was that Mom and Grandma said yes to the idea. But Grandpa had the sense to say no to such nonsense.[17]

My plans quashed, I gave up on escaping Atwater and sought fun in new ways. And sure enough, fun came my way. Vicky and I continued to attend base dances and met a new set of airmen, including nineteen-year-old Burt, who stood out from the rest as a mature, sensitive guy and a particularly good conversationalist. He neither drank heavily nor got into fights. On my sixteenth birthday, he walked me home from the dance and tried to kiss me goodnight. I didn't let him but then felt guilty because he had to walk alone the entire two miles back to the base. By late December, we were dating. Sometime after the New Year, we began going steady. I liked Burt a lot and desperately wanted to be in love with someone other than Earl. I soon filled my secret journal with angst-driven declarations that leapt from being in love to being uncertain that I was truly in love to being certain that I was not in love with Burt.[18]

In June 1964, Burt and I joined Mom on a road trip to Arizona, to visit Aunt Mary Jo and Frank. Mary Jo now tended bar at Glendale's Cantina tavern. Her skin was dark from the Arizona sun, her hair dyed jet black. "It's better that I look Mexican like my customers," she laughed. Booze by now had robbed Frank of all health and dignity. While Mary Jo worked, he tended Barney—as best he could. On a sweltering summer day, as Burt and I drove to the Cantina to meet Mom and Mary Jo, we spied Frank, thin, shirtless, and listless, walking along a downtown street with Barney hoisted up on his shoulders. Later, we visited Mary Jo and Frank's home. The furniture in their small, rented house consisted almost entirely of bare mattresses. We began our long drive home the next morning, depressed by much of what we had seen. I would certainly *not* be finishing high school in Glendale.[19]

Within a month, my ruminations about whether I was in love with Burt didn't matter: I was pregnant, and there was a wedding to be planned—and fast! We set the date for 22 August 1964 and the location in El Cajon, near Burt's hometown of San Diego. Neither set of parents seemed unduly upset by my pregnancy or concerned that we were marrying so young. The fact that Burt had an Air Force income no doubt made the decision easier for all. As for me, I felt keenly my lack of options. Abortion was illegal, and as a Catholic, I would not have sought one anyway. At the same time, marriage frightened me. When I expressed my misgivings to Mom, she snapped, "What the hell else are you going to do?" She was right, of course. I had no good choices. As plans moved forward, our priest, Father O'Friel, took me aside and kindly reminded me that I could still give up my infant for adoption. I quickly brushed him off. That, too, was unthinkable to me. It was too late for options.

The next time I saw Mary Jo and Barney was in July 1966, at Grandma and Grandpa's home in Waconia. By then, Frank had returned to his family in Florida, where he soon died. Burt and I, married now for almost two years, were eager to show off our son, Randy. We were equally excited to meet Mary Jo's long-lost daughter, Jane, the baby she had given up for adoption in 1940. Jane had located Mary Jo earlier that year, and our gathering centered on welcoming her into the Huckenpoehler family.

As I reflect on that 1966 Waconia visit, I'm struck by the ongoing transformation in my own life as much as the impending transformation in the lives of Mary Jo and Jane. An insecure, thrill-seeking teenager five years earlier, I was now a wife and mother about to see her husband off to Vietnam. The following year, while Burt was hunkered down in Da Nang, Carol called from Plattsmouth to tell me that Earl had been killed in a traffic accident while driving home from a late-night poker game. I could barely comprehend the tragedy of my first boyfriend's sudden, violent death or the idea that someone over whom I had obsessed for years was no longer in the world. A year later, Corky Adkins was killed in Vietnam. Those two awful deaths, along with Burt's safe return to the States in late 1967, coincided with the end of my teenage years.[20]

Burt's service in Vietnam proved as important to my future as to his. During the eighteen months during which he was gone, Randy and I lived with my parents, first in Salinas and then in Monterey. During that time, I worked as a department store clerk and as a waitress while Mom babysat Randy. I took an art class that greatly enhanced my pencil and charcoal drawing skills. Then, in the spring of 1967, I attended Monterey's evening adult school and earned my high school diploma. Perhaps more important than the degree itself were the stimulating class discussions and debates about national policies on volatile issues such as abortion, race, and most of all US intervention in Vietnam. Participating in conversations as an adult rather than a teenager fired me up to want more education. By the time Burt returned from Vietnam, I opposed the war and was pleased that his firsthand experiences had turned him against it, too.

Upon his return to the States, Burt was stationed at Andrews Air Force Base in Maryland, where I joined him and our daughter, Erika, was born in 1968. On 15 November of the following year, while still on active duty, Burt was one of half a million people who participated in the Washington, DC, march against the Vietnam War. In 1970, he left the Air Force, and we returned to California, living in the tiny town of Seaside while he attended Monterey Peninsula Community College. In this era of antiwar protests and social movements, we considered ourselves countercultural. I was now a hip wife and mother who publicly condemned the war and reviled corporate capitalism. Mostly, however, I remained a homemaker, though a highly politicized one. My Earth Mother phase included baking whole-grain bread, sewing clothing for myself and Erika, and using my artistic and baking skills to make rather than purchase Christmas cards and gifts for friends and family. After initially relying on Dr. Spock's *Baby and Child Care* and Irma S. Rombauer's *The Joy of Cooking*, I added John Holt's criticism of public schools, *How Children Learn*, to my bookshelf and began supporting progressive, antiracist alternative schools; Ellen Ewald's *Recipes for a Small Planet* soon joined my cookbook collection as well. Burt was an equally hip breadwinner, letting his hair grow to his shoulders while he worked barefoot at the college library. Happy to be free of the military and to have such a liberating job, he quit taking classes altogether when the library offered him a full-time position.

By early 1974, despite our mutual commitment to progressive politics, the end of our marriage was in sight. We permanently separated after Burt fell in love with one of the teachers at our children's alternative school, though we didn't officially divorce until 1980. Looking back, our years together seem like an incubator, a protective time during which I safely grew up, mostly apart from my parents' alcoholic household and removed from the drug culture that swept the United States. I have few regrets. In less than ten years, I learned to care for two children, manage a household, balance a checkbook, wait tables, run a cash register, and be a loyal companion. I also became an amateur genealogist, learning some historian skills along the way.

Most important, I had already begun college and could now give education my full attention. From the summer of 1974 until the fall of 1976, Randy, Erika, and I lived on the outskirts of downtown while I attended San Diego City College full time. In 1975, we moved into a rambling old Victorian home on the other side of town with two friends from City College and their daughter. Our children attended the Exploring Family Alternative School, and I worked part time for the Center for Women's Studies and Services as an illustrator and occasional writer of feminist pieces. Burt and I had no formal child support or custody arrangements, but we took turns raising the kids. Thanks to the remnants of President Lyndon Johnson's Great Society programs, government-funded work-study jobs, student loans, and welfare enabled me to remain in college.

For a sixteen-year-old girl who had silently suffered while a doctor and a nurse callously joked about her pregnancy, I had done okay. Now, Burt's love affair gave me a get-out-of-marriage-free card at age twenty-six. "Life is so wonderful," I wrote in my journal, "I'm glad to have returned!"[21]

13

My Father's Story

My long journey toward understanding my father began in 1958, when I was ten, and he was transferred from MacDill Air Force Base in Florida to Castle Air Force Base in California. Our family's monthlong trip across the country doubled as a vacation that included not only stops at tourist attractions but visits to Dad's home state of Mississippi and Mom's home state of Minnesota, where I tapped into my family's personal histories.

After visiting Dad's relatives in Jones County, we drove further south to have a noon meal with his father, Hiram Solomon (Sollie) Smith, and his fourth wife, whose name I can't remember. And what a meal it was! Soon after we arrived, Mrs. Smith called us to the dining room, where a true southern groaning board greeted us. A huge oblong table held platters of sliced ham and fried chicken, baskets of cloth-covered breads, bowls of steaming vegetables and even a bowl of stewed prunes. I had never been to an indoor meal in which all the food, including desserts, was laid right out on the table from the start. Or where people ate their big meal so early in the day—for us kids, noon typically brought a peanut-butter-and-jelly sandwich. I happily stuffed myself while glancing with anticipation at several nearby fruit pies.

During and after our meal, Grandpa Smith and Dad talked to each other in polite, subdued tones. Billy and I became restless and headed outdoors for some exploring. A shed back of the house caught our attention as a family of feral cats

Sollie Smith (*left*) and Stan Bynum, Poplarville, Mississippi, 1958.

darted out and disappeared into the nearby tangle of bushes and weeds. They were gorgeous wild creatures with tortoiseshell markings that blended perfectly with their surroundings. Back in the house, I told Grandpa Smith about our discovery. That produced a rare smile from him as we talked a bit about the cats. Before we left, everyone gathered in the front yard to take a few photos.

We never again visited the Smiths. Mouth-watering platters of food and feral cats are my only vivid memories of a day that I now realize constituted a journey back in time. Almost eleven years old, I vaguely understood that this grandpa was sort of but not really Dad's father. Dad always called the man a "foster father," but much later I discovered that Sollie and his second wife, Bertie, had legally adopted my father when he was five months old. All this made me curious to know more about Dad's biological father, Aden Gallington Bynum, who lived until Dad was twenty-four years old. Why did Aden give up his youngest son? Did he and Dad ever meet later in life? In 1958, I was a long way from understanding my father's childhood. But the dinner with the Smiths raised questions that a long-overdue conversation would eventually answer.

That conversation came on the heels of the 1966 Huckenpoehler family reunion at my grandparents' home in Waconia. After the visit ended, Dad, Burt, and I split off from the rest of the family (Mom, Aunt Mary Jo, her son Barney, and Burt's and my son Randy) to drive Burt to the training facility in Topeka, Kansas, that would prepare him for duty in Vietnam. After saying goodbye to him the next morning, Dad and I headed to Salt Lake City, where we were to meet up with Mom and Mary Jo and caravan on to California.

As we traveled from Topeka to Salt Lake City, Dad and I had a conversation that has affected me ever since. With fifteen hours of driving through Kansas, Colorado, Wyoming, and Utah ahead of us, we had to talk about *something*, so I asked Dad about his childhood. And he answered. I've always been struck by how my father, who teared up at the corniest TV dramas and bit his nails well below the quick, recounted for me, without tears or a trace of self-pity, his Mississippi childhood. It was as if sharing his story rather than simply feeling it calmed him. The circumstances of his birth, his early years, his running away from home at age sixteen, all came tumbling out. As I quietly listened, I knew I would never feel the same about him again. The man I reviled for his alcoholic rages and blamed for all the evil that ripped at our family became a different person.

"Honey, look what Mama's got," Naoma purred as she held up her newborn baby boy for his sister to see. Four-year-old Merle's eyes popped open wide on this cold November morning in 1917. She had fussed all night after being banished from her Mama's bed for reasons she did not understand. Now she did. The tiny creature Mama held up was her newest brother. Less than six weeks later, Merle was led down the hallway of their house again, this time to view with a child's horror her mother's dead body stretched out on a cooling board. For all her long life, Merle remembered the images of her newborn brother and her newly dead mother. Little Oma Stanley Bynum, of course, never knew the mother for whom he was named. And the boy also did not know his father: in his despair, Aden Bynum left his infant son to be raised by others.

Pretty much all Dad knew was that he had been born into a family that already included six sons (Oran, Cerulian, Wendell, Clifton, Harry, and Conrad) and two daughters (Laree and Ila Murial, known as Merle) and

Aden Bynum and Naoma Shows Bynum, Mississippi, 1899.

that by the time he was six weeks old, a deadly local epidemic had left him with only four brothers and one sister and with no mother. During the epidemic, baby Stanley was taken from the infected home and nursed by his aunt Mat, who was married to Aden's oldest brother, Leonidas Sherwood (Leon) Bynum, and had recently given birth.

The grim specter of death that hung over the Bynum home ravaged the rest of the community as well, leaving many families decimated by an epidemic likely connected to World War I. Beginning in the winter of 1917 and continuing into the early months of 1918, what Aunt Merle remembered as the "bloody flux" (dysentery), combined with measles to devastate the Sweetwater neighborhood of the town of Moselle in Jones County. One by one, members of the Bynum family fell victim, beginning when twelve-year-old Cliff came home sick from uncle Johnnie Shows's farm, where the boy had boarded and worked for some time. By early December, seven children lay in beds lining the walls of a single room. Only Aden; oldest son, Oran; and baby Stanley were spared.

Merle (*left*) and Laree Bynum, Moselle, Mississippi, ca. 1917.

Uncle Cerulian recalled being too weak to lift his legs as he lay helplessly among his younger siblings. He blinked and looked away as he told me that he would never forget the pallor of nine-year-old Laree's face just before she died on 2 December. Next to die was two-year-old Conrad on 6 December. Five days later, seven-year-old Harry succumbed. "The bereaved family has the sympathy of the entire community," declared the *Jones County News* on 20 December, "this being the third child they have lost in ten days."[1]

Naoma Shows Bynum had married Aden on 28 September 1899, and she too, was stricken. For a time, she appeared on the mend, but as her children died one by one, she relapsed and fell "dangerously ill." Six days before Christmas, thirty-seven-year-old Naoma cried out that she could not bear to lose another child. Then she shut her eyes for the final time. "It made us sad to learn that Mr. Aden Bynum lost his dear wife and darling children," reported the *Jones County News* on 27 December. On 3 January 1918, the paper finally reported some encouraging news: the remaining Bynum children—Cerulian, Cliff, Wendell, and Merle—appeared "about to recover." And recover they did, but the family unit did not.[2]

And so began Dad's childhood. His two oldest brothers joined the navy, while the other three children moved in with their Bynum grandparents, William and Sophronia. In the next farmhouse over, two-month-old Stanley thrived with Leon and Mat Bynum. Relatives remembered that Mat wanted to adopt the boy but was overruled by relatives who feared that she could not keep nursing two newborns. Gossip held that Aden didn't much like his sister-in-law, anyway. According to another family member, just before Naoma died, she had asked her older sister Centeola Emma (Teola) Shows Newton to raise the baby but was overruled by Teola's husband. Finally came the good news that Aden's cousin Bertie Mae Bynum Smith and her husband, Sollie, had stepped forward to adopt Stanley. The Smiths lived in Slidell, Louisiana, where twenty-eight-year-old Bertie ran a café and forty-three-year-old Sollie managed the Dixie Ranch Livestock and Farm Company. The Smiths were well-off enough to employ Black "help"—household servant Isaiah Smith and Callie Williams, who cooked for them and for the restaurant.[3]

Stylish and attractive, Bertie hailed from the urban Ellisville branch of the family. Her father, John Hall Bynum, served as the Jones County clerk in the late nineteenth century. In 1875, John built a lovely two-story home for his family that has been restored and still stands today. The Ellisville Bynums even had their own downtown cemetery. Unlike their rural Bynum cousins in nearby Calhoun, who supported the Union during the Civil War and contributed two men to Newt Knight's infamous band of guerrillas in the "Free State of Jones," the Ellisville branch of the family held people in slavery and stuck by the Confederacy. In 1910, when Bertie and Sollie married, they lived in Poplarville, where Sollie served as chancery clerk and Bertie served as his deputy. Sometime before 1916, they moved to Slidell. Although Sollie had a son from a previous marriage, he and Bertie had no children together after eight years of marriage. For them to adopt Stanley must have seemed a good solution to the cash-poor, child-rich Bynums and Showses of rural Moselle and Seminary. On 29 April 1918, five-month-old Stanley Bynum legally became Stanley Smith.[4]

Around the same time, Aden Bynum took off for Alabama, where he remarried in 1920. His oldest sons, Oran and Cerulian, were sailors at the US Naval Reservation in Gulfport, while the rest of the children remained with relatives in Jones County. Only Stanley had been given up for adoption and taken away. For the first sixteen years of his life, he knew neither his father nor siblings and had little information about his Jones County roots. When

Stanley Smith (Stan Bynum),
Poplarville, Mississippi, ca. 1920.

he asked who his "real" father was, Sollie responded that Stanley had a "living father," which confused him. If he had a living father, why then didn't he live with that father? Did Sollie mean that he was Stanley's real father?[5]

Dad loved Bertie and described her as an affectionate, fun-loving woman—the first in their town to have her hair bobbed in the latest style, he proudly told me. He reminisced to my mother that for one Mardi Gras, Bertie dressed him up in a diaper fastened by a giant safety pin and hung a baby bottle around his neck.

Sollie Smith was a very different sort of parent. Stern and quiet, he was quick to take a strap to his son for wetting his bed or for telling a lie. And the whippings were preceded by taunts that Dad found even more difficult to bear: in a mockingly soft voice, Sollie would murmur to the bent-over boy, "Now, Stanley, you're going to be the bass drum, and I'm going to play that drum." Dad referred to Sollie his "foster father" and never spoke of him with even a hint of affection.

Sometime around 1920, Sollie and Bertie moved the family to Sollie's home-town of Poplarville, Mississippi. There, Sollie sold patent drugs while Bertie again managed a café. In 1923, Sollie ran for chancery clerk of Pearl River County and lost. Like most of their neighbors, the Smiths were churchgoing Baptists, although religion never took root with Stanley. In search of mischief, he and his friends liked to peek through the window of the hard-shell Baptist church on Sundays and watch the "holy rollers'" antics. It especially tickled

Dad to tell my brothers and me how the preacher roared at him and his friends and condemned them "straight to hell." Dad had no use for ecstatic religions and claimed to have seen a woman in the throes of such ecstasy "throw her baby into the air." Fortunately, another worshiper caught the child.[6]

Growing up in Poplarville, Dad was unaware he had several siblings living just north of him at the "old Bynum place" in Seminary or with their uncle Leon and aunt Mat. No one told him that his Grandpa Bynum died in 1920 or that his aunt Bessie Mae Bynum had moved back to help Grandma Sophronia raise Wendell, Cliff, and Merle.[7]

Bertie Smith died on 7 February 1932 at age forty-six, setting in motion events that changed Dad's life forever. It is possible that in the wake of her death, perhaps at her funeral, he gathered bits of family news from his Ellisville kinfolk. Losing the only mother he had ever known also reawakened his curiosity about his biological father, especially after Sollie married Rachel House less than a year later. Whereas Bertie had provided a buffer against Sollie's stern ways, his new stepmother made him feel in the way. Bertie was blood kin, an important distinction in the rural South; with her gone, fourteen-year-old Stanley felt alienated from "parents" who neither shared his blood nor won his heart.[8]

On 10 April 1933, Grandma Sophronia died. Merle had married Charles Dial around 1929, and the couple had moved to Rockford, Alabama, where they lived with his aunt and uncle. The marriage failed within a few years, however, and around the time of Sophronia's death, Merle returned to the old Bynum home with her son, Charles Aden (Sonny) Dial, who was born on 31 March 1932. It is not clear whether Dad knew of these events, but he was haunted by the knowledge that he had two living fathers—one who whipped him and one who ignored him. Did his biological father ever wonder about him? Dad decided to find out. He hopped the dummy train going north from the coast and landed in Ellisville. From there, he hitched a ride over to Seminary, where he found Merle, Sonny, and Aunt Bessie living in the old Bynum place. Merle and Bessie were utterly charmed by Aden and Naoma's long-lost baby, who had grown into a handsome young man, tall and slim with black hair and black eyes. Stanley poured on the charm. He playfully sat on forty-three-year-old Bessie's lap, flirting with her like she was his pretty young girlfriend rather than his maiden aunt. He was finally home.[9]

Merle threw a big party to welcome him. Leon and Mat Bynum's granddaughter, sixteen-year-old Laura Frances Bynum, came from next door to gawk at her cousin and even seventy years later remembered thinking that "he was such a handsome man!" She, Dad, and Merle soon began eating supper together, talking late into the night, and going on triple dates. Dad met other relatives, including his uncle Leon, aunt Mat, and aunt Teola. Most members of his extended family were still farmers, wageworkers, or homemakers with more than ten children and were struggling amid the Great Depression. At some point, though I'm not certain when and where, Dad finally met his biological father. During the mid-1920s, Aden Bynum had worked as a cabinetmaker in New Orleans, where he lived with his second wife, Minnie Henderson Bynum. In 1930, they were living in Castleberry, Alabama, and he was working as a carpenter. Dad found it difficult to talk to him.[10]

Dad began to think about his future. He considered settling in Jones County but ultimately decided to follow the same path as all his brothers, who had joined the military and were living elsewhere. Dad took off for New Orleans and on 4 September 1935, two months and ten days shy of his eighteenth birthday, enlisted in the US Navy. Learning that Aunt Bessie had terminal cancer may have hastened his exit from Mississippi. When he arrived in Jones County, he had already lost his birth and adoptive mothers. The impending loss of his aunt might have seemed like more than he could bear. He entered the navy as an apprentice seaman and was assigned to the Naval Training Station in Norfolk, Virginia, where he obtained the tattoos expected of a young sailor: *Mother* and Naoma's death date on his upper left arm, a long-haired and soon-to-be-forgotten girlfriend named Jewel on his right arm.[11]

Dad apparently had a number of "girlfriends" while in the navy, and he later told Mom that he had gonorrhea. On 2 January 1936, he was admitted to the Norfolk Naval Hospital. After his release, he was sent to New York City, and by September 1936, he was aboard the USS *Mahan*. Five months later, he was again hospitalized, this time at the Naval Hospital in Brooklyn. After his recovery from an unspecified "physical disability," he was discharged on 13 May 1937 "under honorable conditions" (the category just below "honorable"). He spent one year, five months, and two days in service, earning no certificates of training and completing no school courses. The navy sent him back to New Orleans with one month's pay and travel money in his pocket.[12]

By 1938, Dad was back in New York, driving buses for the Bee-Line fleet in Long Island's Rockville Centre, about twenty-five miles east of Manhattan. His previous wage work experience, likely in Mississippi, had consisted of driving

Stan Bynum and an unidentified woman, ca. 1940.

a ten-ton semitrailer hauling logs, lumber, stumps, coal, gravel, and some freight. To drive a city bus and to earn northern wages was a big step up.[13]

Living in urban New York also plunged Dad into a far different social world. He thrilled to the sounds of big band music and enjoyed the jazz and blues clubs that hearkened back to his early childhood living near New Orleans. He shed his Mississippi accent and Baptist upbringing. A sharp dresser, he wore carefully tailored shirts and well-shined shoes out on the town. On the dance floor, he threw his partners up over his head, then down between his legs without ever losing the beat. From 1938 to 1942, Stanley Smith was a true city boy. And he began to call himself Stan Bynum.

By 1939, Aden and Minnie Bynum were living in Mobile, Alabama, where he died on 23 March 1942. His body was returned to Mississippi for burial, at which all of his surviving children were present—except one: according to the obituary, "Stanley Bynum" of Brooklyn, New York, was not present. Two weeks later, on 8 April, with labor unrest roiling the transit industry and World War II beckoning, Dad enlisted in the US Army Air Corps. He was soon ordered to Cochran Field in Macon, Georgia, a rural military town bursting at the seams with young people away from home for the first time. Macon may have lacked urban sophistication, but it nevertheless had a rollicking nightlife.[14]

At age twenty-four, Dad, nicknamed "Smitty" by his new friends, was a bit older than most of the soldiers and hit the party scene at full speed. And within a few months, he met a pretty blond from Minnesota and immediately fell in love.

My parents' final years together in Monterey were the most peaceful of their long and troubled marriage. After Dad went to work for the city in 1966, he and Mom bought a small bungalow on David Avenue, just five blocks from Cannery Row and Fisherman's Wharf. He worked the graveyard shift for the city of Monterey and once treated his granddaughter Erika to an exciting late-night ride on the sweeper truck. A stint in alcohol rehab around 1980 kept him sober until Mom began doling out bourbon "short ones" to him from their locked liquor cabinet. During those few sober years, he took predawn walks to the wharf that became scavenging expeditions for memorabilia, jewelry, and spare change lost by busy tourists. Each morning he carefully deposited his treasures into a giant bottle. The walks continued after he returned to drinking, but his declining health eventually ended both. He retired in 1982 and during the last years of his life depended on Mom for physical care and emergency ambulance calls.

In late January 1990, Dad was admitted to Fort Ord's military hospital for treatment of respiratory stress caused by emphysema. Such visits had become common, and within a week his condition was once again stable. This time, however, complications arose. His congestive heart failure, hypertension, and pulmonary disease required extra measures and a longer-than-usual hospital stay. With my brothers and me living far away, my mother became stressed and agitated. She began an affair with the alcoholic next door, a man so damaged, obnoxious, and childish that I could hardly bear his presence. By phone, Mom told me that their affair soothed her nerves and asked me to postpone a planned visit by a few days. Sympathetic to her difficult years with Dad, I complied. Late on the afternoon of 22 February, as I was changing planes in Los Angeles on my way to Monterey, I called Mom and learned that Dad had contracted sepsis and died earlier in the afternoon. The sadness and guilt I felt in that moment remain with me today.

My father's death left a deep void, one that no one in the family had anticipated. Surprised at how much we missed him, we focused on memories leavened by alcohol and laughter. Looking back, I believe Dad's alcoholism united us. When Jim, Bill, and I were growing up, we and Mom made fun of his drunken behavior, though not in his presence. My brothers and I developed a language that parodied Dad in a sentimental, besotted state that infused our conversations long after his death. The laughter seemed healthy at the time, but in hindsight, it is clear that the humor masked our collective anxiety and conflicted relationships with each other. By the time I was a teenager, Mom was more like a teenage girlfriend than a mother. Bill remained her "special child," the baby about whom she felt a secret guilt and the son to whom she could never say no. Rebellious Jim developed a flashy personality at once gregarious and aloof.

As adults, Bill and I initially remained close, sharing insights into our troubled past, but in Mom's final years, his aggressive appropriation of her care destroyed our relationship. In contrast, Jim married young and moved away, distancing himself both physically and emotionally. On family visits, he greeted me with either exaggerated enthusiasm or cold indifference. For most of my life, I remained as uncertain as I had been as a teenager about whether he wanted his younger sister around, but as we aged, we talked more openly about our childhood and the experiences in Vietnam that left him with PTSD. Still, old feelings die hard. Jim's death in 2022 grieved me terribly, yet the insecure child buried deep within me dreamed that he had faked his death to avoid seeing me again. Childhoods filled with shame and our parents' lies and deceptions made it difficult for us to trust each other despite the bonds we shared.

14

My Grandmother's Rage and Sorrow

I want to go home!
I'm lonely here and sick!
My sight is dimming and my speech is thick
These strangers in white gowns are not my kin
Why was I left behind, what was my sin
That I should be here shaken and undone
Deserted and unloved by anyone
Once, long ago by day and night
I cared for my babies and I taught them right
I loved them and bore for them much loss and pain
To see them grow in grace my heart's refrain
But Mammon stole the grace and they have strayed
With faith and fervor for their souls I've prayed
And now I know I've failed my greatest task
Death and deliverance now is all I ask
I have no home on earth I know no soul
My life no longer has an earthly goal
My soul is sick my mind rejects the world
My flag of triumph is forever furled
My body lives I cannot tell you why
When all I really want now is to die.

—MARY DANIEL HUCKENPOEHLER, ca. 1975

From the time her children ventured out into the world, my grandmother Mary struggled to help them build successful adult lives. Whether they needed money, caretaking services, or simply her love, she gave fully of all she had. But what she most desired to give them, the Catholic faith that sustained her through two world wars and the Great Depression, she could not. Feeling defeated and deserted, she wrote a poem from her nursing home bed when she was in her late eighties.

Feelings of inadequacy dogged Mary for much of her life. While she often cited her children's rejection of Catholic doctrine as proof of her failure as a mother, in 1960 she pointedly blamed her own behavior as a parent, asking herself, "What did I do right for my children?" Her answer: "Very little. First of all I had very little to do with. But morally my mental attitude was wrong. I was childish and complaining and lazy. . . . I expected too much understanding and reasoning power from very young children." While she especially regretted allowing Mary Jo to transfer from Catholic school to public school in the eighth grade, she had also "neglected to forbid dangerous things" to her oldest child. All of the children had gone their own ways, she concluded, because "I was too soft-hearted and ignorant of the dangers of their world to bear down hard on them."[1]

Determined nonetheless to keep her family united, Grandma mostly kept her bitter thoughts to herself until the final decade of her life. Family visits were her lifeblood. She particularly enjoyed the 1961 family reunion, which occurred less than a year after she wrote those disparaging words. In 1963, an unexpected reunion with a long-forgotten cousin, Agnes Lewis Bennett, brought her a new and satisfying friendship. When I first encountered Agnes's full name and address, written in a shaky, aged hand on an empty envelope Grandma had repurposed for family history notes, I had no idea who Agnes was. Intrigued, I discovered through further digging that she was the daughter of Mary's uncle, William Henry Lewis, and that the two women had reconnected when they were in their seventies. Mary eagerly traveled by train to Agnes's home in Mason City, Iowa, where they shared mutual stories of childhood alienation from the Lewis family. They became intimates, visiting and writing to each other as long as their health allowed.[2]

In summer 1966, another unexpected family reunion occurred, but this one brought heartache rather than happiness. Jane Frances Baetz Grapper, Mary Jo's daughter whom Grandma had relinquished for adoption in 1940, reentered their lives. In this day of easily obtained DNA kits and online adoption centers and websites, such stories are common, but in 1966, the identities of parents and children given up for adoption were by law closely guarded. Possibly through her adoptive father, Rudolph Baetz, who had been employed by the Catholic Aid Society of St. Paul, Jane obtained enough information to send her to my grandparents' doorstep. Home alone, Grandma answered the door to find a young woman who bore an uncanny resemblance to Mary Jo.[3]

Although Jane's reappearance rekindled my grandmother's guilt over having signed the baby over for adoption, she answered Jane's questions as quickly as Jane asked them, and in July, my grandparents hosted a family reunion that included Jane; her husband, Rudy Grapper; and their four daughters, Mary, Jo, Kathy, and Sandy. Mary Jo came up from Arizona with her four-year-old son, Barney. My parents were there, and so was I, with Burt and eighteen-month-old Randy. The families congregated at Waconia's downtown park for a cookout. The day went well. Husbands played with the children while we women prepared food and got to know Jane. Probably because I was closest to her in age, Jane probed me about my high school experiences. Had I been popular? She asked. Had I attended any proms? Having dropped out of high school two years earlier to marry, I could only answer, "Uh, no." It seemed to me that Jane felt that she had been cheated out of a normal teenage life, and I later learned that she had been educated at a strict Catholic academy.

After the picnic, folks congregated in the Huckenpoehler home to say goodbye. Upon request, Mary Jo played the piano. Jane teared up as we all looked on and listened. Jane soon decided that she wanted more than occasional visits with her birth mother. She and Rudy quarreled over how that might be done, and Jane rather suddenly traveled alone to Arizona. There, according to a letter that Mary Jo wrote to Grandma, Jane visited Mary Jo's son Mike Drumm without telling Mary Jo that she was in town and then rebuffed Mary Jo's efforts to arrange a visit. After that, Mary Jo wrote, "I just gave up." After returning to Minnesota and entering St. Joseph's hospital for a "mental check-up," Jane sent a note of apology to Mary Jo and promised to bring her entire family to Arizona. But from Mary Jo's perspective, "I could care less."[4]

In the summer of 1967, the entire Grapper family moved to Arizona. Desperate for his wife to be happy, Rudy had secured a position with General Electric and rented a home in Phoenix. But from the moment the Grappers arrived, Mary Jo's alcoholism and Jane's mental problems were apparent. Mary Jo could never be Jane's fantasy mother and had no interest in trying.

Jane Grapper with daughters (*left to right*) Kathy, Jo, Mary, and Sandy, ca. 1965.

(*left to right*) Vikki Bynum, Jane Grapper, and Sandy Grapper at a family reunion, Waconia, Minnesota, July 1966.

The two fought bitterly over Mary Jo's alcohol-fueled lifestyle and bartending jobs. Then Jane and Mary Jo's ex-husband Wayne Drumm began having an affair, and by September, she was pregnant with his child. Wayne's current wife immediately left him and their two children, while a devastated Rudy headed back to Minnesota with his daughters, rarely speaking to them of their mother. No doubt intending to stabilize their lives after such trauma, he remarried in haste. The girls resented their stepmother, and she resented them, and they grew up wondering why their mother had abandoned them.[5]

Jane and Wayne soon left for Coalinga, California, where Wayne had friends and a job. Proclaiming themselves happy and in love, they and their newborn baby, Daniel, visited my parents in Monterey. Then, suddenly, Jane was gone, leaving Wayne with his two children from his second marriage and the baby. He enlisted my mother temporarily to take care of Daniel, then turned to Mary Jo. Widowed, practically destitute, and having lost custody of Barney, Mary Jo agreed to join Wayne in Coalinga. For a time, they lived as though they were still married, visiting with my parents just like old times back in Macon. Sometime during this debacle, Daniel was transferred to foster care in Minnesota, where Jane had returned, and she was allowed to have him on weekends until her psychiatric problems worsened again and she was confined to Hastings State Hospital. In mid-August 1970, Grandma stated the obvious: "That whole branch of the family lives like a soap opera."[6]

Wayne, his kids, and Mary Jo soon returned to Glendale. After her release from Hastings, Jane did the same, and she and Wayne resumed their relationship. By April 1971, Jane was again pregnant, and she and Wayne married in Reno, Nevada, on 18 April and set up housekeeping. They regained custody of three-year-old Daniel and on 24 January 1972 welcomed their new daughter, Deanne. With her former husband married to her newly discovered daughter, Mary Jo faced the fact that Wayne had won this round of their long-running game of gotcha. That is, until Jane's mind unraveled again. After "throwing another fit," tearing up Mary Jo's house, and threatening to drown Deanne in a nearby river, Jane was locked up once more. Only Mary Jo's death on 29 July 1978 put an end to the sordid triangle of her relationship with Wayne and Jane. Mary Jo had been not only the source of her mother's greatest sadness but also the engine of her daughter's rage.[7]

Life nevertheless remained conflicted and chaotic for the Drumm family. Mary Jo and Wayne's oldest son, Junior, was particularly upset by his father's marriage to his half-sister. Junior's first marriage failed in 1967, and he lived for a time with Mary Jo, who attributed her son's divorce to the fact that he was too "irresponsible and selfish." In 1976, Junior joined the navy and remarried, and he lived in San Diego, California, until he died of lung cancer in 1994.[8]

Jane's fragile mental state led her to become addicted to alcohol and prescription drugs. Around 1982, she and Wayne divorced, and she quickly remarried Cyril Turf. During these years, her children with Wayne were shuttled back and forth, sometimes living with a parent or grown sibling but often residing in foster homes. In 1985, while the Turfs were living in Tulare, California, Cyril filed for separation, but they reconciled and moved to Arizona. In 1996, Sandy Grapper Troyer, one of Jane's daughters from her first marriage, located her in a mental hospital. For the first time in years, they spoke by telephone, and Jane was happy and hopeful for the future. But they never spoke again. Jane was subsequently diagnosed with pancreatic cancer, and after writing letters of goodbye to Daniel and Deanne, she died at age sixty on 6 February 2001.[9]

Through the mid-1960s, Grandma's letters to her children became increasingly pessimistic about the state of the world in general. In a May 1967 letter to her son Bill and his wife, Betty, she lamented the "bloodshed and cruelty" of war while proclaiming communism the greatest threat to world peace. Adhering to the Domino Theory, which held that the Soviet Union was seeking to dominate the world one nation at a time, she supported US intervention in Vietnam as necessary to prevent that tile from falling. As her Cold War fears of godless Soviet authoritarianism shaded into paranoia, she enrolled in teacher-training classes at St. Joseph's High School of Religion, hoping to be hired as a substitute teacher of religion, although at age eighty, she knew her chances were slim. Nevertheless, she vowed to "be ready if they need me . . . if or when the Communists take over this country after they've bled us white in Vietnam." When that happened, she predicted, "church schools will be closed and the Faith will have to be taught secretly in small groups by dedicated teachers." As one of those educators, Grandma hoped to compensate "for having lost three of my own children to the pagan civilization they now live in."[10]

At this point, the dangers of communism and her children's rejection of the Catholic Church had become inextricably intertwined in my grandmother's mind. Both, she believed, threatened the welfare and progress of her family. The next greatest threat was alcohol, a destructive force in Mary Jo, Wayne, and Jane's shredded personal lives. That the former son-in-law Grandma had long prayed would remarry Mary Jo had instead taken up with her daughter was more than Grandma could bear, and she wished she'd "never let" Jane into the house. Grandma prayed that all her children and grandchildren would put their fate in "God's hands" before it was too late. Nationwide antiwar protests, civil rights marches, and Klan violence in Mississippi convinced her that the world was "writing its final chapter" of history. "I'm old and ready," she wrote, "but I ache for the future of [my] beloved descendants."[11]

By late 1968, Grandma's fears for the world centered on the presidential election amid dramatic political and social upheavals. She was more frightened than ever to stand alone on city streets and bus stops: "It's not the blacks any more than the unruly-class of white folks," she explained in a letter. "It's just an undercurrent of lawlessness." A former New Deal Democrat, she now placed her hopes in the "law and order" Republican Party. Though she had previously disliked Richard Nixon and the "stiff and bigoted" Republicans, she deplored the Democrats' "scandalous" Chicago convention, which erupted in violence. She considered the Democratic candidate, Senator Hubert Humphrey, too weak to govern, whereas Nixon was "firm and confident and experienced." She even had a good word for the American Independent Party's candidate, Alabama's segregationist former governor, George Wallace. In the end, she voted for Nixon but admitted she was not "thoroughly sold" and was still "scared for America."[12]

I would have been disheartened by my grandmother's political views had I known them. Perhaps because she suspected that my mother had far more liberal views, Grandma confined her political pronouncements mostly to letters to her daughter Jeanne. In 1968, Mom and I supported neither Nixon nor Humphrey for president but were great fans of Senator Robert F. Kennedy. In June, just two months after the horrifying assassination of the Reverend Martin Luther King Jr., a ringing phone roused me from sleep. In shock, I listened as my sobbing mother, watching live news coverage on TV, described Bobby Kennedy's murder. I was six months pregnant with Erika and stayed glued to the television the entire day, getting up only to relieve the "morning" sickness that kept me vomiting all day. Looking back, I realize the political differences among the branches of our family were representative of those of the nation writ large.

Though our political choices were different, I now have a better understanding of my grandparents' urgent need to feel safe. They had weathered the Great Depression and two world wars, and they remained poor for the rest of their lives. They benefited from Social Security and Medicare after 1965, but they worked intermittently for wages into their seventies. Still, as Christmas 1968 approached, Grandma remained philosophical: "I might say 'it's Hell to be poor,' but we are *lucky yet*," she wrote. "We have a warm place to live, enough to eat, all the clothes we need to be decently dressed." Noting that many people were much worse off, she regretted her inability to help the "millions in *this land* who are sick and cold and hungry and out of work." She included Mary Jo in that group. Bill, Mom, and Jeanne sent my grandparents checks on birthdays and holidays; Grandma, in turn, sent a small check to Mary Jo every Christmas.[13]

In the spring of 1969, my mother traveled alone to Minneapolis and spent ten days visiting her parents. Mom rarely traveled overnight, since Dad generally got drunk when left alone and ended up calling her. She also feared that he would drive drunk and be arrested. But despite his calls, she had a wonderful visit with her parents, relatives, and childhood friends. Mom permed and styled Grandma's hair, which delighted her. Grandpa was relieved that she paid for their gravestones: he had worried that they would only be able to afford tiny metal markers and had even threatened to sell the antique writing desk that had belonged to Grandma's stepmother, Jeannette, and that Grandma later passed on to me.[14]

Marge Daniel Jones, the formidable woman who had hosted our family at the Kenwood home in 1958, passed away of colon cancer in early 1968, when she was ninety-one. With Marge's death, Grandma's only remaining sibling was her younger brother Doddy, with whom she had little contact in old age. The most attentive members of her extended family were Rod Peck, the son of her sister Lillian and brother-in-law Horace for whom she had babysat so long ago, and Agnes Bennett.[15]

In mid-July 1968, Mary Jo wrote to Grandma that she was sick and unable to work. Barney had been adopted by his foster parents, and Mary Jo proposed moving to Waconia and living with her parents indefinitely. She swore she had not had a drink since doctors warned her that alcohol would kill her. Grandma did not sleep for days, her mind "running in circles" about what to do. By now, she knew to be wary. She attended a Franciscan retreat and took great comfort when the priest advised that under no circumstances should she and Grandpa allow Mary Jo to live with them and that their deeply troubled daughter's care was now the responsibility of her four grown sons. Calmed by the priest's words, Grandma nonetheless sympathized with Mary Jo's predicament. "I feel so bad for her and so utterly helpless about it," she wrote to Jeanne. "I think Jane's visit there was very bad for her." Grandma was greatly relieved that Jeanne and her husband, Jack, were "sober folks."[16]

Yet two months later, she let loose on Jeanne for having left the Catholic Church: "Of course, I know you don't believe in prayer anymore," she wrote, "So this all seems foolish to you, as it does to Pa. . . . My having lost you and all your children and Bill's family, too, is a heartbreaking thing to me, but I still *love* you all and God still loves you too." At least nominally still Catholic, Mom and Mary Jo escaped Grandma's fire on this occasion.[17]

In the grip of her Cold War fears, Grandma expressed fear of being hijacked by Russians if she dared to board a plane to travel to Bill and Betty's home for Christmas. Disappointment with the world's political leaders dampened her enthusiasm even for the family history that Bill urged her to finish: "It seems kind of pointless to write a family history when we read and hear so much about the air, earth, and water pollution that is going to snuff out all life on the beautiful Earth in about twenty-five years." The world was full of "discarded *things*," she continued, while the air was choked with vehicle exhaust fumes and "sulphurous smoke" from chimneys and burning garbage. She deplored the dumping of lead and mercury into lakes, "not to mention turning our Great Lakes and coastal waters into open sewers." Who, she wondered, would be left to read a family history?[18]

Waconia's Senior Citizen Center provided a safe if limited vehicle for my grandparents' engagement with the larger world. The center organized group bus trips and reduced-price entry to many events. In July 1970, Grandma was eagerly looking forward to attending the county fair, where the board "has rented a booth to Hippies and one to the John Birchers," she wrote to Jeanne. "So I'm going to visit each one just to get both of the 'far out' messages." She was also excited about the state fair and the opportunity "to see how the world of industry and farming and education has changed since I last went . . . over a quarter of a century ago," though she later changed her mind as a consequence of too many meal expenses and too many "purse snatchers and pick pockets." Both she and Grandpa were great fans of the Minnesota Twins but also passed on a trip to a baseball game because stadium officials always consigned seniors to the upper deck, reserving the best seats for the highest-paying customers. With no railings on the steep steps, "we have decided we are too old to risk breaking our necks climbing down."[19]

A few weeks before Christmas 1970, right around the time of her eighty-third birthday, Grandma fell on the ice outside her home and cracked her hip—her second such injury in fifteen years. To the surprise of everyone including her doctors, she made a rapid recovery. At Christmas, Grandpa reported that "she was driving around the hospital in a wheelchair." She soon graduated to crutches and on 16 January 1971 was transferred to the Nightingale Nursing Home, where she spent four-plus months.[20]

Grandma remained in good spirits throughout her time there, enjoying her escape from housework and cooking—and likely from Grandpa's criticisms. Harrigan's conviction that no workingman should come home to an untidy house or an unsatisfying meal continued well beyond his retirement from the workforce. In a letter written when he was ninety-four, Harrigan assured his daughter Jeanne that although "ma is not feeling so good now," she was getting better. The proof? She still "does the housework." Small wonder Grandma told Jeanne that "I like this Nursing Home so much that I plan to come back here if I ever find myself alone and unable to keep house by myself." Should that happen, she imagined, "I would be free to go out visiting—even to travel to spend a week or more with one of my children." And "no one will ever have

to have me settle in with them." That she might find herself alone was realistic, but the idea that she could live in a place like Nightingale while still in
good enough health to travel long distances was pure fantasy, as she bitterly
discovered when she returned to Nightingale in 1975.[21]

Despite their remarkably good health, my grandparents rarely traveled after
1970. By then, Grandpa was in his nineties and determined that he would die
in his beloved Waconia. Since he no longer could be left alone for extended
periods, Grandma became tied to the home as well. Their children would have
to come there. In between such visits, she continued writing devoted letters
to family members, with Grandpa occasionally contributing brief missives.

In June 1971, my grandparents hosted a mini family reunion. My mother
and I attended, and so did Mary Jo, Jeanne, and Jeanne's two youngest children, Ruth and Mary. Mary Jo, taking a break from her constant wrangling
with Wayne and Jane, arrived courtesy of Jeanne, who bought Mary Jo a
one-way plane ticket after she insisted that her health was too poor for a long
bus ride. Her health was indeed poor—she was recovering from multiple
bouts with the flu and was nursing a swollen leg and ankle—but soon after
she got to Waconia, she headed to the taverns and began flirting with her
old boyfriend Ray, who had fathered her first child, Michael, but who was
now married. Plus she was still angling to make Waconia her permanent
home: she boldly announced her goal of becoming the manager of Maggie's
Saloon—Grandpa's favorite downtown tavern—and of living right there in
the family home. Grandma was none too pleased with Jeanne.[22]

But Grandpa and Grandma refused to allow Mary Jo to live with them,
recognizing that their oldest child had physically and emotionally lost her
bearings. During her visit two years earlier, my grandmother had written to
Jeanne that "Mary Jo had a bad spell from alcoholism but I think she's pulling
out of it now"; by June 1971, however, Grandma understood that alcoholism
was a physical addiction requiring medical attention: Mary Jo was "still, *of
course*, an alcoholic and has not minded the doctors' advice that her life
depends on her staying completely off alcohol." Back to Arizona she went.[23]

In May 1972, my grandparents moved into Waconia's brand-new federally
subsidized housing complex for senior citizens. Their apartment, though
tiny, relieved them of climbing stairs and shoveling snow. Housekeeping was

minimal, and the complex's community center provided social activities. They were very happy there. In October, my parents visited, sleeping on the apartment floor in sleeping bags. During the visit, Mom assured Grandma that if Pa died first, she would have a home with them and would not be consigned to an "old people's home."²⁴

With sociable neighbors close by, Grandma frequently apologized to her children for being late in answering their letters. To Bill and Betty, she described the new apartment as "a little bit of heaven. . . . I hope we both live a few years longer to enjoy it." Her main complaint was that nosy towns-people occasionally came by to investigate how their "tax dollars" were being spent and whether the tenants were "keeping up" their apartments. Having always enjoyed solitary pursuits, Grandma also occasionally wearied of too much company. "Any six-year-old kid" can play Kings in the Corner, a card game that was all the rage among women tenants. "I'd rather spend that time reading, mending, writing letters, or trying to write my autobiography, or composing poems or other things."²⁵ Grandpa, ever the social man about town, enjoyed daily chats with their neighbors. In a letter to Jeanne, Grandma described him as "cock of the walk, being the only male in the settlement and a nice friendly gentlemanly one at that." Grandpa exclaimed to Bill and Betty that "I eat good, sleep good, and feel like 50. I drive the car down town to stop by stores and have one brandy a day and sometimes play a couple of games of pool. So Thank God."²⁶

In February 1974, after a particularly harsh, snowy winter of confinement, Grandma was briefly hospitalized after experiencing dizzy spells. The following June, Grandpa suffered a heart attack. In the aftermath of his return home, Mary Jo came to Waconia to serve as his live-in caretaker. Two years earlier, Mary Jo had ridden a Greyhound bus to my parents' home in Monterey and arrived drunk. She fell in the driveway, broke her wrist, and was taken to the hospital. There, suffering from alcohol withdrawal, she lapsed into delirium tremens and hallucinations and tore off her bandages. At their wit's end, Mom and Dad put her on a bus back to Arizona, and Mom told her brother Bill, that Mary Jo "needs psychiatric help" and "is beyond any help I can give her!" She had not sought that help, and now she was supposedly going to take care of two elderly and frail people.

In a carefully crafted letter to Bill, Mary Jo described dutifully monitoring Grandpa's urine and blood sugar to make sure his diabetes was under control, admitting only to a brief visit to a downtown tavern on the Fourth of July.

"Pa" was getting along fine, she wrote cheerily, "stubborn as ever" and driving his car against doctor's orders; "Mama" was "still her sweet, absent-minded self." Nine days later, Mary Jo admitted to visiting Waconia's taverns every Friday night despite her father's disapproval: Pa was so "stingy" that she was forced to shoot pool—and win—to buy cigarettes, leading "these hicks in Waconia" to call her "Minnesota Fats." I was twenty-six and newly separated from Burt, and she invited me to join her in Waconia: "We would have a ball. I know some nice-looking young dudes."[27]

By mid-October, Mary Jo was back in Arizona, apparently, according to Grandpa, because Jane "wanted her back." Disgusted by his daughter's frequent trips to downtown taverns, Grandpa was glad to see her return to her Arizona family where "she really belongs." When Jeanne offered to come to Waconia, Grandpa was hesitant to have more company and warned, "If you come, don't bring children along." However, he noted proudly, "I still drive my car."[28]

Despite his fierce independence, Grandpa and Grandma did need help. A concerned neighbor, Agnes Olin, began performing light cleaning for them in December 1974, which sufficed until April 1975, when Grandpa suffered a second heart attack. His hospitalization sent Grandma into a panic. Initially uncertain about whether Grandpa would be able to return home, she wrote to Bill in early April, "I need help! I can't *cope* alone!" The tone of her letter then abruptly changed, calmly discussing the help Agnes was providing and asking Bill to "please write and let us know how you all are and if you would be able to visit us on your next vacation." Bill then received three more similar letters in rapid succession. The day after the first letter to Bill, Grandma wrote to Jeanne, "I know you can't come to help me because of the cost of the trip and because you can't leave your family." By the end of the month, Jeanne had received four more letters that said essentially the same thing. As the calendar turned to May, Grandma reported that Grandpa was home and doing well and that Agnes and Josephine Zahler Hansen, the daughter of Grandpa's older sister, were helping my grandparents manage their affairs and "think straight."[29]

In fact, my grandparents' financial affairs were a mess and Grandpa's health remained precarious. In late April 1975, Mom received an official letter from the Carver County Family Service Department explaining that my grandparents had received overpayments from Social Security and that the government was consequently withholding payments for their mounting medical bills. When county agents visited their home to correct the problem, they found Grandpa "confused" about the situation and reported that he had reluctantly concluded that they could no longer live on their own. The county advised Mom and her siblings that they needed to get involved and recommended that my grandparents be placed in a nursing home. Mom added a cover letter and sent the county's letter on to Bill and Betty, endorsing the nursing home recommendation.[30]

But my mother did not clearly communicate the gravity of the situation, telling her brother and sister-in-law, "I certainly hope that nothing interferes with your plans" for a vacation in the United Kingdom. And so they proceeded as planned. Only Jeanne seemed to perceive that her presence was required back home, flying to Minnesota sometime between late April and early June. After Grandpa told her that he and Grandma should enter a nursing home, Jeanne visited Nightingale but was told that no space would likely be available for a few months. She flew home to Virginia, expecting to return to Minnesota in the fall.[31]

My grandparents managed in their apartment through most of July with help from Josephine and Agnes but then were suddenly admitted or forced to move into the Nightingale Nursing Home. None of their children were present to help with the move, and being abruptly moved by strangers proved a terrible shock for the couple. In addition, they learned that Nightingale was sex-segregated, meaning that they could not share a living space. Grandpa was so rattled that after one night at the nursing home, he tried to walk back to their apartment. Grandma dashed off a letter in which she told Jeanne that they felt "like lost souls" and that "no matter how competent these strangers are, they are not family." On a more practical level, Grandma warned her youngest daughter, "For God's sake! Keep enough in the bank so you can always *take care* of yourselves."[32]

The geographic distances and lack of intimacy among the Huckenpoehler siblings hampered the coordinated response needed for their parents' end-of-life health emergencies. To make matters worse, Mary Jo was an indigent alcoholic, my dad was an alcoholic, and Jeanne's travel was hampered by family finances and her three relatively young children. Bill and Betty also had young children, having adopted a daughter, Elizabeth Cheine Huckenpoehler, in 1963 and a son, William Christopher Huckenpoehler, four years later. Bill and Betty returned from Europe in July 1975 and immediately wrote to see how Grandma and Grandpa were faring and what they might need. She

answered that a robe for her and a robe and slippers for Pa "would be nice."
In response to the information that Bill was working too hard and losing
weight, she asked, "Is he losing weight because of his long hours of mental
and physical labor? As I remember him, he could lose a few pounds without
becoming a 'living skeleton,' haha!"[33]

By August, Grandma was complaining to Jeanne about the "sanctimonious
do gooders" who visited Nightingale to urge residents to display "patience
and fortitude" and to obey God's will. Listening to one such speaker on
"Christian duty" made Grandma "just itch to slap her across the mouth and
tell her to go mind her own business and leave me alone!" Declaring herself
an "inmate" of "forced idleness," she grudgingly admitted that Grandpa had
adjusted to their new home: "He acts as if he's glad to be batching it again,
occasionally playing his violin for the other residents.[34]

Grandma expected her children to gather up the belongings she and
Grandpa had left behind in their apartment. To Mom, she wrote, "I think
you have been officially notified to come and dispose of all the things we
can't have here. . . . It's kind of like dying but not quite official." Mom believed
that Bill should take on that responsibility since he held power of attorney
for their parents. Bill, in turn, asked Josephine Hansen to oversee the task.
She did her best to gather and disperse my grandparents' possessions, but she
was seventy-four and could only do so much. Many items were put up for
auction, and a few, including two family photograph albums, were purchased
by friends and later returned to Mom and her siblings.[35]

Josephine was not pleased by their seeming lack of interest in their parents' welfare. By the time she heard from Bill, she had visited Grandma and
Grandpa five times in the nursing home, and Josephine chided Bill, "I really
thought you would write and ask about your folks before this, after all that
has happened since you were here last." Though she could not provide extensive details because it was "just too nerve wracking to go through it all," she
assured him that the nursing home was clean and well staffed and that his
parents were being cared for. Grandpa had adjusted "alright" to his lodgings
"across the hall" from Grandma, but Grandma was extremely depressed about
the small room she shared with three other women: "She was really down and
I went out crying," Josephine wrote. And in response to Bill's inquiry about
a bill he had received for the cleaning of his parents' apartment, Josephine
replied that because of the circumstances, no one had been available to clean
the apartment: "I couldn't do it and it was not my responsibility." She was not
happy to have to "write this to you, but that's the way it is."[36]

Grandma was indeed "down," and by mid-August 1975, her sorrow and hopelessness turned to bitter anger. "Don't fret about not being here to help us get incarcerated," she wrote to Jeanne:

> I will never *accept* this situation as long as I live and I pray to God it *won't be long* before we are safely dead and out of everybody's way! . . . I was *born free* and I had 4 children—3 girls and 1 boy. And they were *born free* and still are free I *hope*. But Pa and I are not free anymore and if he can accept this state of affairs well and good. I am still free to earnestly beseech God to "give me *liberty* or give me *death*."

She signed the letter "Your angry Mom."[37]

Grandma likewise shamed Bill for abandoning his parents in their old age. In addition to being their only son and their principal guardian, he was the most successful and wealthy of their children, and she held him primarily responsible for their fate:

> I suppose you are powerless to free us from this God-damned prison they call a "nursing home." . . . So far as I know, the crime I'm in here for is just the crime of living too long, or maybe the crime of neglecting to use birth control measures and so bearing four strong healthy children, all of them together unable or unwilling to give us a real home. . . . I still love you and so I pray daily for God to teach you the error of your ways while you still live so you won't burn in Hell! . . . Your loving Mother.[38]

And she sent Bill more than one such letter. On another occasion, she again referred to the nursing home as "God-damned"—a blasphemous phrase for a devout Catholic to use—and described days that dragged by "in this lonely Godforsaken hole" on this "barren, loveless planet." Finally she told him, "I should have proved my love for you by giving you a good thorough thrashing every so often. . . . I hope someone wiser than I was will beat the Hell out of you someday soon, for your vast improvement." Like the first letter, this one too had an incongruous closing: "Lovingly, Mama."[39] She believed that she had been abandoned by both the God and the family she had so long served and for whom she had sacrificed so much.

During my childhood, Grandma presented me with an alternative to the chaotic, alcoholic life I experienced with my parents—a life of sobriety, education, and purpose. Now, at the end of her life, she felt defeated. The reasons are easy to identify: the toil and struggle of raising four children in Great Depression poverty; the intellectual isolation of rural small-town Minnesota; the husband who disdained her love of books, poor housekeeping skills, and devout Catholicism and found enjoyment in the arms of other women. The final blow to Grandma's peace of mind was the rapidly changing world that threatened her core values. She, who had rebelled against Gilded Age temptations of wealth, watched helplessly as the flowering of modern capitalism transformed post–World War II America into a militarized industrial world of tract homes, highways, and mass-produced goods. Lured outward by the promise of adventure and prosperity—the "Mammon" to which she referred in her poem—not one of her children remained in Minnesota past the age of seventeen. Two of her three daughters' lives were blighted by adultery and alcoholism, and all her children rejected her religious faith. The last years of my grandmother's life were marked by despair, anger, and finally dementia.

EPILOGUE

Memories and Reflections

One of the most disturbing dreams of my life occurred when I was ten years old. It began with me wandering lost and alone in a wide-open field. As I struggled to find my way, a helpful old woman appeared and pointed me toward an opening in the ground. Slowly, I entered the opening and descended further and further into darkness. Each time I reached a new landing of sorts, I wondered if I should turn back. Each time, a voice in my head urged, "You must keep going; you can't go back." Nervously, I trekked ever further into the center of the Earth before ascending into the light of day. I somehow realized I was in China, probably because a popular American story claimed that's where you would end up if you dug all the way through the Earth. I was no longer afraid. I knew I had completed a necessary journey but felt shaken when I awoke. Though still a child, I sensed the dream's importance and never forgot it. As an adult, I considered this Big Dream a prompting from my subconscious to seek new experiences and knowledge no matter how frightening the unknown might appear.

The dream occurred in 1958, the same pivotal year that our family moved to California with stops along the way in Mississippi and Minnesota. The visit to Mississippi, which included dinner with Grandpa Smith, piqued my interest in Dad's murky childhood and planted the seeds for our revelatory conversation eight years later. Our family's equally significant dinner in the

Minneapolis house in which my grandmother was born and raised followed. The stately old Kenwood home where we dined revealed her roots in a world far different from the rural German American community in which she had lived for nearly fifty years.

My dawning awareness of worlds beyond my own did not prevent the long journey of conflict and hard struggle that lay ahead of me. My parents' continual breaching of the boundaries of a healthy family life left me vulnerable and insecure. Not surprisingly, I was drawn to Grandma's old-fashioned life of purpose, order, and sobriety. Yet despite her intellectual influence and my years spent studying, writing, and teaching history, I, like my parents, used alcohol and sex to spice up my life. I lived by Grandma's lessons by day but practiced Mom and Dad's habits by night.

Because of Dad's alcoholism, I grew up strongly identifying with Mom and her Minnesota heritage. I never considered myself a southerner even though I had lived in the South with a Mississippi-born and -raised father. No, I was an Air Force kid whose family happened to be stationed in the South. My disdain only increased after we returned to California. By the early 1960s, national TV news shows regularly displayed the brutality deployed against Black citizens who challenged the Jim Crow South. I sympathized with the civil rights movement and equated my explosive, alcoholic father with the racist, violent South I saw on television. Mississippi was his fatherland, but it was not mine. Only after I learned my father's life story could I see myself in him. Only after studying the South as a historian did I understand that both inhumanity and humanity formed its regional identity.

Until then, Mom was the parent I listened to. From her, I learned that reading made you smart whether or not you went to college, that religious chauvinism was a form of bigotry, and that racial integration was morally just. But alongside her social justice principles were unspoken messages. Over the years, I watched her endure Dad's drunken rages by drinking too heavily herself and roaming from sexual affair to sexual affair. Growing up amid my parents' blighted dreams led predictably to my own teenage marriage, early motherhood, and divorce. Years of single parenthood, welfare checks, and broken relationships followed. At the same time, I persevered with college, my emotional and intellectual lifeline.

I was fortunate to enter San Diego City College in the immediate aftermath of my failed first marriage rather than before it. For my grandmother, a rebellious marriage brought to an abrupt end the exciting world of intellectual and social engagement she had only recently discovered at Winona Normal School. In turn, my mother's rebellion amounted to eagerly trading her Depression-era small town for the exciting nightlife of a World War II military community. Although the sexual revolution was not declared until the 1960s, she and her sister Mary Jo enjoyed unprecedented sexual freedom before embracing the Cold War promise of middle-class marriages. The same sexual "freedom" later landed me in a teenage marriage, but the end of that marriage and the political movements of the early 1970s inspired me to enter education. College transformed the possibilities of my life as much as boarding a ship across the ocean had for my Welsh great-great-grandmother, Margaret Davies Lewis.

In 1971, the raw lyrics from Joni Mitchell's song "Blue"—"Acid, booze, and ass, needles, guns, and grass, lots of laughs"—captured the dual sense of liberation and danger felt by many women of my generation. For me, however, those feelings were delayed by my marriage to Burt. Even though I attended the 1967 Monterey Pop Festival while he served in Vietnam, and even though we sat together, transfixed by the movie *Woodstock* in a Washington, DC, theater in 1970, I only vicariously experienced the angst and excitement of the 1960s youth revolution. When Burt went to DC to participate in the 1969 march against the Vietnam War, I heartily approved—but stayed home with the kids. In 1973, I watched the televised Watergate hearings alone at home. Enthralled by the revelations of John Dean and delighted by the southern wit and tenacity of Sam Ervin, I nonetheless remained cloistered away from the centers of action. Then the breakup of my marriage suddenly thrust me into the world of urban college life, feminist politics, and volatile relationships. At age twenty-six, I reveled in my new freedom.[1]

On days when I attended classes and Randy and Erika were with Burt, I enjoyed drinking beer with friends and professors at the Cottage Inn bar across the street from the college. One night, I partied into the night and walked home in the dark. When I reached my apartment, I foolishly stopped to check my mail. From out of nowhere, a young man appeared at my side and asked, "You wanna get high?" "Nope," I said, affecting an air of confidence as I shut and locked my mailbox. "Oh, clean Momma, huh?" He whispered, lightly touching my hip. Struggling to remain calm, I turned and walked quickly up the stairs to my apartment. To my relief, he did not follow. With the door locked behind me, I felt shaken but safe. I realized that this man—a boy, really, looking no more than sixteen years old—might not be so passive the next time he approached a lone woman out at night. I now avoided walking alone on the streets of downtown San Diego after dark.

At times, my contradictory impulses and personalities so jangled my brain that they threatened to derail what I had worked so hard to achieve. But in 1983, seven years after temporarily trading San Diego for the small northern town of Rohnert Park, California, my realization of the special dangers faced by women became horrifyingly graphic. Noelle, my closest friend and running partner while in Rohnert Park, was murdered after a late night of drinking and barhopping that ended with her accepting a ride from a man she either did not know or knew only slightly. For forty years, her killer remained unidentified, but in 2023, as I was finishing this book, advances in DNA testing finally enabled police to make an arrest.[2]

Grandpa died on 2 June 1976 at the age of ninety-seven. All of his children except for Mary Jo, who was too sick to travel, attended the funeral. While in Waconia, Bill, Mom, and Jeanne visited Grandma in the nursing home and witnessed in person her misery and mental decline. There was one light-hearted moment when Grandma mistook Bill for my dad and said delightedly, "You're not looking so sporty as you used to, Stan," but the tortured state of her mind caused my mother great pain.

After listening to Mom's account of the visit, I urged her to transfer Grandma to a California nursing home so she could be near our family. After all, Mom had long cited Grandpa's refusal to leave Minnesota as the only barrier to moving Grandma closer. Mom discussed the possibility with her brother, but Bill vetoed the idea. Perhaps that was best, considering Grandma's age and state of mind. Whatever the case, family members who wanted to see her again would have to travel to the Nightingale Nursing Home.

Jeanne and her family made a difficult visit to Grandma in the spring or early summer of 1978. Grandma recognized Jeanne's husband, Jack, immediately, and soon recognized Jeanne, too. She begged them to take her back to Virginia with them and refused to discuss anything else. Later that summer, I went to Waconia with Randy, age thirteen, and Erika, age nine, who barely knew their great-grandmother. As we self-consciously approached the wheelchair where she awaited us, I noticed her distant expression. Not certain if she would recognize me, I nervously greeted her. To my great relief, so did the children. Grandma looked directly at Randy and Erika and asked if they had ever seen a "real witch." They smiled a bit, not knowing how to answer. She leaned forward with her eyes narrowed and her thin lips pursed and exclaimed, "Well, my sister Marge was a *real* witch!" Time had not softened her anger.

The next day, I went back to the nursing home alone. I had high hopes that my grandmother would recognize me as she had the Van Sises. Instead, she relived the past, at one point imagining herself and nine-year-old Jeannie on their 1942 bus ride to Macon, Georgia. Familiar with the story, I smiled and nodded as though I were Jeannie as Grandma rocked back and forth in her bus seat, scratching and swatting at the insects buzzing around them. Disappointed, I took solace from the fact that she at least recognized me as a family member. Before leaving, I told her how much I loved her and how much she had meant to me over the years. She accepted my words with a quiet smile. Then I hugged her, kissed her forehead, and said goodbye, blinking back tears as I walked toward the exit. On the way, I stopped and thanked the floor nurse for helping to take good care of my grandmother, and she replied, "We do our best."

Shortly after my return home, news arrived that Aunt Mary Jo was dead. On a hot July day, a farmworker discovered her body in a field about three miles from her home in Arizona. Police at first suspected homicide, but an autopsy revealed that Mary Jo had died of natural causes. Several family members speculated that she had tried to walk home from the tavern where she once tended bar. Some wondered if she had been dropped off near the field, maybe following an argument. Others remained convinced that she had been murdered. Her obituary gives her date of death as 29 July 1978, but when she actually died is uncertain.[3]

Mercifully, Grandma's descent into dementia spared her the agony of learning of her eldest daughter's death. When Mom and I visited the Nightingale Nursing Home in May 1979, Grandma shut her eyes and refused to speak to us. She died on 10 November, less than a month shy of her ninety-second birthday.

Since my grandmother's death, I have not returned to Minnesota. Mom never went back there either, though she maintained regular contact with her siblings. In 1995, Uncle Bill, age seventy-one, died of melanoma. His daughter, Inga, believes the melanoma likely resulted from his participation in nuclear testing during World War II. In 2004, seventy-two-year-old Aunt

Jeanne died after a recurrence of colon cancer. My mother died of heart failure at age ninety-three in 2017.

In 1979, the same year my grandmother died, I entered graduate school. Though still hoping to transcribe, annotate, and publish Grandma's memoir, I became immersed instead in the demands of coursework and doctoral exams. In 1981, I became friends with a fellow graduate student, Gregg Andrews. The following year, I left for North Carolina to research my dissertation, and he transferred to Northern Illinois University. We met again in 1988 as faculty members in Texas State University's history department. In 1990, we married.

Our marriage furthered my commitment to facing life's downturns with courage rather than seeking solace in alcohol or via other vices. In Gregg, I discovered a loving companion who had endured a childhood of poverty with an alcoholic father as well as a failed teenage marriage. We based our relationship on love, our similar backgrounds, and our shared intellectual interests. As historians, we devoted our lives to researching people from the past who struggled against circumstances of birth and choices that set them at odds with dominant forces in American society. With Gregg's ongoing encouragement and mentorship, I decided against merely annotating my grandmother's memoir and instead chose to use her work as the centerpiece for this microhistory of the social and economic forces that shaped her life, those of our forebears, and me. In a sense, my grandmother and I became coauthors of the history we shared for thirty-two years.

NOTES

Abbreviations

B&BH	Bill and Betty Huckenpoehler
Bynum Diary	Victoria Bynum Diary, 1961–65
Daniel Letters	Roderick Evan Daniel Letters, 1864–92, Mary Daniel Huckenpoehler and Family Papers, Minnesota Historical Society, St. Paul
DFP	*Detroit Free Press*
JVS	Jeanne Van Sise
MB	Margaret Bynum
MDH	Mary Daniel Huckenpoehler
MDH Daybook	Mary Daniel Huckenpoehler Daybook, 1925, Mary Daniel Huckenpoehler and Family Papers, Minnesota Historical Society, St. Paul
MDH Memoir, 1920–42	Mary Daniel Huckenpoehler Memoir, 1920–42, Mary Daniel Huckenpoehler and Family Papers, Minnesota Historical Society, St. Paul
MDH Notes and Drafts	Mary Daniel Huckenpoehler Notes and Drafts in Preparation for Memoir/History
MEL	Mary Ellen Lewis
MJK	Mary Jo King
"Notes on My Life"	Mary Daniel Huckenpoehler, "Notes on My Life and the Lives That Touched It [1864–1920]," unpublished memoir, Mary Daniel Huckenpoehler and Family Papers, Minnesota Historical Society, St. Paul
RED	Roderick Evan Daniel
RRL	Huckenpoehler Family Round Robin Letters, in possession of Inga McArdle
VB	Victoria Bynum

Prologue: Discovering Mary Daniel

1. "Notes on My Life"; MDH Notes and Drafts.

2. Mary seemed quickly to recover from her crush in the wake of Hazel's marriage ("Notes on My Life"). The classic work on homoerotic female relationships in the nineteenth century is Smith-Rosenberg's "Female World of Love and Ritual." On turn-of-the-century crushes among college women like Mary Daniel, see esp. Inness, "Mashes, Smashes, Crushes, and Raves." Faderman explores the connection of such relationships to the development of lesbian culture in *Odd Girls and Twilight Lovers*.

Chapter 1: The Welsh Roots of an American Civil War Love Story

1. "Notes on My Life"; MDH Notes and Drafts; Daniel Letters.

2. Frank Jones to VB, 29 September 1971, 26 March 1972; Nancy Jones to VB, 18 November 1971, 24 February 1972. Unless otherwise indicated, all documents and photographs are in possession of VB.

3. Kathryn Williams, "Short Bio, Drych, Apr 1918," 19 April 2019, Ancestry.com; James, "Introduction."

4. Susannah Davies and her infant died in 1819 in Blaen Cowny, Llangadfan, Wales, Geneanet Community Trees Index, Ancestry.com.

5. "Rees Davies and His Family." One of John and Margaret Lewis's daughters, designated on the *Orpheus* manifest as *M*, died during the passage (New York Passenger Lists, 1820–1957, Ancestry.com).

6. The Rees Davies family sailed on the *Atlantic* (New York Passenger Lists, 1820–1957, Ancestry.com). Baptismal records of Rees and Gwen's children identify them as members of the Bethel Calvinistic Methodist Church of Llanwddyn, Montgomeryshire, Wales (England and Wales, Non-Conformist and Non-Parochial Registers, 1567–1936, Ancestry.com). The great revivalist leader Charles Grandison Finney popularized the term *burned-over district* in 1876.

7. David Moore, "Wales and the Slave Trade"; Evans, *Slave Wales*; Sanders, *Wales, the Welsh and the Making of America*, 19–29; Hammond, *Woven Histories*. On Jones in India, see especially Andrew J. May, *Welsh Missionaries and British Imperialism*.

8. Sanders, *Wales, the Welsh and the Making of America*, 33–43, 48–87; Hunter, *Sons of Arthur, Children of Lincoln*, 50–53.

9. Hunter, *Sons of Arthur, Children of Lincoln*, 50–58. According to Hunter, the Welsh belief that their distant ancestors had been sold into slavery in the "markets of Rome" (65) helped fuel Welsh abolitionism. See also David Moore, "Wales and the Slave Trade."

10. Hunter, *Sons of Arthur, Children of Lincoln*, 77–84.

11. Van Vugt, "Welsh Emigration"; U.S. Census, 1900, Minneapolis, Minnesota; "Notes on My Life."

12. Bagley and Bagley, *Welsh Families—Wisconsin Pioneers*, 67–68.

13. Hunter, *Sons of Arthur, Children of Lincoln*, 14–15, 63–65. J. P. Harris was the editor of *Y Seren Orllewinol*.

14. Edward Jones, a shoemaker, also lived in the Lewis Jones household. The census listed Roderick and Thomas Daniel in both this household and that of Roderick and Catharine Evans (US Census, 1850, Racine, Wisconsin; "Notes on My Life").

15. In Utica, John Lewis claimed $1,000 in property in 1850. The thirty-four-year-old carpenter in his household, William Lewis, is identified as William Davis in the 1855 New York State Census, suggesting that he was Margaret's younger brother. The major breadwinners in the household of Rees and Gwen Davies, ages seventy-one and fifty-two, respectively, were their twenty-six-year-old son, Rees Davies Jr., and their son-in-law, Evan Owens, whose wives and children also resided in the household. The Davies household also included two apparently unrelated artisan families (US Census, 1850, Utica, New York). Sixty-two-year-old Gwen Davies's 1860 New York City household included her daughters, Elizabeth, twenty-eight; Mary, twenty-seven; and Catherine, twenty-one, all of whom were dressmakers (US Census, 1860, New York, New York).

16. After Rees Davies's death, Gwen Davies never remarried and lived with one or another of her daughters for the remaining thirty-seven years of her life (Gwen Davies obituary, *Cambrian*, ca. 12 January 1895).

17. Barrington Moore, *Social Origins of Dictatorship and Democracy*, 129–42; Foner, *Free Soil, Free Labor, Free Men*; Oakes, *Crooked Path to Abolition*.

18. Between 1855 and 1858, Elizabeth James's husband Erasmus and their two daughters died of undisclosed causes. In 1860, after she and Evan married, Elizabeth Daniel's home was valued at $1,300 and Evan's property at $800. Their Norwegian blacksmith employee, Loss Ergrude, and his family of seven lived with them. The 1870 US Census valued Elizabeth's real estate at $12,000, including four homes that she rented out. Her will specified that she was the sole owner of all the couple's real estate (US Census, 1850, 1860, 1870, Racine, Wisconsin; Will and Probate Record for Elizabeth [James] Daniel, 14 December 1878, Ancestry.com).

19. On immigrant support for Lincoln, see Holzer, *Brought Forth on this Continent*.

20. Hunter, *Sons of Arthur, Children of Lincoln*, 57, 103–4; RED Military Records. Utley was a Democrat from Massachusetts who moved to Racine and joined the Free Soil Party in 1848. Roderick's earliest surviving letter is dated 23 April 1864.

21. Byrne, *Uncommon Soldiers*, 9–11; Fliss, "Wisconsin's Abolitionist Regiment"; Groves, *Blooding the Regiment*, 57.

22. Byrne, *Uncommon Soldiers*, 14–15; Hunter, *Sons of Arthur; Children of Lincoln*, 397.

23. Giles and Guelzo, "Colonel Utley's Emancipation."

24. Byrne, *Uncommon Soldiers*, 15–16.

25. RED to MEL, 1 August 1864, Daniel Letters; RED Military Records; Byrne, *Uncommon Soldiers*, 60. Groves describes the capture and imprisonment of the 22nd Wisconsin Regiment in *Blooding the Regiment*, 88–159.

26. MDH Notes and Drafts; Byrne, *Uncommon Soldiers*, 49, 62–63.

27. RED Military Records; RED to Mary Ellen Lewis, 3 April 1864, Daniel Letters.

28. In April 1864, some fifteen members of the Knight Band were captured and forced back into the 7th Battalion, Mississippi Infantry. The 7th Battalion was soon sent to Georgia with the Army of Tennessee, where at least eight of the men were captured on 3 July by General Sherman near Kennesaw Mountain and sent to Union prisons for the duration of the Civil War (Bynum, *Free State of Jones*, 124).

29. RED to MEL, 1 August 1864, Daniel Letters.

30. RED to MEL, 1 August 1864, Daniel Letters.

31. RED to MEL, 14 April 1865, Daniel Letters.

32. "Notes on My Life"; MDH Notes and Drafts; Evan O. Jones obituary, *Racine Journal*, 24 April 1906.

33. "Notes on My Life." Roderick may have been recovering from typhoid at the time of his discharge (MDH Notes and Drafts).

34. RED to MEL, 9 June 1866, Daniel Letters.

35. RED to MEL, 9 June 1866, Daniel Letters.

36. RED to MEL, 11 July 1866, Daniel Letters.

37. RED to MEL, 28 November 1866, Daniel Letters; RED to MEL, 7 December 1866, Daniel Letters.

38. RED to MEL, 7 December 1866, Daniel Letters.

39. RED to MEL, 7 June 1867, Daniel Letters.

40. Handwritten marriage record, in the Mary Daniel Huckenpoehler and Family Papers, Minnesota Historical Society, St. Paul.

41. On the impact of the War of 1812 on national identity among frontier people, see Bynum, *Free State of Jones*, 32–37. On the democratizing effects of Reconstruction, see Doyle, *Age of Reconstruction*.

42. Marx and Engels, *Civil War in the United States*.

Chapter 2: Class Matters in the Gilded Age

1. "Notes on My Life."

2. On Nekimi, see Davies, *Oshkosh, Wisconsin, Welsh Settlement Centennial, 1847–1947*. The 1870 US Census for Nekimi, Winnebago County, Wisconsin, lists John and Margaret Lewis and their son, William [Henry], as residents.

3. Katie Lewis to Mary Ellen Daniel, 29 May 1872, Mary Daniel Huckenpoehler and Family Papers, Minnesota Historical Society, St. Paul.

4. US Marriage Records, 1820–2004, Ancestry.com. The 1860 US Census for Racine, reports Frederic Ullmann's father, Isaac J. Ullmann, as sixty-one years old; born in Strasburg, Germany; and working as a "Deputy U.S. Collector." Henry Johnson Ullmann, age thirty-four, Daniel Ullmann, thirty-five, and James John Ullmann, twenty-seven, were reported as bankers.

5. *Chicago Tribune*, 11 October 1871; 18 October 1871. The former president of the Bank of Racine and more recently vice -president of the Manufacturers National Bank in Chicago, Henry Johnson Ullmann had replaced his deceased brother James at the Chicago banking house of Wrenn, Ullmann, & Co. less than six months earlier (Racine city directory, 1858; *Racine Journal*, 26 April 1871).

6. In 1870, Anna Lewis taught music in Oshkosh (US Census, 1870, Oshkosh, Wisconsin). Her memorial at Milwaukee's Forest Home Cemetery states that she studied voice in New York City and Berlin, Germany, and served on the faculty of the Evanston Conservatory of Music. Born in Milwaukee in 1850, Mather Dean graduated from Northwestern University in 1873. He was descended from the colonial Mather family of Puritan Connecticut through his abolitionist father, Alonzo Kimball (Hobbs, *Kimball-Weston Memorial*. See also Alonzo Kimball obituary, 7 August 1900, Green Bay, Wisconsin, Ancestry.com).

7. *Chicago Tribune*, 4 July 1875; *Green Bay Weekly Gazette*, 10 July 1875.

8. *Chicago Tribune*, 4 July 1875; *Green Bay Press-Gazette*, 31 December 1875.

9. The *Oshkosh Northwestern*, 29 February 1876, reported that Katie Lewis, "sister of Mrs. R. E. Daniel," had died that morning. On 16 August 1876, the newspaper noted the death of John D. Lewis. Tuberculosis also claimed Jennie Lewis Jones six years later (*Racine Journal Times*, 6 January 1882).

10. Roderick's insurance partnerships included Daniel and McCurdy, Daniel and Gile, and Daniel and Luscher (*Oshkosh Northwestern*, 7 October 1879, 15 May 1880, 3 March 1882). For his musical and lecture activities, see *Oshkosh Northwestern*, 8 September, 6 November 1875; 29 September 1876; 13 September, 28 December 1878. For his political involvement, see *Oshkosh Northwestern*, 9 February 1876; 19 July, 16, 21 August 1879; 5 January 1880.

11. US Census, 1880, Minneapolis, Minnesota.

12. *Oshkosh Northwestern*, 24 January 1887.

13. *Oshkosh Northwestern*, 23 March 1886; George, "Reformer Deplores the Poverty Caused by Industrial Progress." Three of the convicted Haymarket activists were hanged; the fourth died by suicide. The men were later exonerated by Chicago mayor John Altgeld.

14. *Oshkosh Northwestern*, 24 June 1887.

15. On the emergence of formerly enslaved Black Americans as part of the urban South's working class, see Andrews, *Shantyboats and Roustabouts*. On immigrant working conditions in the early nineteenth century, see Andrews, *City of Dust*.

16. Andrews, *Shantyboats and Roustabouts*, 120–21.

17. Horowitz, *Rereading Sex*; Gordon, *Moral Property of Women*; Brodie, *Contraception and Abortion*.

18. For an overview of this era from the perspective of American employers and workers, see Pearson, *Reform or Repression*.

19. Dalen et al., "Epidemic of the 20th Century"; "Notes on My Life."

20. Tyrrell, *Woman's World, Woman's Empire*. For evidence that Mather edited *Good Form* and that the Kimballs and Willard were close friends, see Jack Rudolph, "Old Weekly Globe Colorful Sheet," *Green Bay Press-Gazette*, 1 May 1965. The *Chicago Tribune*, 10 August 1892, reported that Anna organized the music and sang the opening hymn at the funeral of Willard's mother.

21. "Notes on My Life"; MDH Notes and Drafts.

22. *Oshkosh Northwestern*, 3 December 1887.

23. "Notes on My Life"; MDH Notes and Drafts. Jones boarded the *Adriatic* in Liverpool, England, on 4 May 1889 (Frank Jones to VB, 29 September 1971).

24. "Notes on My Life."

25. Margaret Daniel Jones obituary, *Minneapolis Star Tribune*, 21 March 1968. According to the 1940 US Census for Minneapolis, Minnesota, Lillian completed four years of college, but I have found no further evidence that she did so.

26. "Notes on My Life."

27. "Notes on My Life."

28. In 1880, Robert Williams boarded at Susannah's home; sometime during the next decade, they married. See U.S Census, 1880, 1900, Minneapolis, Minnesota.

29. MDH Notes and Drafts; *Mason City Globe Gazette*, 1 August 1942; John Arthur Lewis obituary, *Pasadena Independent Star-News*, 31 January 1968. Agnes studied under Clara Williams in Minneapolis, Oscar Saenger of the Metropolitan Opera in New York, and Henry Pepper of London. She and Bennett married on 14 September 1916 and went on to have two sons. She died in Mason City, Iowa, in October 1978.

30. "Notes on My Life"; *Chicago Chronicle*, 20 November 1897; *Chicago Tribune*, 11 December 1898; *Chicago Inter Ocean*, 3 January 1899.

31. "Notes on My Life"; *Chicago Tribune*, 8 June 1901.

32. Frederic Ullmann's will valued his real estate at $116,534.73.

33. "Notes on My Life."

34. "Notes on My Life"; MDH Notes and Drafts; Margaret Ullmann to Hamlin Garland, 13 April 1913, Hamlin Garland Correspondence, University of Southern California Digital Library, Los Angeles. The 1910 US Census for Chicago lists the occupations of thirty-two-year-old Bessie and twenty-eight-year-old Daisy as "none," although enumerators were instructed to list the occupations of all individuals, whether a child, woman, or man (see "1910 Census Instructions to Enumerators," US Census Bureau website, accessed 23 July 2024, https://www.census.gov/programs-surveys/decennial-census/technical-documentation /questionnaires/1910/1910-instructions.html). Daisy Ullmann's papers, 1894–1956, which include a childhood scrapbook and myriad published and unpublished poems and essays, are at the Newberry Library, Chicago.

35. Daisy Ullmann shared snippets of her life in occasional notes to her alma mater (Bryn Mawr College Publications, Alumnae Bulletins, 1928–1931). For her care packages to Jennie Jones, see Frank Jones to VB, 29 September 1971. Margaret died on 7 January 1961 at the age of seventy-eight. In her will, she distributed her large estate among cousins, friends, and her beloved Bryn Mawr College. Cousins unconnected to Margaret socially, including MDH, received token bequests of one hundred dollars (Margaret Ullmann, Last Will and Testament, 6 October 1957).

36. "Notes on My Life"; MDH Notes and Drafts; MDH to VB, 18 July 1971.

Chapter 3: Building a Family Dynasty

1. "Notes on My Life."

2. "Notes on My Life."

3. Roderick Daniel to Jeannette May Jones, 13 September 1889, Daniel Letters.

4. Roderick Daniel to Jeannette May Jones, 16 February 1890, Daniel Letters.

5. Roderick Daniel to Jeannette May Jones, 16 February 1890, Daniel Letters.

6. Dubnow, *History of the Jews in Russia and Poland*; Clark, *Sleepwalkers*.

7. "Notes on My Life."

8. Roderick Daniel to Jeannette May Jones, 13 September 1889, Daniel Letters. On anti-Semitism among nineteenth century American elites, see Okrent, The Guarded Gate, pp. 33-41.

9. Veidingler, *In the Midst of Civilized Europe*; North, *Russian Revolution*, 289–90.

10. "Notes on My Life"; MDH Notes and Drafts.

11. "Notes on My Life"; MDH Notes and Drafts. Mary nevertheless "loved that kindergarten" and was that rare child who "who ran away to school." She lamented that kindergartens of her childhood were too formal and believed that they should have "followed each child's natural lead" (MDH Notes and Drafts).

12. "Notes on My Life." Mary misdated her visit to the Williams home as mid-June 1893 rather than 1892.

13. "Notes on My Life." Margaret Lewis died at the home of her daughter Elizabeth Ullmann in Chicago on 27 January 1903.

14. "Notes on My Life."

15. *Minneapolis Star Tribune*, 3 August 1895; "Notes on My Life."

16. "Notes on My Life."

17. "Notes on My Life." Unperfumed and made from olive oil, Bocabelli castile soap is still produced today according to the same formula and process.

18. "Notes on My Life."

19. MDH Memoir, 1920–42; "Notes on My Life."

20. "Notes on My Life"; *Minneapolis Star Tribune*, 17 June 1897.

21. Herbert N. Peck's father, Horace Merriman Peck, was a farmer from Waterford, Connecticut, who became one of the richest bankers in Kalamazoo, Michigan. Sara Edsell Peck's father, Wilson C. Edsell, was born in Pennsylvania, attended Oberlin College in Ohio, joined the Prohibitionist Party after the Civil War, and cofounded the National Bank of Otsego, Michigan, with his son-in-law Herbert N. Peck (Michigan Legislative Biography, Library of Michigan, Lansing).

22. Loren Fales obituary, *DFP*, 6 November 1909.

23. *Sioux City Journal*, 23 August 1896.

24. *DFP*, 21–22 August 1898, 25 January 1900.

25. *DFP*, 15 May 1900, 31 December 1901. In 1900, Bingley celebrated his all-American roots by joining the Sons of the American Revolution (Bingley R. Fales, application to the Sons of the American Revolution, 1900, Ancestry.com).

26. *Minneapolis Star Tribune*, 13 August 1899; *DFP*, 15 May 1900, 5 March 1902.

27. *Minneapolis Star Tribune*, 13 August 1899.

28. *DFP*, 8 April 1886, 29 March 1936.

29. US Census, 1880, Kalamazoo, Michigan; *Minneapolis Star Tribune*, 15 February 1891, 5 March 1952; *DFP*, 3 March 1900.

30. Horace and Lillian's marriage indirectly aided Lillian's brother Lewis in finding an elegant new wife when his first marriage went sour. Esther Edsell Martindale, an aunt of Horace and Alice Peck from Michigan, attended both siblings' weddings. Twenty years later, after Esther's first husband had died of cancer and Lewis Daniel's wife had left him for another man, they married ("Notes on My Life").

31. See especially Horace's full-page spread in the *Minneapolis Journal*, 30 August 1902.

32. Horace, Herbert, and Georgia Peck invested almost $50,000 in the Carbon Paper and Plate Company, which "deal[t] in photographic supplies" and thus dovetailed nicely with Horace's photography (*Minneapolis Star Tribune*, 22 September 1899).

33. *DFP*, 3 March 1900.

Chapter 4: The Misfit and the Millionaires

1. "Notes on My Life." On the life and career of Marge's brilliant teacher, see Hogstad, "Anna Schoen-René."

2. "Notes on My Life."

3. Roderick L. Daniel and Margaret Grimes marriage record, 1901, Custer County, Nebraska, Marriage Records, 1855–1908, State Library and Archives, Nebraska State Historical Society, Lincoln. Mary misdated Llew's western adventure by almost a decade ("Notes on My Life").

4. "Notes on My Life"; Horace E. Peck obituary, *Minneapolis Star Tribune*, 26 August 1916. The 1907 Jackrabbit was a two-passenger roadster with top speed of seventy-five miles per hour ("Apperson").

5. Horace's other photographs in the *Minneapolis Journal*, 14 December 1901, included E. C. Tolley of Minneapolis on horseback as "A Prairie Centaur," Tolley branding a steer, and various hunting scenes. The 1900 US Census for Minneapolis, Minnesota, listed Horace's occupation as "photo paper manufacturer."

6. "Notes on My Life." Mary reported Roderick Daniel Peck's birth date as 5 February 1899, but records show he was born on 5 February 1902 (World War II draft registration card, 1942).

7. *Minneapolis Daily Times*, 29 June 1902; *Minneapolis Star Tribune*, 27 September 1903. In 1906, Horace bought a fully appointed barber shop in Kenmare that he promptly advertised for rent in the *Minneapolis Star Tribune,* 23 September 1906.

8. *Wahpeton Times*, 17 October 1907. On North Dakota's alliance with Texas populism and socialism, see Alter, *Toward a Cooperative Commonwealth*, 7, 93, 209, 165–77.

9. According to Mary, Horace and Lillian Peck had moved to the Dupont Avenue apartment by February 1904. Indicative of their dual households, the 1910 US Census reported the family as residents of Kenmare, while the 1920 Minnesota Census listed Lillian still living in the Dupont Avenue apartment.

10. See "Bank for Mohall," *Bottineau Courant*, 17 April 1903. Minneapolis city directories indicate that Herbert and Horace Peck ran the State Loan Company from their Hawthorn Avenue residence until around 1903.

11. *Minneapolis Star Tribune*, 16 February 1903; "Notes on My Life." Rental ads for the mansion appeared in both the *Minneapolis Journal* and *Star Tribune* between 1906 and 1907.

12. *Minneapolis Star Tribune*, 9 May 1909. The article noted that Horace's automobile was rated at fifty horsepower and had thirty-four-inch wheels.

13. *Bottineau Courant*, 18 July 1913; "Dickinson G. C.," 279; "Off to Alaska to Hunt Bear: North Dakota Banker Will Have Interesting Trip to North Country," *Bismarck Tribune*, 28 April 1915. For shooting tournaments, see *Ward County Independent*, 16, 23 August 1913, 22 July 1915; *Grand Forks Herald*, 27 June 1913, 16 March 1914; *Bismarck Herald*, 13 August 1913, 23, 30 June 1915.

14. *Ward County Independent*, 9 August 1906; *Williston Graphic*, 4 September 1913; *Bismarck Tribune*, 13 August 1913; "Hunting with Gun and Graflex," 13. After Horace's death, the University of North Dakota obtained his collection of mounted birds (*Grand Forks Herald*, 20 June 1919).

15. *DFP*, 30 March 1899.

16. *DFP*, 9 May 1901, 17 March, 13 May 1903, 14 June 1904, 4 July 1906. Herbert Peck bought 150 shares in the CHC, while Bingley bought 50. Edison Illuminating Company, for which Bingley served as assistant general manager, assured the public that it did not stand to profit if the CHC won the city's franchise. Despite concerns, the Detroit City Council approved the franchise. In June 1904 Bingley urged the council to choose the CHC over the Murphy Heating Company to lay the city's conduits and pipes. In July 1906, the CHC merged with the Edison Company.

17. *Williston Graphic*, 1 September 1904; *DFP*, 6 March 1905, 4 July 1906. For a study of how industrial titans viewed themselves as "progressive reformers and benevolent guardians of America's economic and political institutions," see Pearson, *Reform or Repression*.

18. The house was expanded to encompass fifteen thousand square feet after Bingley's death, and its address was changed to 1771 Seminole Street.

19. "Notes on My Life"; MDH to JVS, 10 March 1973. Mary and Rod remained close for the rest of their lives. At age eighty-five, Mary told her daughter Jeanne, "Rod is the only one back home who keeps in touch with me" (MDH to JVS, 10 March 1973).

20. "Notes on My Life."

21. "Notes on My Life."

22. "Notes on My Life." Mary spelled his name *Brombach*. Gordon was the grandson of German immigrants and, like Harrigan Huckenpoehler, went on to become a locomotive fireman (US Census, 1910, 1920, 1930, Minneapolis, Minnesota).

23. "Notes on My Life"; MDH to JVS, 13 August 1970.

24. "Notes on My Life"; MDH to JVS, 11 July 1970.

25. "Notes on My Life."

26. "Notes on My Life." On Gustavus Johnson and the Johnson School of Music, see Laudon, "Minnesota Musicians of the Cultured Generation."

27. "Notes on My Life."

28. "Notes on My Life." Founded in 1858, Winona State Normal School became Winona State Teachers College in 1921, Winona State College in 1957, and Winona State University in 1975.

29. "Notes on My Life."

30. "Notes on My Life."

31. "Notes on My Life."

32. "Notes on My Life."

33. "Notes on My Life."

34. "Notes on My Life."

35. *DFP*, 15 February 1909.

36. *DFP*, 24 February, 15 December 1907, 23 April 1908.

37. *DFP*, 8 April, 8 November 1908. The following November, Bingley attempted to defend the CHC in a speech before Detroit's Wholesalers' Association on "The Practicality and Economy of the Central Heating Plant" (*DFP*, 8 November 1908).

38. Bingley Fales death certificate, Ancestry.com. In 1912, Herbert N. Peck sold the Hawthorn Avenue mansion to a men's organization, the United Commercial Travelers (*Minneapolis Star Tribune*, 16 January 1912).

39. *DFP*, 6 November 1909, 3 August 1910; *Minneapolis Star Tribune*, 16 January 1912.

40. "Notes on My Life."

41. "Notes on My Life."

42. "Notes on My Life."

43. *Bowbells Tribune*, 8 March 1912, 11 July 1913; *Fargo Forum and Daily Republican*, 22 April 1913.

44. *Ward County Independent*, 13 July 1913; *Bowbells Tribune*, 1 August 1913. The "boom town" of Kenmare never developed into the thriving industrial and agricultural center that its boosters predicted, and today it has population of around twelve hundred.

45. *Ward County Independent*, 13 July 1913; *Bowbells Tribune*, 3 October 1913. Gardner's suit apparently was thrown out after Horace's death.

46. *Fargo Nonpartisan Leader*, 2 December 1915. For an in-depth history of the NPL, see Lansing, *Insurgent Democracy*. For the North Dakota NPL's connections with Texas radicalism, see Alter, *Toward a Cooperative Commonwealth*, 174–211.

47. *Bismarck Tribune*, 25 August 1916; *Ward County Independent*, 24 August 1916; *Grand Forks Herald*, 25 August 1916.

48. *Ward County Independent*, 24, 31 August, 21 October, 2 November 1916; "Notes on My Life."

49. *Los Angeles Times*, 28 April 1918; *Minneapolis Star Tribune*, 10 February 1920. Alice and Charles's marriage ended in 1934, and she died in New York City on 2 March 1952 (*Minneapolis Star Tribune*, 5 March 1952).

50. Pacific Coast Architecture Database, accessed 17 June 2024, https://v2039.host.s.uw
.edu/building/19026/.

51. *Pasadena Post*, 13 February 1928; *Chicago Tribune*, 14 February 1928. Funds to build
the Playhouse Theater had been raised by wealthy Pasadena citizens transplanted from the
East Coast (see Pasadena Playhouse website, accessed 2 June 2024, https://www.pasadena
playhouse.org/about/).

52. Frederic Ullmann Jr. obituary, *Chicago Tribune*, 24 August 1942.

53. Thomas R. Daniel obituary, *Pasadena Post*, 17 April 1926.

Chapter 5: Mary's Great Rebellion

1. "Notes on My Life."

2. "Notes on My Life."

3. "Notes on My Life."

4. Kitch, *Girl on the Magazine Cover*, 48–55; "Notes on My Life."

5. "Notes on My Life."

6. New York, U.S., Arriving Passenger and Crew Lists (including Castle Garden and
Ellis Island), 1820–1957, Ancestry.com. Though the Huckenpoehlers' oldest child was known
as Christina, she was actually named Anna Maria, after her mother, Anna Marie Rump
Huckenpoehler, Heinrich's first wife. Anna Marie died in 1850, shortly after the birth and
death of the couple's second daughter, Theresia (Heinrich Huckenpoehler and Anna Marie
Gertrud Rump marriage record, 29 February 1848, Westphalen, Prussia, Germany, Germany,
Select Marriages, 1558–1929, Ancestry.com; Germany, Select Births and Baptisms, 1558–1898,
Ancestry.com).

7. James Huckenpahler, unpublished history of the Huckenpahler/Huckenpoehler family,
courtesy of James Huckenpahler.

8. Neill and Bryant, *History of the Minnesota Valley*, 391; obituary of Anton Claesgens Sr.,
Waconia Patriot, 6 October 1905; Josepha Claesgens death registration, 19 December 1871,
"Carver [County] Death Records Index," FamilySearch.org.

9. Berg, *38 Nooses*; Mitchno, *Dakota Dawn*.

10. Berg, *38 Nooses*. Lincoln approved the convictions of thirty-nine men found guilty of
either rape or massacre; one of those men received a last-minute reprieve. On the rules of
war used to hang the men, see Haymond, "How the U.S. Used 'Laws of War.'"

11. Elizabeth Bleichner Bahr (daughter of Louisa Claesgens), conversation with VB, June
1971, Waconia, Minnesota; Mary Claesgens and Moritz Wagner marriage record, Minnesota,
U.S. Marriages Index, 1849–1950, Ancestry.com).

12. *St. Paul Globe*, 22, 24, May 1878.

13. *St. Paul Globe*, 22, 24, May 1878.

14. "Notes on My Life."

15. "Notes on My Life."

16. "Notes on My Life."

17. "Notes on My Life." In 1910, both Harrigan, thirty-one, and Walter, twenty-two, were
single, and they boarded in neighboring homes; Harrigan tended bar in the sample room of
a hotel, while Walter worked as a store clerk (US Census, 1910, Waconia, Minnesota).

18. "Notes on My Life."

19. "Notes on My Life."

20. "Notes on My Life."

21. "Notes on My Life."

22. "Notes on My Life." Mary wrote that she moved to Onamia in September 1915 but also said that the move occurred directly following Horace Peck's death, which occurred on 24 August 1916. Harriet Van Rhee's marriage also took place in August 1916 (www.familysearch. org, accessed 18 June 2024, entry for Harriet Van Rhee, person ID LR1R-VRD).

23. "Notes on My Life."

24. "Notes on My Life." Mary misdated the year as 1916.

25. "Notes on My Life."

26. "Notes on My Life"; Lubotina, "Corporate Supported Ethnic Conflict."

27. Okrent, *Guarded Gate*; Lubotina, "Corporate Supported Ethnic Conflict."

28. "Notes on My Life."

29. "Notes on My Life."

30. "Notes on My Life."

31. Barry, "Site of Origin of the 1918 Influenza Pandemic"; *Minneapolis Star Tribune*, 9, 16, 18 April 1918.

32. "Notes on My Life."

33. "Notes on My Life." Her daughter Mary Jo's suggestion that Harrigan ultimately married Mary because she was "so hard to get" certainly has a ring of truth to it (Mary Jo Drumm, conversation with VB, ca. 1966).

34. "Notes on My Life."

35. "Notes on My Life."

36. "Notes on My Life."

37. Josephine Huckenpoehler to William Bernard Huckenpoehler, 1 December 1918; "Notes on My Life."

38. "Notes on My Life."

Chapter 6: Schooled by Life

1. Gordon, *Second Coming of the KKK*. The movie was based on Thomas Dixon Jr.'s novel *The Clansman: A Historical Romance of the Ku Klux Klan*. Exceptions to Lost Cause history before the 1950s include Du Bois, *Black Reconstruction*; Williams, *Capitalism and Slavery*; Schlesinger, "Causes of the Civil War." Groundbreaking works of the 1950s include Woodward, *Origins of the New South*; Stampp, *Peculiar Institution*.

2. White, *Under the Iron Heel*; Pearson, *Capital's Terrorists*; Mackaman, *New Immigrants and the Radicalization of American Labor*; Hudelson and Ross, *By the Ore Docks*; Lubotina, "Corporate Supported Ethnic Conflict."

3. On the Bolshevik Revolution, pogroms, and international anti-Semitism, see Veidingler, *In the Midst of Civilized Europe*; North, *Russian Revolution*.

4. "Notes on My Life." During the same month when Harrigan visited Mary, a Red Scare erupted in numerous industrial cities, bringing arrests and deportations (Murray, *Red Scare*; Cohen, "Study in Nativism").

5. "Notes on My Life."

6. "Notes on My Life."

7. "Notes on My Life."

8. "Notes on My Life."

9. "Notes on My Life."

10. "Notes on My Life."

11. US Census, 1900, Waconia, Minnesota; Josephine Huckenpoehler File, Records of St. Peter Hospital, Minnesota Historical Society, St. Paul.

12. Josephine Huckenpoehler File. For the history of Anoka State Hospital, see "Preserving Anoka Asylum," *Minneapolis Star Tribune*, 25 June 2014.

13. "Notes on My Life."

14. "Notes on My Life."

15. "Notes on My Life."

16. "Notes on My Life."

17. "Notes on My Life"; MDH to JVS, 14, 15 August 1975.

18. "Notes on My Life" gives no indication that Harrigan was in Duluth, but Mary does not identify his place of employment during this period.

19. Fedo, *Lynchings in Duluth*.

20. Fedo, *Lynchings in Duluth*; *Duluth News Tribune*, 20 March 1920; *Duluth Labor World*, 19, 26 June 1920.

21. "Notes on My Life."

22. "Notes on My Life."

23. MDH Memoir, 1920–42.

Chapter 7: Motherhood Gone Awry

1. "Notes on My Life."

2. "Notes on My Life."

3. MDH Daybook; "Notes on My Life"; MDH Memoir, 1920–42.

4. MDH Daybook; US Census, 1930, Waconia, Minnesota.

5. MDH Daybook.

6. MDH Daybook.

7. MDH Daybook.

8. MDH Daybook.

9. MDH Daybook.

10. MDH Daybook.

11. MDH Daybook.

12. MDH Daybook; MDH to JVS, 16 January 1970; MDH Memoir, 1920–42.

13. MDH Memoir, 1920–42.

14. MDH Photograph Album, in possession of Inga McArdle. The US Census, 1930, Waconia, Minnesota, assessed the value of the Huckenpoehler home at $6,000.

15. MDH Memoir, 1920–42.

16. MDH Memoir, 1920–42.

17. MDH Memoir, 1920–42. Jeanne's name was originally spelled *Gene*.

18. "Notes on My Life"; US Census, 1940, Waconia, Minnesota.

19. MDH Memoir, 1920–42.

20. MDH Memoir, 1920–42.

21. MDH Memoir, 1920–42.

22. MDH Memoir, 1920–42; Lewis F. Daniel obituary, *Minneapolis Star Tribune*, 30 August 1936.

23. MDH Memoir, 1920–42; Hibbing city directory, 1938.

24. MDH Memoir, 1920–42.

25. MDH Memoir, 1920–42.

26. William B. Huckenpoehler to JVS, 18 May 1973.

27. *Minneapolis Star Tribune*, 27 March 1927; *Minneapolis Star*, 10 January 1930, 27 April, 17 October 1933. For a history of the Woman's Club of Minneapolis, see Madison, "Happiness Harnessing Itself to Good." Founded in 1907, the club was at the forefront of Progressive reform and featured Helen Keller as its speaker in 1914.

28. *Minneapolis Star Tribune*, 6 February 1935.

29. MDH Memoir, 1920–42. After his adoption, Michael Dennis became Michael Joseph.

30. MDH Memoir, 1920–42.

31. MDH Memoir, 1920–42; Herbert William Jones Obituary, *Minneapolis Star Tribune*, 11 July 1940.

32. MDH Memoir, 1920–42. Consistent with my grandmother's statement that Mary Jo changed her name, I have been unable to locate her in the 1940 US Census.

33. Born and raised in St. Paul, Rudolph was forty-three and Mary was thirty-seven in 1940 (US Census, 1940, St. Paul, Minnesota).

34. MDH Memoir, 1920–42.

Chapter 8: "A Lonesome Mother's Futile Hobby"

1. MDH Memoir, 1920–42.

2. MDH Memoir, 1920–42; US Indian Census Rolls, Pine Ridge Reservation, 1885–1940.

3. MDH Memoir, 1920–42; MDH Photograph Album, in possession of Inga McArdle.

4. MDH Memoir, 1920–42.

5. MDH Memoir, 1920–42.

6. MDH Memoir, 1920–42; Mary Champagne to VB, 16 August 2012.

7. *Minneapolis Star Tribune*, 5 August 1945; William B. Huckenpoehler Jr. identification card, Joint Task Force One, in possession of Inga McArdle; W. H. P. Blandy to William B. Huckenpoehler Jr., letter of commendation for meritorious service to Joint Task Force One, 13 March–30 September 1946, in possession of Inga McArdle.

8. Photo caption, MDH Photograph Album, in possession of Inga McArdle.

9. OkraJoe, "History of Muroc, CA (Now Edwards AFB)," 22 December 2011, https://www.youtube.com/watch?v=D3qsbO8GDsw; Edwards Air Force Base website, accessed 2 June 2024, https://www.edwards.af.mil/.

10. MDH Photograph Album, in possession of Inga McArdle; Victoria Elizabeth Bynum certificate of baptism,, 11 January 1948. Although the name on my birth certificate is *Victoria Lee Bynum*, by the time I was baptized, my mother had changed my middle name to *Elizabeth*.

11. MDH Notes and Drafts.

12. MDH, 3 October 1955, RRL.

13. *Tampa Tribune*, 25 July 1959.

14. William Bernard Huckenpoehler Jr. obituary, *Baltimore Sun*, 21 February 1995; Betty Huckenpoehler, 16 February 1962, RRL.

15. MB, 19 November 1955, RRL.

16. MB, 19 November 1955, RRL.

17. JVS, 25 November 1955, RRL; Mary Champagne to VB, 16 August 2012.

18. Mary Jo Drumm, 12 October 1955, RRL.

19. MDH, 30 November 1955, RRL.

20. B&BH, ca. 1 November 1955, RRL; MDH, 10 February 1956, RRL; Betty Huckenpoehler, 16 February 1962, RRL.

21. MDH, 17 January 1956, RRL; JVS, 29 December 1955, RRL; Mary Jo Drumm, [December 1955], RRL. Wayne remarried in 1956 and by 1962 had two children with his new wife.

22. William B. Huckenpoehler Sr., 17 January 1956, RRL.

23. Mary Jo Drumm, 24 January 1956, RRL.

24. MDH, 10 February 1956, RRL.

25. MB, 13 February 1956, RRL; JVS, 17 February, 23 May, 7 November 1956, RRL.

26. MB, 15 May 1956, RRL; JVS, 23 May, 7 November 1956, RRL. Clark Van Sise was born in February 1957, after the family moved to Crimora (Mary Champagne to VB, 16 August 2012).

27. MDH, 2 December 1956, RRL

28. MDH, 2 December 1956, RRL.

29. MDH, 1957, RRL.

Chapter 9: My Mother's Secrets

1. US Indian Census Rolls, Pine Ridge Reservation, South Dakota,1915, 1922, 1923; US Indian Wills, Book 3, Will of Ida Bone Necklace Morrison, 12 August 1915; Esther Yellow Hair Marshall, Public Member Trees, Ancestry.com; US Census, 1930, Bennett County, South Dakota; US Census, 1940, Fort Snelling, Hennepin County, Minnesota; Esther Marshall, application for Benjamin W. Marshall, Headstone Applications for Military Veterans, 28 June 1948.

2. MB to VB, 13 September 2012.

3. Oma Stanley Bynum and Margaret Huckenpoehler marriage license, 19 August 1942, Houston County, Georgia; Stan Bynum Military Records.

4. Stan Bynum Military Records; Margaret Bynum Photograph Album. On the history of the 345th Bombardment Group, see Hickey, *Warpath across the Pacific*.

5. MB to VB, 13 September 2012; Stan Bynum Military Records. Muroc Army Airfield became Muroc Air Force Base on 10 February 1948 and was renamed Edwards Air Force Base in December 1949.

6. Oma Stanley Bynum, last will and testament, 21 July 1950.

Chapter 10: Lifting the Curtain of Guilt and Shame

1. Unidentified newspaper clipping, 29 August 1951.

2. Georgia, U.S., Catholic Diocese of Savannah Cemetery Records, 1853–1975, Ancestry.com; Stan Bynum Military Records.

3. *Tampa Tribune*, 8 December 1953.

4. MB, 19 November 1955, RRL.

Chapter 11: Children Unattended

1. *Tampa Times*, 27 April 1955, 27 January 1959. Even when the school was officially desegregated in the fall of 1955, no Black children attended Tinker Elementary because none of the African Americans stationed at MacDill Air Force Base had grade-school-aged children (*Tampa Times*, 6 September 1955). See also Kimmel, "Hillsborough County School Desegregation."

2. Hitchcock, *Age of Eisenhower*; Simon, *Eisenhower vs. Warren*.

3. For a positive assessment of Eisenhower's civil rights accomplishments, see Nichols, *Matter of Justice*. On violence and the civil rights movement in Mississippi, see esp. Moody, *Coming of Age in Mississippi*. On the general effects of region and class on Blacks' experience of racism, see Reed, *The South*, 15–39; Eubanks, *Ever Is a Long Time*, 3–79.

4. Elaine Tyler May, *Homeward Bound*.

5. *Tampa Morning Tribune*, 16 August 1956.

Chapter 12: Islands of Refuge

1. *Atwater Signal*, 31 August 1958.

2. Bynum Diary, 13, 14 August 1962.

3. *Plattsmouth Journal*, 23 April 1962.

4. Bynum Diary, 1961.

5. Krugler, *1919*.

6. Menard, "Lest We Forget"; Loewen, *Sundown Towns*; *North Platte Daily Telegraph*, 13 July, 23 July 1929; *Grand Island Daily Independent*, 15 July 1929.

7. *Plattsmouth Journal*, 23, 26 July 1923, 10 October, 21 November 1932.

8. Bynum Diary, 8 July 1962.

9. Bynum Diary, 15 July 1962. The FDA had banned amphetamines in nasal inhalers in 1959, but a loophole allowed Valo and other companies to continue including methamphetamines (Gal, "Amphetamines in Nasal Inhalers").

10. Bynum Diary, 24 June, 19 September 1962.

11. Bynum Diary, 21 October 1962; *Plattsmouth Journal*, 22 October 1962.

12. Bynum Diary, 27 October, 1 November 1962.

13. Bynum Diary, October–December 1962.

14. Bynum Diary, 28 December 1962, 7 January 1963; VB Journal, 27 August 1963.

15. Bynum Diary, esp. 22 November, 23 December 1962; MJK to MDH, 27 October [1963?].

16. Bynum Diary, 13 October, 15 October 1963.

17. Bynum Diary, 16, 24 October 1963.

18. Bynum Diary, 21 November 1963; VB Journal, 8 January–7 May 1964.

19. Two months later, Mary Jo wrote to Grandma that "Frank is his usual drunken self. Not working & is drawing unemployment." Working nights left her tired during the day, so Barney was "staying with" the family of her son Mike's girlfriend. MJK to MDH, August 1964.

20. *Plattsmouth Journal*, 14 August 1967, 5 September 1968.

21. VB Journal, 24 April 1974.

Chapter 13: My Father's Story

1. Merle Breazeale to VB, 6 February 1972; *Ellisville Jones County News*, 20 December 1917.

2. *Ellisville Jones County News*, 27 December 1917, 3 January 1918.

3. Juanice Walters, "Shows Family History"; Juanice Walters to VB, 6 February 2002; US Census, 1920, St. Tammany Parish, Louisiana; Hiram S. Smith, World War I draft registration card, 12 September 1918. In 1900, before his marriage and divorce from Mary Elizabeth "Mollie" Stewart, Sollie had been superintendent of education in Poplarville (US Census, 1900, Poplarville, Mississippi). Mollie Stewart, the mother of Daniel Terrell Smith, is identified as "divorced" in the US Census, 1910, Poplarville, Mississippi.

4. US Census, 1900, Ellisville, Mississippi; US Census, 1910, Poplarville, Mississippi; Mississippi, US, Compiled Marriage Index, 1776–1935, Ancestry.com. The Ellisville home that John Hall Bynum built in 1875, today known as the Bynum-Anderson House, was listed on the National Register of Historic Places on 15 September 2022, the second oldest home in Ellisville after the infamous Amos Deason home, where Newt Knight allegedly shot Confederate Major Amos McLemore during the Civil War (Paula Moore-Hollowell [great-granddaughter of John Hall Bynum] to VB, 27 June 2022, 30 March 2023; Bynum, *Free State of Jones*, 105. John Hall Bynum's obituary in the *Jones County News*, 15 June 1916, identified Bertie as living in Slidell.

5. US Census, 1920, Harrison County and Jones County, Mississippi.

6. US Census, 1920, Poplarville and Seminary, Mississippi; *Poplarville Free Press*, 4 Jan 1923.

7. US Census, 1920, Poplarville and Seminary, Mississippi.

8. Bertie Bynum Smith gravestone, Find a Grave, accessed 1 July 2024, https://www.findagrave.com/memorial/41501417/bertie-mae-smith;

9. Sophronia Tisdale Bynum gravestone, Find a Grave, accessed 1 July 2024, https://www.findagrave.com/memorial/76729876/sophronia-a.-bynum; US Census, 1930, Coosa County, Alabama; Wayne Wingate to VB, 27 September 2004.

10. Laura Frances Bynum Sanford to VB, September 2004; New Orleans city directories, 1925, 1927; US Census, 1930, Castleberry, Alabama.

11. Stan Bynum Military Records.

12. Stan Bynum Military Records. Dad's discharge papers describe sores on various parts of his body, which would be consistent with gonorrhea.

13. Stan Bynum Military Records.

14. Mobile, Alabama, city directories, 1939, 1940, and 1941; Aden G. Bynum obituary, unidentified newspaper clipping. The reference to Brooklyn was probably a mistake: when Dad enlisted in the US Army Air Corps, he was living in Lynbrook, New York (Stan Bynum Military Records).

Chapter 14: My Grandmother's Rage and Sorrow

1. MDH Notes and Drafts.

2. MDH Notes and Drafts; RRL, 1963–64. Agnes died in October 1978 at age ninety-five.

3. MDH, conversation with VB, Waconia, Minnesota, July 1966.

4. MJK to MDH, 1966. Mary Jo's letter to her mother is one of several that are extant because Mary wrote notes for her family history on the backs of the letters (MDH Notes and Drafts).

5. MDH to B&BH, 17 May 1967, 7 July 1967; JVS to B&BH, 6 July 1967. MDH to JVS, 23 February 1968, 10 July 1968; Sandy Troyer, conversation with VB, 29 December 2022.

6. MDH to JVS, 3 June 1969, 19 March, 13 August 1970. It is likely that Jane's adoptive mother, Mary Baetz, brought Jane and Daniel to Minneapolis.

7. MDH to JVS, 26 July 1971.

8. MDH to Bill Huckenpoehler, 7 July 1967; W. Joel Drumm record, US Department of Veterans Affairs BIRLS Death File, 1850–2011.

9. *Tulare Advance-Register*, 9 April 1985; *Phoenix Arizona Republic*, 9 February 2001.

10. MDH to Bill Huckenpoehler, May 1967; MDH to JVS, 6 October 1967.

11. MDH to JVS, 25 January, 10 July 1968. On the civil rights struggle in southern Mississippi during the 1960s, see especially Boyett, *Right to Revolt*.

12. MDH to JVS, 6 August, 4 October 1968.

13. MDH to JVS, 22 November, 10 December 1968.

14. MDH to JVS, 16 May 1969, 7 May 1970.

15. MDH to JVS, 26 March 1968, 16 January, 10 July 1970, MDH to VB, 18, 26 July 1971.

16. MDH to JVS, 11 July 1970.

17. MDH to JVS, 26 September 1970.

18. MDH to JVS, 13 August 1970.

19. MDH to JVS, 12 August, 13 August 1970.

20. Josephine Hansen to JVS and Family, 9 December 1970; Harrigan Huckenpoehler to JVS, 1970; MDH to JVS, 1970; MDH to JVS, 15 January 1971.

21. Harrigan Huckenpoehler to JVS, 18 May 1973; MDH to JVS, 6 March 1971.

22. MJK to MDH, 7 May 1971; MDH to JVS, 8 June 1971.

23. MDH to JVS, 12 April 1969, 8 June 1971.

24. MDH to JVS, 3 October 1972.

25. MDH to B&BH, May 1972; MDH to JVS, 24 May, 17 June 1972.

26. MDH to JVS, 24 May 1972; Harrigan Huckenpoehler to B&BH, 1 May 1973.

27. MB to B&BH, 14 May 1972; MJK to B&BH, 5, 14 July 1974; MJK to VB, 24 [July] 1974.

28. Harrigan Huckenpoehler to JVS, 17 October 1974.

29. MDH to Bill Huckenpoehler Jr., 2 April 1975; MDH to JVS, 3 April 1975.

30. Cora Dixon to MB, 22 April 1975.

31. JVS to VB, n.d.

32. MDH to JVS, 21 July 1975.

33. MDH, RRL, 1963; William Christian Huckenpoehler record, US Cemetery and Funeral Home Collection, 1847–Current, Ancestry.com; MDH to B&BH, 30 July 1975.

34. MDH to JVS and Jack Van Sise, 7, 14, 15 August 1975.

35. MDH to MB, 8 August 1975; Bill Huckenpoehler Jr. to JVS and Jack Van Sise, 18 November 1976.

36. Josephine Hansen to B&BH, n.d.

37. MDH to JVS, 15 August 1975.

38. MDH to Bill Huckenpoehler Jr., n.d.

39. MDH to Bill Huckenpoehler Jr., n.d.

Epilogue: Memories and Reflections

1. VB Diary, 1973.

2. *Santa Rosa Press Democrat*, 3 October, 27 December 2023.

3. "Body Found in Glendale," *Phoenix Arizona Republic*, 30 July 1978; "Autopsy Shows Woman Died of Natural Causes," *Phoenix Arizona Republic*, 1 August 1978.

BIBLIOGRAPHY

Manuscript and Record Collections

Bryn Mawr, Pennsylvania
Bryn Mawr College
Alumnae Association Publications
Chicago
Newberry Library
Margaret Ullmann Writings, 1894–1956
Los Angeles
University of Southern California Digital Library
Hamlin Garland Correspondence, 1864–1941
St. Paul, Minnesota
Minnesota Historical Society
Mary Daniel Huckenpoehler and Family Papers, 1864–2013 (bulk 1887–1943), Gale
Family Library, Manuscripts (P2858)
Records of St. Peter Hospital

Newspapers

Atwater (CA) Signal
Baltimore Sun
Bismarck (ND) Herald
Bismarck (ND) Tribune
Bottineau (ND) Courant
Bowbells (ND) Tribune
Chaska (MN) Weekly Valley Herald

Chicago Chronicle
Chicago Inter Ocean
Chicago Tribune
Detroit Free Press
Duluth (MN) Labor World
Duluth (MN) News Tribune
Ellisville (MS) Jones County News
Fargo (ND) Nonpartisan Leader
Grand Forks (ND) Herald
Grand Island (NE) Daily Independent
Green Bay (WI) Press-Gazette
Green Bay (WI) Weekly Gazette
Los Angeles Times
Mason City (IA) Globe Gazette
Minneapolis Star Tribune
North Platte (NE) Daily Telegraph
Oshkosh (WI) Northwestern
Pasadena (CA) Independent Star-News
Pasadena (CA) Post
Phoenix Arizona Republic
Plattsmouth (NE) Journal
Poplarville (MS) Free Press
Racine (WI) Journal
Racine (WI) Journal Times
St. Paul (MN) Globe
Santa Rosa (CA) Press Democrat
Sioux City (IA) Journal
Tampa (FL) Morning Tribune
Tampa (FL) Tribune
Tulare (CA) Advance-Register
Waconia (MN) Patriot
Wahpeton (ND) Times
Ward County (ND) Independent
Williston (ND) Graphic

Published Works

Alter, Thomas, II. *Toward a Cooperative Commonwealth: The Transplanted Roots of Farmer-Labor Radicalism in Texas*. Urbana: University of Illinois Press, 2022.

Andrews, Gregg. *City of Dust: A Cement Company Town in the Land of Tom Sawyer*. Columbia: University of Missouri Press, 2002.

Andrews, Gregg. *Shantyboats and Roustabouts*. Baton Rouge: Louisiana State University Press, 2022.

"Apperson: America's First Sports Cars." ClassicSpeedsters.com, 6 December 2019. https://www.classicspeedsters.com/blog/2019/12/5/apperson-americas-first-sports-cars.

Bagley, Cynthia Barkley, and Loren D. Bagley, comps. *Welsh Families—Wisconsin Pioneers, 1845–1920.* Vol. 1, *The Sociology of a Wisconsin Welsh Community.* Albany, WI: Albertson Memorial Library, 2001–8. https://content.mpl.org/digital/collection/AML/id/3542.

Barry, John M. "The Site of Origin of the 1918 Influenza Pandemic and Its Public Health Implications." *Journal of Translational Medicine* 2 (2004). https://doi.org/10.1186/1479 -5876-2-3.

Berg, Scott W. *38 Nooses: Lincoln, Little Crow, and the Beginning of the Frontier's End.* New York: Vintage, 2013.

Boyett, Patricia Michelle. *Right to Revolt: The Crusade for Racial Justice in Mississippi's Central Piney Woods.* Jackson: University Press of Mississippi, 2015.

Brodie, Janet Farrell. *Contraception and Abortion in Nineteenth-Century America.* New York: Cornell University Press, 1997.

Bynum, Victoria. *The Free State of Jones: Mississippi's Longest Civil War.* Chapel Hill: University of North Carolina Press, 2001.

Byrne, L. Frank, ed. *Uncommon Soldiers: Harvey Reid and the 22nd Wisconsin March with Sherman.* Knoxville: University of Tennessee Press, 2001.

Clark, Christopher. *The Sleepwalkers: How Europe Went to War in 1914.* New York: Harper Perennial, 2014.

Coben, Stanley. "A Study in Nativism: The American Red Scare of 1919–20." *Political Science Quarterly* 79, no. 1 (March 1964): 52–75.

Dalen, James E., Joseph S. Alpert, Robert J. Goldberg, and Ronald S. Weinstein. "The Epidemic of the 20th Century: Coronary Heart Disease." *American Journal of Medicine* 127, no. 9 (September 2014): 801–96.

Davies, David. *Oshkosh, Wisconsin, Welsh Settlement Centennial, 1847–1947: A Translation of Hanes y Cymry (History of the Welsh). The Jubilee Book of 1897, Giving the History of the Welsh of Winnebago and Fond Du Lac Counties, Wisconsin, 1847–1897.* Translated by Howell David Davies. Oshkosh, WI: n.p., 1947.

"Dickinson G. C." *Forest and Stream* 81 (30 August 1913): 279.

Dixon, Thomas, Jr. *The Clansman: A Historical Romance of the Ku Klux Klan.* New York: Grosset and Dunlap, 1905.

Doyle, Don H. *Age of Reconstruction: How Lincoln's New Birth of Freedom Remade the World.* Princeton: Princeton University Press, 2024.

Dubnow, S. M. *History of the Jews in Russia and Poland.* Vol. 2, *From the Death of Alexander I, until the Death of Alexander III (1825–1894).* Translated by I. Friedlaender. Philadelphia: Jewish Publication Society of America, 1918.

Du Bois, W. E. B. *Black Reconstruction.* New York: Harcourt, Brace, and Howe, 1935.

Eubanks, W. Ralph. *Ever Is a Long Time: A Journey into Mississippi's Dark Past.* New York: Basic Books, 2003.

Evans, Chris. *Slave Wales: The Welsh and Atlantic Slavery, 1660–1850.* Cardiff: University of Wales Press, 2010.

Ewald, Ellen Buchwald. *Recipes for a Small Planet: The Art and Science of High Protein Vegetarian Cookery.* New York: Ballantine, 1973.

Faderman, Lillian. *Odd Girls and Twilight Lovers: A History of Lesbian Life in Twentieth-Century America.* New York: Columbia University Press, 1991.

Fedo, Michael. *The Lynchings in Duluth.* St. Paul: Minnesota Historical Society Press, 2000.

Fliss, William M. "Wisconsin's Abolitionist Regiment: The Twenty-Second Volunteer Infantry in Kentucky, 1862–1863." *Wisconsin Magazine of History* 86 (Winter 2002–3): 2–17.

Foner, Eric. *Free Soil, Free Labor, Free Men: The Ideology of the Republican Party before the Civil War*. Oxford: Oxford University Press, 1970.

Gal, Joseph. "Amphetamines in Nasal Inhalers" (letter to the editor). *Journal of Toxicology: Clinical Toxicology* 19, no. 5 (1982): 517–18.

George, Henry. "A Reformer Deplores the Poverty Caused by Industrial Progress" (1879). *SHEC: Resources for Teachers*, https://shec.ashp.cuny.edu/items/show/584.

Giles, Jerrica A., and Allen C. Guelzo. "Colonel Utley's Emancipation—or, How Lincoln Offered to Buy a Slave." *Marquette Law Review* 93, no. 4 (Summer 2010): 1263–82.

Gordon, Linda. *The Moral Property of Women: A History of Birth Control Politics in America*. Urbana: University of Illinois Press, 2002.

Gordon, Linda. *The Second Coming of the KKK: The Ku Klux Klan of the 1920s and the American Political Tradition*. New York: Liveright, 2017.

Groves, Richard H. *Blooding the Regiment: An Account of the 22d Wisconsin's Long and Difficult Apprenticeship*. Lanham, MD: Scarecrow, 2005.

Hammond, Charlotte. *Woven Histories of Welsh Wool and Slavery*. E-book. United Kingdom: Common Threads Press.

Haymond, John A. "How the U.S. Used 'Laws of War' to Hang Dakota Indians after 1862 Uprising." 16 November 2021. https://www.historynet.com/how-the-u-s-used-laws-of-war-to-hang-dakota-indians-after-1862-uprising/.

Hickey, Lawrence J. *Warpath across the Pacific: The Illustrated History of the 345th Bombardment Group during World War II*. 5th ed. Boulder, CO: International Historical Research Associates, 2008.

Hitchcock, William J. *The Age of Eisenhower: America and the World in the 1950s*. New York: Simon and Schuster, 2018.

Hobbs, William Herbert, comp. *Kimball-Weston Memorial: The American Ancestry and Descendants of Alonzo and Sarah (Weston) Kimball of Green Bay, Wisconsin*. Madison, WI: n.p., 1902.

Hogstad, Emily E. "Anna Schoen-René: Soprano, Conductor, Minnesota Pioneer." *Song of the Lark* (blog), 15 November 2017. https://songofthelarkblog.com/2017/11/15/anna-schoen-rene/.

Holt, John. *How Children Learn*. New York: Pitman, 1968.

Holzer, Harold. *Brought Forth on This Continent: Abraham Lincoln and American Immigration*. New York: Penguin Random House, 2024.

Horowitz, Helen Lefkowitz. *Rereading Sex: Battles over Sexual Knowledge and Suppression in Nineteenth-Century America*. New York: Vintage, 2002.

Hudelson, Richard, and Carl Ross. *By the Ore Docks: A Working People's History of Duluth*. Minneapolis: University of Minnesota Press, 2006.

Hughes, Thomas E., David Edwards, Hugh G. Roberts, and Thomas Hughes, eds. *The History of the Welsh in Minnesota, Foreston and Lime Springs, Ia., Gathered by the Old Settlers*. N.p., 1895.

Hunter, Jerry. *Sons of Arthur, Children of Lincoln: Welsh Writing from the American Civil War*. Cardiff: University of Wales Press, 2007.

"Hunting with Gun and Graflex." *Minnesotan: An Illustrated Monthly Magazine about Northwest People, Products, Possibilities* 2, no. 3 (September 1916): 13–15.

Inness, Sherrie A. "Mashes, Smashes, Crushes, and Raves: Woman-to-Woman Relationships in Popular Women's College Fiction, 1895–1915." *NWSA Journal* 6, no. 1 (Spring 1994): 48–68.

James, E. Wyn. "Introduction to the Life and Work of Ann Griffiths." Accessed 31 May 2024. https://www.anngriffiths.cardiff.ac.uk/introduction.html.

Kimmel, Elinor. "Hillsborough County School Desegregation Busing and Black High Schools in Tampa, Florida, April 1971–September 1971." *Sunland Tribune*, vol. 18, art. 7 (1992). https://digitalcommons.usf.edu/sunlandtribune/vol18/iss1/7.

Kitch, Carolyn. *The Girl on the Magazine Cover: The Origins of Visual Stereotypes in American Mass Media*. Chapel Hill: University of North Carolina Press, 2001.

Krugler, David F. *1919, the Year of Racial Violence: How African Americans Fought Back*. Cambridge: Cambridge University Press, 2014.

Lansing, Michael J. *Insurgent Democracy: The Non-Partisan League in North America*. Chicago: University of Chicago Press, 2015.

Lappé, Frances Moore. *Diet for a Small Planet*. New York: Ballantine Books, 1971.

Laudon, Robert Tallant. "Minnesota Musicians of the Cultured Generation: Gustavus Johnson, Pianist-Composer of Minneapolis." 2001. https://conservancy.umn.edu /bitstream/11299/48398/1/0015uarc.pdf.

Loewen, James W. *Sundown Towns: A Hidden Dimension of American Racism*. New York: New Press, 2018.

Lubotina, Paul. "Corporate Supported Ethnic Conflict on the Mesabi Range, 1890–1930." *Upper Country: A Journal of the Lake Superior Region* 3 (2015): 29–52.

Madison, Cathy. "Happiness Harnessing Itself to Good." *Minnesota Monthly*, 12 September 2006. https://www.minnesotamonthly.com/archive/ happiness-harnessing-itself-to-good/.

Mackaman, Thomas. *New Immigrants and the Radicalization of American Labor, 1914–1924*. Jefferson NC: McFarland, 2017.

Marx, Karl, and Friedrich Engels. *The Civil War in the United States*. New York: International Publishers, 1969.

May, Andrew J. *Welsh Missionaries and British Imperialism: The Empire of Clouds in North-East India*. Manchester: Manchester University Press, 2012.

May, Elaine Tyler. *Homeward Bound: American Families in the Cold War Era*. New York: Basic Books, 1988.

Menard, Orville D. "Lest We Forget: The Lynching of Will Brown, Omaha's 1919 Race Riot." *Nebraska History* 91 (2010): 152–65.

Mitchno, Gregory F. *Dakota Dawn: The Decisive First Week of the Sioux Uprising, August 1862*. El Dorado Hills, CA: Savas Beatie, 2011.

Moody, Anne. *Coming of Age in Mississippi*. New York: Dial, 1968.

Moore, Barrington. *Social Origins of Dictatorship and Democracy: Lord and Peasant in the Making of the Modern World*. Boston: Beacon, 1993.

Moore, David. "Wales and the Slave Trade." National Library of Wales/Llyfrgell Genedlaethol Cymru Blog, 23 August 2021. https://web.archive.org/web/20240201195642/https://blog .library.wales/2021/08/.

Murray, Robert K. *Red Scare: A Study in National Hysteria, 1919–1920*. Minneapolis: University of Minnesota Press, 1955.

Neill, Edward D., and Charles S. Bryant. *History of the Minnesota Valley Including Explorers and Pioneers of Minnesota and History of the Sioux Massacre*. Minneapolis: North Star, 1882.

Nichols, David. *A Matter of Justice: Eisenhower and the Beginning of the Civil Rights Revolution*. New York: Simon and Schuster, 2007.

North, David. *The Russian Revolution and the Unfinished Twentieth Century*. Royal Oak, MI: Mehring, 2014.

Oakes, James. *The Crooked Path to Abolition: Abraham Lincoln and the Antislavery Constitution*. New York: Norton, 2021.

Okrent, Daniel. *The Guarded Gate: Bigotry, Eugenics, and the Law That Kept Two Generations of Jews, Italians and Other European Immigrants out of America*. New York: Simon and Schuster, 2020.

Orr, Patti. "History of Muroc and North Muroc, Calif." *Mojave Desert News*, 7 September 2021. https://www.desertnews.com/news/article_5a3aa2e4-0ff0-11ec-8936-ff255d9309a7 .html.

Pearson, Chad. *Capital's Terrorists: Klansmen, Lawmen, and Employers in America's Long Nineteenth Century*. Chapel Hill: University of North Carolina Press, 2022.

Pearson, Chad. *Reform or Repression: Organizing America's Anti-Union Movement*. Philadelphia: University of Pennsylvania Press, 2016.

Reed, Adolph L., Jr. *The South: Jim Crow and Its Afterlives*. New York: Verso, 2022.

"Rees Davies and His Family, 1844." Accessed 31 May 2024. https://www.peoplescollection. wales/items/576039.

Sanders, Vivienne. *Wales, the Welsh and the Making of America*. Cardiff: University of Wales Press, 2021.

Schlesinger, Arthur, Jr. "The Causes of the Civil War: A Note on Historical Sentimentalism." *Partisan Review* 16, no. 10 (October 1949): 969–81.

Simon, James F. *Eisenhower vs. Warren: The Battle for Civil Rights and Liberties*. New York: Liveright, 2018.

Smith-Rosenberg, Carroll. "The Female World of Love and Ritual: Relations between Women in Nineteenth-Century America." *Signs* 1, no. 1 (Autumn 1975): 1–29.

Stampp, Kenneth. *The Peculiar Institution: Slavery in Ante-Bellum America*. New York: Basic Books, 1956.

Tyrrell, Ian. *Woman's World, Woman's Empire: The Woman's Christian Temperance Union in International Perspective, 1880–1930*. Chapel Hill: University of North Carolina Press, 2010.

Ullmann, Margaret. *Pocahontas*. Boston: Poet Lore, 1912.

Ullmann, Margaret. *Tone-Poems*. Chicago: Lakeside, 1908.

Van Vugt, William E. "Welsh Emigration to the United States in the Mid-Nineteenth Century." *Welsh History Review* 15, no 4 (1991): 545–61.

Veidingler, Jeffrey. *In the Midst of Civilized Europe: The Pogroms of 1918–1921 and the Onset of the Holocaust*. New York: Metropolitan, 2021.

White, Ahmed. *Under the Iron Heel: The Wobblies and the American War on Radical Workers*. Oakland: University of California Press, 2022.

Williams, Eric. *Capitalism and Slavery*. Chapel Hill: University of North Carolina Press, 1944.

Woodward, C. Vann. *The Origins of the New South, 1877–1913*. Baton Rouge: Louisiana State University Press, 1951.

INDEX

Page numbers in **bold** indicate illustrations.

ABOUT THE AUTHOR

Photo courtesy of the author

Victoria Bynum is distinguished professor emeritus of history at Texas State University, San Marcos. A scholar of class, gender, and race relations in the Civil War–era South, she is an award-winning author and a National Endowment for the Humanities Fellow. Her book *The Free State of Jones* inspired the movie of the same title. Other publications include *The Long Shadow of the Civil War: Southern Dissent and Its Legacies* and *Unruly Women: The Politics of Social and Sexual Control in the Old South*. She is the creator and administrator of the blog *Renegade South*.